Praise for Blissfully Blended Bullshit

Rebecca Eckler's direct and honest approach to storytelling makes for a refreshing and often hilarious read. Eckler has an undeniable talent for weaving in touching stories of relationships, motherhood, and the reality of blended families that gives her writing real humanity.

— Heather Dixon, editor-in-chief of SavvyMom

A touching and telling modern love story between husband and wife and mother and daughter and the balance of all the relationships in between. Eckler weaves her story of vulnerability and painful truths to reveal the unfiltered reality of blending families. With her raw sense of honesty and self-awareness, Rebecca Eckler provides an invaluable human approach. This is a valuable and eye-opening read for anyone contemplating a life of blended and splendid.

— Daniella English, founder of The Not So Single Life

Inspiring, touching, and raw.... What a great read by Rebecca! Once again she continues to help all those going through "inventional" blending.

— Marni Sky, co-founder of Divorce Angels

Another totally entertaining and relatable read by Rebecca Eckler. As a blended family survivor, I had a visceral reaction to so many of the anecdotes. It is real and it is uncomfortable. This book is a must read for anyone considering (or living through) blending worlds.

— Joanna Track, founder and executive publisher of Bullet

BLISSFULLY

BLENDED

BULLSHIT

BLISSFULLY

BLENDED

BULLSHIT

THE UNCOMFORTABLE TRUTH
OF BLENDING FAMILIES

REBECCA ECKLER

DUNDURN
TORONTO

Cover image: stock.com/Robert Daly
Printer: Webcom, a division of Marquis Printing Inc.

Library and Archives Canada Cataloguing in Publication

Title: Blissfully blended bullshit : the uncomfortable truth of blending families / Rebecca Eckler.
Names: Eckler, Rebecca, author.
Identifiers: Canadiana (print) 20190054476 | Canadiana (ebook) 20190054484 | ISBN 9781459743939 (softcover) | ISBN 9781459743946 (PDF) | ISBN 9781459743953 (EPUB)
Subjects: LCSH: Eckler, Rebecca. | LCSH: Eckler, Rebecca—Family. | LCSH: Stepmothers—Biography. | LCSH: Stepfamilies. | LCGFT: Autobiographies.
Classification: LCC HQ759.92 .E25 2019 | DDC 306.874/7—dc23

1   2   3   4   5   23   22   21   20   19

We acknowledge the support of the **Canada Council for the Arts**, which last year invested $153 million to bring the arts to Canadians throughout the country, and the **Ontario Arts Council** for our publishing program. We also acknowledge the financial support of the **Government of Ontario**, through the **Ontario Book Publishing Tax Credit** and **Ontario Creates**, and the **Government of Canada**.

Nous remercions le **Conseil des arts du Canada** de son soutien. L'an dernier, le Conseil a investi 153 millions de dollars pour mettre de l'art dans la vie des Canadiennes et des Canadiens de tout le pays.

Printed and bound in Canada.

VISIT US AT

 dundurn.com |  @dundurnpress | dundurnpress | dundurnpress

Dundurn
3 Church Street, Suite 500
Toronto, Ontario, Canada
M5E 1M2

For everyone out there reinventing what family means, whether it's the one you start out with, the one you end up with, or the family you gained along the way.

"Come home! Your kids and my kids are
picking on our kid!"

· PROLOGUE ·

Where the fuck is my confetti? Where is my celebratory dinner? Oh, right. I've forgotten about the less-than-thrilled response I received from some members of my blended family when I told them I'd signed a book deal. I suppose breaking the news that it was about them might have had something to do with that. They didn't seem overjoyed that I was going to write about the cold, hard, uncomfortable truth of what really happens behind the closed doors of blended families. Welcome to my life. Even before I sat at my computer to compose my thoughts on what this book would look like, certain members of my blended family already had their backs up, wondering what the hell I would be writing about and, of course, how they would be perceived. It's not that they weren't happy that I'd got a book deal. They just weren't exactly enamoured with what they thought, or assumed, I was going to share. They were anxious. And, honestly, they should be.

I was "gently" advised by my partner to "be cautious" when writing about all of us — all of us being myself, my partner and his two biological children, the son we have together, and my daughter from my first common-law marriage. One big happy-ish family! I felt like a child being told to think before I speak. I "gently" reminded him that I'm a grown woman. So, no, there was no dinner, no champagne toast, not even dying roses from a gas station in my honour when I got the go-ahead to tell my story about what it's like to be in a blended family.

It's a story worth telling. Holy shit, have my experiences opened my eyes, not just to the gargantuan reality of adjusting to life in a blended family, but also because of what I've learned about myself and relationships while blending. You kind of get a crash course in reality when trying to manage all the bullshit that comes along with this rapidly growing family dynamic.

Sometimes what happens in a blended family really is stranger than fiction. The fights and slights can be so ridiculous, I'm not sure anyone would actually believe me. Which is why I've never truly shared, nor have I found any book out there that can commiserate with me about what a shit show it is to be in a blended family.

This is *not* a memoir about being a step-parent or having stepchildren or the step-parent–stepchild relationship. Not that I don't touch on it. But this is more my account of how blending families affects everyone, including people you'd never consider, like our exes, or our ex-in-laws, our new in-laws, and even the dog.

The truth about blending families can be fucking harsh. Those who haven't gone through it and are dating others with children, are thinking about blending, are embarking on blend-ing, or are just curious about what it's like to blend families prob-ably just figure it's an … *adjustment*? Perhaps a process to learn, a path to travel, a mountain to climb, a field to plant, a knot to unravel, a Coen brothers movie to fully understand. In other words, a difficult but seemingly surmountable challenge.

Ha! *Challenge.* Living it, I'd probably use a *much* different word. Every single one of us in my blended family has our own perception of our roles in each other's lives and in our blended household. We may all live under the same roof, but our experiences are totally different and can even be contrasting at times. Our truths may have discrepancies and may even have zero basis in reality. Everyone else's sense about what it's been like for them to blend is a reflection of them, just as my reactions while blending reveal a lot about me.

My family — the kids, the grandparents, the Boyfriend, and the exes — know that honesty and candour are my MO. This memoir is *my* truth, and, unfortunately, truth can sound an awful lot like criticism. Some people — yep, I'm gonna go there — can't handle the truth. Or, at the very least, they would prefer to ignore it than to admit and confront it. Believe me, I've been on that side, too. But I know my truth from talking to others in blended families — some successful, some not so much, some not at all — and comparing notes to see if I'm just batshit crazy, or if they could relate to a lot of the bullshit I've found comes along with blending. I mostly know about the bullshit of blending from living it, from being honest about the way I feel in certain situations and the way I think everyone else feels in my blended family, and, also, from the hundreds of texts and email exchanges over the years with the cast of characters in my blended family. Thank you, iCloud!

So, yeah — *blah, blah, blah* — the truth will set us free. But first it will piss someone, or everyone, off. Or, who knows? Maybe everyone in my blended family will let out a huge sigh of relief that it's *not just us* who thinks navigating our new roles is a bit of a shit show. Maybe they'll even have a good giggle. What screws most of us up is a picture or the fantasy in our heads of how a family is supposed to be, how we are supposed to treat each other, and how we are supposed to look. I hope that when my family looks back on the most difficult times, we'll also remember the awesome memories we've created and continue to create. I know I will. Even for all of our scars and bumps and bruises and imperfections and missteps, it hasn't all been all bad.

There is one thing I'm pretty sure we'd all agree on, though — and I do mean just one! The process of blending families comes with a considerable amount of bullshit.

Still, knowing that the people who have been in my life now for years — the family I've gained after blending and as we continue to blend — are, for lack of a better word, *perturbed* over what I'm going to write kind of stings. I'm not going to lie. I'm legit hurt by their lack of enthusiasm.

So, okay, I don't exactly have a cheering section. There is no confetti. No bouquet — flower, fruit, balloon, or otherwise — in my future. But maybe, just maybe, this book will be like blending families: completely unexpected, with some WTF, but also a whole lot of, "Oh, really? I hadn't thought of it that way!" My family need not fear that they will come off looking like assholes while I come across all roses and rainbows. Quite the opposite, actually. Many times I'm the one who comes across as the schmuck. Many, many times, my dark, jealous, resentful side surfaces, and often my feelings are completely irrational and immature, to the point that it horrifies even me.

But I'm not one to shy away from sharing *my* account of the hard truths, the less-than-ideal realities, and all the bullshit I was completely unprepared for by blending. I wouldn't be me if I held back. So I don't plan to.

· ONE ·

I'm not averse to a good old-fashioned rebound screw. Honestly? I just want to get laid. Cinderella never asked for a prince. She asked for a night off and a dress. I'm not looking for a future husband, nor am I too bothered over what I should wear for this first — and most likely last — date. Cute outfit or not, it doesn't really matter. I want a one-night stand, some therapeutic physical action, to help distract me from the emotional pain of my recent breakup. I'm not desperate to jump into another serious relationship, especially after the roller coaster of a ride, that had finally ended, with a ridiculously handsome man who was also ridiculously underemployed for someone his age. What I'm looking for is a diversion and, yes, I'll admit, a bit of an ego boost. If a relationship does happen to fall in my lap, I won't run away, arms flailing. But I am also more than okay being on my own and raising my daughter as a single mom, as I have been doing for years. I guess I am like a cat. I appreciate attention, but only when I want it. I'm very multidimensional.

Also, I'm all about the Theory of Least Effort when it comes to dating. After a girlfriend shows me how one of the most popular dating apps work, using her profile to log on, all I come away with after swiping is, "Fuck, that was entertaining!" Also, I'm left wondering, Why do so many men post photos with waxed chests, on boats, holding giant fish? But I digress …

When another girlfriend asks if I want to be set up on a blind date with a recently single man, her boyfriend's childhood friend who is also back on the market after separating from his wife of twelve years, I immediately say *yes*! I also make it clear to my girlfriend that I'm not really looking for anything more than some (hopefully) mind-boggling action.

My phone rings, and the man I'm being set-up with is on the other end. Yes, he actually calls. Yes, I actually "accept" the "unknown caller." We are both, clearly, dinosaurs. We make a plan to meet up later in the week. Of course, I immediately call my girlfriend after the plans are set, as girls do, and reiterate that all I'm looking for is someone to screw the sadness out of me. I can't get a lobotomy. A one-night stand it is.

"Don't worry," my friend laughs. "I don't think *that's* going to be a problem." I don't know much about my anticipated one-night stand. But I trust that my friend and her boyfriend aren't fixing me up with a subpar blind date. Apparently, he's cute. Check! And single. Check! And he has a grown-up job. Check! I don't even put in the effort to investigate him on social media. I'm not holding auditions for boyfriends, nor am I auditioning to be someone's girlfriend. So, before we even meet, I already doubt he'll get a callback after this date. I have no expectation that I'll get one either. I know the basics: he's recently separated, in the process of divorce, and he has two children he has shared custody of. This will be my first time going on a date with a *father*. Still, I have zero — Z-E-R-O — intention of ever meeting his offspring, so that part of his life isn't really on my radar. I'm guessing he is equally invested in the fact I'm a single mom. It probably doesn't occur to him he'll meet my daughter on our very first date.

You mean not everyone lets their children meet their one-night stands?

·   ·   ·   ·   ·

Rowan, my daughter, who lives with me full-time, is more excited than I am about this mystery date, who shows up exactly on time. Before I can stop her, my daughter rushes to the door to greet my bed-buddy, like a dog who hasn't seen its owner in a month.

Mericol, Rowan's nanny, and I have already role played an escape route for me in case I can't stand the guy. She's been directed to say, in front of my blind date, "Rebecca, I'm really sorry, but I can only stay until ten." We have rehearsed this line. Thanks to this ruse, if I don't like the dude, I will only be wasting three hours *tops* with him. I feel pretty fucking clever about this plan.

"Rebecca," Mericol says, on cue, in front of my potential one-night stand as he waits inside my front door, my daughter looking him up and down, beaming. "I forgot to tell you, but I have to leave by ten. I'm so sorry."

"Oh, really?" I respond, biting my lip. I feign disappointment, with a side of surprise. "That's okay, right?" I ask One-Night Stand, to make sure he's heard her.

"Sure, that's fine," he responds. I think he appreciates having the option of a way out as much as I do.

Mericol and I also have another plan in place. If I invite him in after our date and scratch my nose, that means I *do* like the guy, and she can disappear, knowing that all is good.

Rowan rushes to hug my one-night stand's legs, again, as we head out the door. She's seven. She hugs everyone. For a nanosecond, I wonder if One-Night Stand is going to suddenly remember he left the stove on or forgot to feed his hamster. Maybe he has his own escape route planned out in case he doesn't like *me*. As I pry my daughter off his legs — "The sooner I leave, the sooner I'll be back," I tell her — I worry that he worries that my kid is in the market for an Insta-Daddy, which couldn't be further from the truth. Even worse, I fear that he now thinks that *I'm* looking for an Insta-Daddy for my daughter, which also couldn't be further from the truth.

But he doesn't run. He simply looks slightly uncomfortable. Maybe he's just nervous. Most guys aren't dying to have a kid they met forty-five seconds earlier attach to them like an annoying acquaintance you can't get away from at a cocktail party. It's not very sexy, that's for damn sure. Should I tell One-Night Stand he shouldn't take this hug personally? The other day, my daughter hugged the pharmacist. Yesterday, she hugged a bus driver. I inwardly roll my eyes, thinking that my chances of getting laid have dropped significantly. But at least he has seen proof that I have a child. I refuse to hide my daughter, who is by far the most important person in my life. I don't feel reckless or irresponsible for allowing my daughter to meet my date. We come as a package deal. Might as well let this guy know he's hooking up, or at least going on a date, with a *mother*.

· · · · ·

I take One-Night Stand to the premiere of a movie, possibly one of the worst movies ever made, that one of my PR friends had offered me tickets to. The movie isn't even the good type of bad — it's just bad bad. But my date and I have fun moaning throughout it, laughing at parts that aren't meant to be funny at all. My potential one-night stand is sweet, easy to talk with, and, I'll admit, easy on the eyes. And he likes popcorn. I like popcorn! We have so much in common! Plus, as my friend has already disclosed, he's on a bit of a hook-up tour himself. After the movie, he drives me home and I "lure" him inside, not with my feminine wiles, but with the promise that my daughter's nanny makes a mean meatloaf.

"There are leftovers," I say, as we pull into my driveway. "Would you like to come in and try some?" Some people invite dates in to "Netflix and chill." I offer leftover meatloaf. I'm all class.

"Sure, I would love to," my date replies as he gets out of his pimped-out sports car. Like a gentleman who knows he is likely going to get laid, he comes around and opens the passenger door for me, and then walks slightly behind me, waiting as I unlock my door. Chivalry is not dead! I'm impressed.

"Fabulous!" I say, hearing my tone, which is *way* too enthusiastic for fucking leftovers. I mean, it's meatloaf. It's not *that* good. I'm comforted, though, that he recognizes that "meatloaf" is code for ... obviously something else. Mericol greets us at the door. I scratch my nose. She smiles brightly, tells me that my daughter is fast asleep in my bed, as usual, and makes a quick exit. Guess my bed is taken, then. Noted.

As soon as we walk into my kitchen, we start kissing. He's a good kisser. I'm inwardly relieved he isn't really just there for the meatloaf. One never knows. Our clothes quickly come off, as if they are on fire, as we work our way from the kitchen to the living room, the promise of meatloaf forgotten. My blind date and I have mind-boggling sex on my living room couch, and I thank the sleeping gods for giving me a child who sleeps so soundly that not even fire alarms wake her. My friend was bang-on. One-Night Stand was, indeed, on the prowl, obviously delighted to be single again, celebrating his newfound freedom by getting laid as much as possible. *What a coincidence!*

One-Night Stand and I get back into our clothes, which form

a bread crumb trail from the kitchen to the couch. I offer him a beer from a six-pack left behind by my recent ex, the ridiculously handsome yet ridiculously underemployed man who was *definitely not father material.* I crack open one of the cans and take a couple of sips. I don't even like beer. But here I am, pretending to be a girl who likes beer and who is also up for a one-night stand. *How fun am I? So fun!*

It is, um, shall we say, a satisfying night, on many levels. I don't think of my ex once. Rebound accomplished! I thank my date for the evening and tell him I need to go to bed, meaning "Bye-bye! Time to get the hell out!" I'm so romantic. Even though I had a surprisingly enjoyable time — yes, the hook-up was cathartic — I just want to crawl into bed with my sleeping daughter. The only warm body this girl needs in her bed is Rowan.

"I'll walk you to the door," I tell him, trying to speed up the process of getting him out. He looks surprised that I've asked him to leave. But I'm a mother! I have a sleeping child upstairs! Did he think he was going to sleep over and we were all going to sit around the table in the morning eating eggs and toast and drinking orange juice? It's time to exit.

We kiss again at the door. Neither of us mentions the leftovers. What meatloaf? But when I open the refrigerator the next morning and see the casserole dish covered with tinfoil, I can't help but laugh. Did I really offer my one-night stand meatloaf last night? Oy!

· · · · ·

It's been two days since the night of mind-blowing sex, and One-Night Stand just called and asked if I'd like him to come over after an event he has to attend. He doesn't ask about the meatloaf. You'd think he'd be curious to know if it's as good as I pumped it up to be. Nope.

He clearly is suffering from playboy-itis. But I can tell he also genuinely wants to see me again. I'm game. I appreciate his enthusiasm and initiative, and I wouldn't be averse to another go-around, if you know what I mean …

He says he can be at my door in thirty minutes.

"Come whenever," I say, all breezy. A second after we hang up, I'm upstairs, madly looking through my drawers for some cute casual clothes to change into. I'm trying to look sexy without looking like I've spent any time at all trying to look sexy. *Oh, this old thing?* is the "look" I'm going for.

The night goes very well. A few days later, we are at it again, and now we've also started talking on the phone every night, for hours, after our respective kids are asleep. We start going out for dinners. I'm starting to like him, more than a little, and not just because he is good in bed. I start looking forward to his calls and texts and our dates, though I'm still not looking to be in a relationship. Or maybe I'm kidding myself. I'm probably kidding myself. But that was never the plan with this guy.

Oh. Shit.

Are we dating? Is that what's going on here? That was not the plan! Am I even ready to date someone seriously so soon? Is he? The answer is probably no, for both of us. Aren't we supposed to take some time to reflect on our recent breakups, and where we went wrong, and what we learned from them? Meh. At this point, I don't really give enough of a shit to analyze myself. But I also can't control my brain, which is racing faster than a coked-up hamster on an exercise wheel. I can't stop fantasizing about the so many what-ifs. The more time I spend with One-Night Stand, the more I try not to think about the what-ifs of this turning into something more permanent. I start imagining our families meeting. I even start imagining what our baby would look like.

There is no Mr. Clean Magic Eraser for thought doodles, and I'm drawing images and scenarios in my mind whenever I see or think about One-Night Stand.

I am so fucked.

. . . . .

Well, shit. As it turns out, I am falling for One-Night Stand, and no amount of denial is going to change it at this point. Now what? Can I really see a future with him? I kind of do want to move forward to see where this might go. So does he, apparently.

The friends who set us up are one part happy for us and three parts cocky as fuck, as if this was their plan all along. I almost don't want to tell them just how well their set-up worked, because now they're already practically offering their services to co-emcee at our wedding. "Rebecca was rebounding. He is a notoriously good lay, so we figured they'd make a great match." What a wonderful love story! My parents would shed tears of pride.

So yeah, we are officially dating exclusively. I'm now living my what-if scenarios and allowing myself to indulge in imagining what our life might look like together. Who knew that a one-night stand and a promise of leftover meatloaf could turn out to be something ... *meaningful*?

It makes sense to invite our friends to go on a double date, and to pick up the tab to thank them, since they were our matchmakers. *Let them see the fruit of their efforts!* Their own relationship also moved at lightning speed. They started dating only a few months before we did, but they're already living together, blending their families — she with her two children and he with his two. Both share fifty/fifty custody of their respective kids with their former spouses, and they have arranged with their exes to be on the same custody schedule. At least a couple of nights a week, and every other weekend, they are completely kid-free. The other times? Well, they have four children, two his and two hers, under the same roof, living a splendid blended life.

At least that's what I thought … until our double date.

At the restaurant, after the four of us are seated and have ordered our drinks, my girlfriend and I head outside to share a cigarette. We need a few moments away from our men, who of course we are going to gossip about. We're passing the cigarette between us, and she erupts like Mount Vesuvius. Turns out that not all is splendid in blended land. Behind closed doors, behind all the social media posts of their picture-perfect blended family on some fun-looking outing with all their kids, my friend is miserable.

"We almost bailed on you guys tonight," my girlfriend admits, inhaling the cigarette madly. They are in a major stand-off tonight. They do a great job of hiding it. I seriously had no clue. "We haven't said one word to each other in two or three days now." My girlfriend, as always, looks beautiful. But tonight she does look bummed out. "I don't want to get into it right now," she answers when I ask her what the hell is going on. "It's too long and complicated. I'll tell you some other time … when we're alone."

Meanwhile, One-Night-Stand-turned-Boyfriend and I are busy being blissfully, deliriously, disgustingly happy. We are that couple that has posted numerous barf-worthy photos of us kissing and of me sitting on his lap at candlelit dinners. In this day and age, if you don't post photographs of how fucking happy you are in your relationship, does the relationship really even exist? Though, given the bombshell my friend just dropped, it clearly doesn't actually mean anything, either.

After dinner, we head back to my place, where we continue to drink and share a joint in my backyard. It's a beautiful night, the kind of warm summer evening when you should be sitting in your backyard and drinking with friends. We are all drunk

and now we are stoned too. Our friends, thanks to the flow-
ing alcohol at dinner, are speaking to each other again. Sort of.
Boyfriend and I exchange WTF glances as they constantly throw
casual digs at each other. They're not as subtle as they think
they are. Maybe they don't care to try to be subtle. All I know
is, Boyfriend and I feel like we're in the middle of two smiling
assassins, waiting for the next verbal bullet to be shot, as we try
to laugh it all off, take cover, and not get hit in the crossfire. I tell
myself their bickering is just how their relationship is. Who am
I to judge? Maybe this is their foreplay. It wouldn't be the first
time that a volatile relationship actually worked for a couple.
For many of my long-married friends, volatility seems to be the
foundation of their relationship.

Still, shit is awkward tonight. Boyfriend and I don't want to
be spectators to their foreplay, if that's what this is. We are beyond blissfully happy, damn it! They are a total buzzkill.

Eventually, they're gone, back to their own home, which is
really *his* home. My girlfriend has shared with me that he always
annoyingly seems to be reminding her of this fact, much like
when that red check engine light turns on every time you start
your car, and it has for months, and any time anyone sits in the
passenger seat, they can't help but point it out and announce,
"Do you know your check engine light is on? You should really
get that checked out." *Of course* I know the check engine light
is on! Yours isn't? Likewise, my friend doesn't need a constant
reminder of whose house she lives in. She moved in with him!
She's not an idiot. She signed a cohabitation agreement, which
clearly states that she has no rights to the property.

I'm relieved the night is over. It was all so fucking awkward.

"That was really uncomfortable. I feel like I need a shower.
I feel dirty," I say to Boyfriend after they leave. "Did you notice
how they were arguing all night?"

"Yeah, I'm not sure what's going on there," he says, pulling me onto his lap and giving me a long kiss. I have a gut suspicion that blending households has resulted in a slight change of status in their relationship. When did they start bickering like two shrill Yorkshire terriers?

Maybe I am a little smug now, too. Boyfriend and I send nightly poems to each other, which, unlike that shit movie we saw on our first date, are so bad they are good. I'm embarrassed to share that, on a night while he's out playing poker with his friends, I send him this high-quality poetry:

> *You are about to play a game*
> *I'm realizing life without you would be very lame*
> *I miss your smile*
> *Thank god I can dial*
> *Because your voice calms me*
> *Like a sunset over the sea*
> *I hope you win big tonight*
> *I wish even more we never fight*
> *With you I only want happiness*
> *And every day one big kiss*
> *Go forth and play poker*
> *When you're with me, you can play poke-her (me)*
> *With your big hard cock*
> *We definitely need to get a lock*
> *I love you the most*
> *So let's make a toast*
> *To US ... always and forever. xo Me.*

I'm fucking mortified, both as a writer and a human. I don't see a Pulitzer Prize for poetry anywhere in my future. At least it's not a haiku! Though, who doesn't love a good haiku?

But it's all true. Boyfriend and I have yet to have our first argument. While we send each other nightly barf-inducing poems, we're still just dating. We haven't discussed next steps. The idea of moving in together hasn't come up in any conversation, even though I'm now so in love, I want to inhale him. But there are a few steps between where we are and packing up a moving truck. I haven't met his children yet. He hasn't really hung out with my daughter. Our children haven't met each other. We are still acting like freewheeling teenagers, spending as much time as we can together in our blissful little bubble of two on the nights we are both kid-free. So maybe I am a little smug, with my new relationship, but at the same time, when I think of our bickering friends, I'm not all like, "This will never happen to us." I'm old enough, and have dated enough, to know that life has a funny way of proving us wrong. But clearly we're not fighters. Right? Because we haven't yet, so that's a good sign!

I am finally admitting to myself, and to Boyfriend, that I'm falling in love. Of course, I wait until he says the words before I do. I'm not *that* out of my mind with love. At the same time, though, I kind of am.

After that fateful night, when my friend's shit relationship makes me see how awesome mine is, Boyfriend and I go full steam ahead with our blissful union. There are regular sleepovers now. We spend as many weekends together as we can, just the two of us, when our kids aren't with us. We set up camp in his bedroom, eating junk food, then fucking, then watching a movie, then eating more junk food, then fucking again, then watching another movie. *Rinse, repeat.*

This is a bigger deal than it sounds, me sleeping over and waking up in someone else's bed. I rarely, if ever, slept at my previous boyfriend's apartment in the three years we were on and off together. I like my bed. But mostly I like sleeping with my daughter beside me. I like waking up with my daughter in my bed. Also, I'm not great with change. I could eat the same three meals for the rest of my life without ever getting bored. I know what makes me comfortable and satisfied. I very, *very* rarely mess with the formula I've figured out to ensure my happiness.

But Boyfriend is fucking that all up ... in a good way, mind you. I'm getting to the point of embracing change. I want to meet his children. I want my daughter to get to know him and him to get to know her, beyond the spider-monkey episode on our first date. I'm eager for our children to meet. I want to meet his parents. I want him to meet mine. It doesn't even occur to me how crazy it is, the list of combinations and permutations of who has to meet whom, who has to like each other, and who has to get along for this whole mash-up of families to work. It's not even on my radar.

I must really like him.

· TWO ·

It's move-in day! Boyfriend and I have decided to blend homes. Today, my house becomes *our* house. Rowan, my daughter, who has been the only child in this home ever, will now have two other girls to share her space with. There will be a new adult male figure in the home. I'm giddy, like a six-year-old experiencing her first pony ride, as I wait for the moving truck to arrive. We are blending! My bed will now be our bed. My kitchen, everyone's. There will be other people's food in my fridge, other people cooking at my stove, using my laundry, walking my halls, using my bathrooms, watching my television, sitting on my couch ...

Ten minutes later, I'm desperately looking for my stash of Ativan, prescribed to me by my doctor for use on an "as-needed basis."

Boyfriend has rented a U-Haul, and I see him backing it into the driveway, from the living room window where I'm standing, for the last time, in *my* house. I'm there, surrounded only by my things, in pure, clutter-free, blissful quiet.

It's kind of a turn-on to see him manoeuvre the truck, which, I'll soon see, is stuffed to the brim. *It's all happening*, I think. *It's happening!*

And then I think, *What have I done? What are we doing? Where's that damn bottle of Ativan?* Seriously, where the fuck is it? It's "as needed" right now.

I wish I could remember the moment or conversation in which Boyfriend and I decided that it was time to live together and blend households, but there really was no ah-ha moment. We didn't sit down and have a long meeting to hash out issues that could arise if and when we were to move in together. There was no sitting down and talking about the logistics, no discussion of how it would affect the kids, no dialogue over who would pay for what, no talk of disciplining each other's children or if the ugly leather chair he is so attached to would be better left on the side of the road. You'd think we'd lay out ground rules and expectations and financial responsibilities and discuss the pros and cons and all of the fun logistics. Or that we'd discuss, possibly with the help of professionals, how to help our children adjust.

Of course, none of that has happened. Because we are so in love, none of that seems to matter. It will all just, you know, naturally work out. There is one enormous reason he is moving in. But, mostly, moving in together just feels right. We are both still in a happy daze at the speed at which our relationship has moved, now both literally and figuratively. We are in love! I've hung out with his two children numerous times. He's hung with my daughter. We have all hung out together. My daughter and I have spent weekends sleeping over at his home, located outside the city in the suburbs, where every house kind of looks the same and there's a Taco Bell on every corner. I've seen Boyfriend in father mode. He's seen me mothering.

One of the reasons I think Boyfriend and I also both came to the conclusion that we wanted to live together was because driving to see each other was time consuming. The planning of getting together was becoming more challenging as we tried to carve out even more time to spend together, fitting that in with all of our children's schedules and activities. Might as well make it more convenient! It was becoming ludicrous figuring out how to see each other as much as possible.

> *I know you're probably sleeping, but I thought I would send you a quick email to go over our days this week. Anal, I know, but it seems to work well. Lol. Wednesday? Free after work, so maybe yoga class — would love it and need it. Thursday night I have the kids and they have soccer. Friday? I know you like to sleep early so I can either come to your house Friday night with the girls and we can lay low and go to bed at a decent time or the girls and I can just stay at my place. Saturday? Wide open. Would be nice to obviously spend the day, after Rowan's ballet, and evening together, with all the girls and the dog. Sunday? All we have is my daughter's soccer practice at 2 p.m. so we can do yoga near my place if you guys sleep over on Saturday. Oh and one more thing, I am so totally and utterly in love with you and I am so looking forward to tomorrow night. I can't wait!*

This was our life before we moved in together — emails from Boyfriend trying to find a sliver of time in our ridiculous lives to see each other.

Our relationship has progressed so far (and accelerated so fast), it just seems dumb not to take the logical next step at our age: sharing real estate. Like I've mentioned, there is a huge reason he's really moving in, which I'll get to in a minute. But, now, we can see each other every day! We can wake up next to each other and go to sleep together. I am genuinely euphoric that Boyfriend is moving in, with his children here 50 percent of the time. I'm overjoyed that I've found my soulmate, or at the very least someone who I actually want to live with full-time. I've lived in this house, alone with my daughter, for about five years. Boyfriend is the only man, after my split-up with my daughter's father, I've ever even *entertained* the idea of living with.

And so we are blending households. But my high spirits are overshadowed by fear and a little bit of dread when Boyfriend opens the back of the U-Haul and I can see all that he's brought — an entire fucking household. I am aghast and alarmed. Is Boyfriend a hoarder? I already have a fully furnished, clutter-free house. I take in all the stuff he brought from the house he had been renting and had fully furnished after his separation, and I feel my heart start to pound madly, as if I've just finished a half-marathon. Suddenly, it's hard to breathe. Where is all his stuff going to go? Where is all his daughters' stuff going to go? Do we really need three microwaves and two kitchen tables and eighteen spatulas? Does anyone?

While Boyfriend and his mom figure out the logistics of blending two households, unloading and unpacking box after box, I make up a lame excuse to get the fuck away from the madness of moving. I'm riding on a roller coaster of emotions — from excitement to fear, delight, and worry. My mood seems to swing faster than an Olympic gymnast on the high bar. Even though this is such a monumental day — blending families is a big fucking deal and I should probably stick around to help — I know I have to escape and leave Boyfriend and his saintly mother to figure out where to fit all his stuff in my house, which now will become *our* house.

To be honest, "my" house is really only *half* mine. The other half belongs to my ex, who pays the mortgage, it being his daughter's primary residence. I'm sure Rowan's father would prefer that we were moving into a house that Boyfriend and I paid for on our own. Why, after all, should my ex pay for Boyfriend and his children to live in a home that is half his? I may have been romantically challenged in the past, but I know this much about men: they have egos, especially when the issue is tied to money. Let's be honest. How much a man makes or has in his portfolio is directly tied to his self-esteem, whereas a woman's self-esteem is often tied to how well her relationships are going.

Except, oddly, for Boyfriend. He doesn't seem to care that he'll be living in a house he doesn't technically have any rights to and never will. I mean, we never signed a cohabitation agreement like our friends did. We will get around to it, but do we really need one? This relationship is for keeps!

Long after he moves in, we will both realize that you can never truly be the king of someone else's castle, even if it's just half a castle.

Figuring out how to fit two fully furnished houses into one house is beyond daunting, like having to sit on a suitcase while someone else zips it up because you couldn't help but buy too many souvenirs on your vacation and you're not checking your bag, *no matter what*. My emotions simply can't bear witness to what Boyfriend and his mom are going to do. So I disappear — not admitting to Boyfriend that I'd rather chew on broken glass than watch this — and head to a coffee shop. For the first time it hits me that this really is going to be a huge change. It probably should have occurred to me before now, but ... love!

By now, Boyfriend knows I'm not exactly good with change, so he understands my need to escape. So, yes, Moving Day is harder than I thought it would be. For a person who resists change, this is a lot to take in. Blending our families, with new routines to follow and new people in my territory, will not just involve an adjustment period. Change will open new wounds, which will have a ripple effect on everyone else involved.

Still, we are blending households. We are blending families. We are throwing a shit ton of random ingredients into a small appliance, pressing the "on" button, and crossing our fingers and toes that it doesn't turn into shit. Although Boyfriend has not yet proposed and we haven't walked down an aisle or made any official vows, we are in this for the long haul, from this day forward, for better or for worse, to love and to cherish. We are now *for better ... or for blended.* Plus, I'm pregnant. So, of course, we want to live together.

·   ·   ·   ·

My ex, because he's the father of my child, needs to know about this huge life development that's going to affect his daughter. Oh, and he should also know that I'm pregnant. I might not want to forget to mention that. I can only sit in this coffee shop for so long without feeling antsy. My emotions are all over the place, and my life feels like that dream where you show up to an exam having never attended a single class. I'm flying blind, and I could really use a cheat sheet. I'm both beyond excited to start this new chapter in our lives and, I admit, also terrified. Not just about how my life is changing. I'm also terrified of the fact that other people's lives are changing. And they don't even know it yet.

I need to call my ex. I need to call Boyfriend's ex.

I have been procrastinating over making these two calls since the day Boyfriend and I made this decision for everyone. I've always worked better under deadlines anyway, even if it's in a deadline-induced panic. Now the deadline has arrived, like seeing "Final Notice" on a bill. I've put it off as long as I can, but once I get home, it will be official. I have to break the news to my ex that another man is moving into his daughter's house, along with two other children.

Long before "positive co-parenting" became part of our societal vernacular, Rowan's father and I have practised it from the day we parted ways. We are way ahead of our time. I often join them for dinner when he's in town to visit Rowan, and we sit beside each other during her recitals and graduations, even saving seats for each other. We have always made our daughter our priority.

This should be interesting.

· · · · ·

I sit in my car, which I've parked on a quiet side street. I'm nervous as fuck. Thanks for nothing, Ativan. I have no clue how my daughter's father will respond to my call, but I hope he takes it better than I did when I saw Boyfriend's entire house jammed into one large truck and had to leave for fear of having a breakdown.

Much like the bulge of fat that has started to form around my midsection thanks to the baby growing inside me, Boyfriend moving in is not something I could have hidden much longer, anyway. Nor do I want to. I love my daughter, and by extension I will always love her father. He deserves to know. Besides, it's happy news that Boyfriend and I have decided to blend families and are having a baby! But I feel like puking, and not because of morning sickness. While I'm thrilled to have found someone who I actually want to live with, *who I'm having a baby with*, I worry Rowan's father may have a different opinion on the choices I've made. I almost feel like I should have asked his permission before Boyfriend and I got knocked up and decided to blend. Not actually, but kind of, which is ridiculous since I'm an adult and we haven't been together in nearly a decade. My loyalty to my daughter's father will irk Boyfriend after we blend houses — it undervalues my relationship with Boyfriend, he will imply — but for now he is just happy to be with me.

Fuck it. I need to just press the call — Oh shit. It's ringing. I should have prepared a speech or at least some talking points.

"Hey, Beck, what's up?" he asks.

Deep breath, Rebecca. He'll be thrilled. You have nothing to worry about, I tell myself.

"I have something to tell you," I say, and then I immediately blurt out that Boyfriend is moving in. "I'm also pregnant," I add, like it's an afterthought, attempting to play down the hugeness of this announcement.

If there is a better or more ironic time for a pregnant pause, I'm not sure when that would be. A deafening silence follows. It feels like a lifetime before he finally responds.

"Wow, Beck. Um, congratulations?" he says, sounding shocked.

I'm pretty damn sure this was *not* the phone call he was expecting to get at eleven in the morning while he was working in his office. I hear a catch in his throat.

"I don't know what else to say," he says.

Fuck. Neither do I.

I can tell he's choked up, and not with tears of joy for me. Of course, blending families is also going to affect him. A million thoughts are probably racing through his head right now. There will now be another adult male in the house, a man who will, unlike her biological dad, see his daughter every day. How could this not affect him? How could he not worry that another man may form a bond with his only child? His daughter will also have a new baby sibling in a few months and two sisters living with her part-time. This is a big deal for me, but it's a big deal for him, too.

"You'll always be Rowan's father and she loves you so much and that will never change," I say, not only because I believe it, but also because there's no fucking manual called *How to Tell Your Ex that a New Man Will Be Living in the Same House as His Kid and You Are Also Pregnant with That Man's Child.*

I don't know how to protect him from this. This is a choice I've made for him. The last thing I want is to hurt him. So why do I feel like I'm the one who got sucker-punched? It's that damn catch in his throat. I think I've crushed him, and it's killing me. I blink back tears. I'm pretty sure he's doing the same.

Ex doesn't ask about the logistics or if Boyfriend is chipping in to live in the house that he half owns. I'm kind of grateful for that, given that I don't even know the answer yet. I'm not totally irresponsible, though. I did have my lawyer draw up a cohabitation agreement. So I have one, hidden away in one of my purses, high on a shelf in my closet. I said I *have* one. I didn't say Boyfriend *knows* anything about it. I asked my lawyer — the lawyer who handled my divorce, who is the human equivalent of a pit bull — to draw one up because isn't that what people do nowadays, whether it's a first-time marriage, a common-law marriage, or a second-chance relationship?

It seems a growing number of divorced men don't seem to mind moving into a woman's house when blending, because our self-esteem is also based on how well our partners treat us.

"No, we did not discuss money before we blended," one of my male friends admits when I ask him why he and his kids moved into his second wife's home instead of finding a new house. "I don't know. Given that my wife came from a very wealthy family and a very bad first marriage, her focus wasn't on my ability to provide financially, as much as on my being a good father figure, a good husband, and someone who had a stable job." Being a healthy role model for her children and a good husband were much higher priorities for his new wife. He admits, too, that from a financial contribution standpoint, for the lifestyle that she was used to living, it would be unreasonable, if not impossible, for her to expect any man who isn't also very wealthy to be her equal when it came to finances in their home.

When my lawyer sent over a draft of the cohabitation agreement by email and I didn't immediately respond, she wrote back and insisted I get Boyfriend to sign it. I promised her I would get it done. That was weeks ago. Now she's stopped reaching out to me. Her accountants, however, have not.

I think the ex needs to process all this information that I've just thrown to him out of left field. "Okay, well, thanks for telling me. Congratulations," he says again. "We'll speak soon." I can tell he is eager to end this conversation, as if I were suddenly contagious and he could catch a virus from me over the phone, four thousand miles away.

After the phone call ends, I allow myself to sob — the ugly kind of sob where tears seem to be coming out of your ears and nose, and after you look like you've been punched in the face and also have pink eye — even though I *think* my ex is genuine with his well wishes. I should be overjoyed that he reacted so well. If he was upset, or angry, or anything other than happy for me, he spared me from knowing. Ex went easy on me, and for that, I am grateful. Many others can't say the same.

Blending families affects people you'd never think of instantly, like our exes, the other biological parents of our children. Yes, it's a little late for this lightbulb moment, yet here I am, more concerned with Rowan's dad's feelings than I am about the changes Boyfriend is about to face as well.

I cry because Rowan's father is a great dad and I don't want him to feel, even for a second, that there is a risk he will be forgotten, or less loved, by his daughter. I cry because I think the fact another man gets to see his daughter every day must sting, and I'm empathetic to that. I cry because I am reminded that we didn't work out, because I was young and stupid. I cry because, in many ways, I still love him. I cry because four hundred times the normal amount of estrogen is coursing through my fucking body, and things that would never have bothered me pre-pregnancy are now sending me into full-blown meltdowns. I cry because by now, that ugly brown leather chair has probably found a place in my house. Mostly, I cry because I'm relieved Ex now knows.

It's not just that three more humans (oh, and one dog), all complete strangers to him, moving into my house affects my ex. Boyfriend and I have been planning this move for a little while now, but today, right now, at this second, it has hit me like a ton of bricks — the gravity of what we're doing. It's not just a U-Haul filled with crap. It's not just a house that is being shared. It's our lives. And those lives started before we met. There were partners — partners who we share children with.

Even though I'm allergic to change, I'm ready to take this challenge on, blaming my pregnancy hormones again for getting irritated over a chair and not being able to handle watching the process of Boyfriend moving in and for bawling uncontrollably in my car. Anyway, it's a little too late to turn back now. Still, I can't stop thinking about that catch in my daughter's father's voice. It will haunt me, not just in the following days, but for years.

· · · · ·

The only people Boyfriend and I have told about the baby are our children and our parents (and now Rowan's dad). We want to keep it a secret until we're out of the first trimester. I'm superstitious, like many women. We've asked the kids to keep our secret, though when we are all together we spend hours deliriously discussing potential baby names, wondering if it will be a girl or a boy, talking about whether we want a girl or a boy, and planning how we should decorate the baby's room. Boyfriend and I, it turns out, are fucking living in a delusional world, one where young girls can actually keep secrets.

Since I've already made one uncomfortable phone call, I figure why not make 'em all?! I had asked Boyfriend for his ex-wife's phone number, explaining that I don't just want to tell her about the pregnancy. I also think it would be a kind gesture — an olive branch, if you will — to invite her over to the house where her two children will be living half of the time. I figure that would be the respectful thing to do. She should hear that I'm pregnant from me first. It's better than coming from Boyfriend, who can barely remain civil when talking to her these days.

It doesn't occur to me that news of me being knocked up by her ex might not land well. Unlike my daughter's father and me, who managed to work out a separation agreement via our lawyers over lunch, Boyfriend is still in an ugly battle with his soon-to-be-ex-wife. My pit bull divorce lawyer is the one who first suggested that I call his ex, in the hope it will move their divorce along quicker. She thinks if I call Boyfriend's ex, it may make things better, if she and I can at least be civil to each other and on the same page about raising her children. I should have remembered that the advice came from a lawyer, not a therapist. *Ugh.*

I want Boyfriend's ex to know that if she ever has a problem, she can always call me to discuss it. And, if she's ever worried about her children when they are with us, she is welcome to reach out. Now that I've got telling my ex out of the way, you'd think I'd be well practised and more confident making this call. I'm not. When she picks up, I say my name, knowing I sound like a bumbling idiot. She knows *exactly* who I am.

"First, I just want to let you know that I'm pregnant," I start. Seems like a reasonable way to begin the conversation, no? Radio silence follows.

"Yes, I know," she responds.

Another pregnant pause. I hate pregnant pauses! So I continue with my speech.

"Also, I wanted to know if you'd like to come over to the house to see where and how your girls are living when they aren't with you," I continue.

My voice wobbles. I'm nervous as fuck. My heart is beating a mile a minute. This is the same feeling I get when a police officer pulls me over for speeding or because of my outdated sticker on my licence plate. As with any dealings with the police, I feel the need to immediately say I'm sorry, agree with everything they say, and cry. I just know the rest of this call is gonna suck. This woman, after all, has the power to make our lives hell. Why do I feel like apologizing? I didn't steal Boyfriend away from her. I just hooked up with him and am starting a new life with her ex-husband. But she sounds ... I'm not sure. Pissed? Annoyed? Aggravated?

I don't hold my breath waiting for a hearty congratulations. She seems as interested in seeing the house and in my pregnancy as a child in the back seat of the car on the twentieth hour of a road trip. Disapproval seeps through the phone. Or maybe it's not disapproval. Maybe it's just a total lack of fucks. Either way, I'm not expecting her to show up with a bottle of wine for us to share any time soon. There will be no future scenes of us leaning over my kitchen counter, laughing about Boyfriend's quirks.

I find it slightly bizarre she seems to have no inclination to take me up on my invitation to see where her girls will be living part-time. I kind of admire her for not seeming to care. But I'm equally baffled and dumbfounded. If she's looking to hurt me, her weapon is indifference.

If my ex invited me to meet a serious girlfriend, one who was going to move in with him and who would be a big part of my daughter's life, there's no way I'd turn down the invitation. I'm way too curious. Why wouldn't Boyfriend's ex-wife want to visit so she could have the opportunity to size me up and judge me? Doesn't she have any feelings about the changes that her children are going through? If she does, she doesn't share them with me.

"When we first blended," a friend tells me, "we constantly argued about the amount of phone calls his ex made to him daily." I hear this a lot. So maybe I should be relieved, if anything, about her indifference.

"Well, the invitation is always open," I say when it's clear the call is going nowhere, and like that, the call is over. I'm pretty sure she pressed "end" before I said "bye." Whatever. I did the best I could. I followed my lawyer's advice. I was attempting to be the Bigger Person.

"The truest thing about blended families is that saying, 'You're marrying the ex,'" my girlfriend tells me over the phone after I relay the mostly one-sided conversation I had with Boyfriend's ex. "I realized very early on that if I was going to have a happy, easy family life, I was going to have to find a way to get her to trust me. I wouldn't say we're best friends now, but we are friendly and respectful. It's been hugely helpful in opening up lines of communication after what was a very painful divorce for both my husband and his ex."

At least I can say I tried, right? Maybe she'll like me some-day. Today, though, is not that day.

If nothing else came out of that call, one very valuable lesson did: do not tell Boyfriend's children anything that I don't want their mother to know.

·   ·   ·   ·

While Boyfriend didn't exactly offer to chip in with some sort of rent or buy out my ex's half of the house before moving in, I haven't said anything about it either. I'm still wrapping my head around what we are going to do with five couches and nine televisions, where the fuck he'll store his clothes, and where the hell I'm going to hide his poker table so it's not in the kitchen.

I *assume* he'll start offering to share the gas bills, the hydro bills, and the cable and internet bills and contribute in some sort of monetary way now that we're living together. But I'm not the only one, thank *gawd*, who didn't discuss money before blending households, which will later come back to bite both Boyfriend and me in the ass. I know I sound totally irresponsible, but I'm not the only one I know who avoided this topic like the plague before blending.

"We didn't discuss too much about money when we got married," admits one of my friends. She has three children and her partner has two children, and they all moved into her house. "We knew we were going to be living in my house, as it was much bigger than his." Like me, she admits she "probably" should have had more conversations. "But I definitely was upfront about my expectations. For example, a nanny and a housekeeper and getting away a couple of times a year is not considered a luxury to me, but a necessity. There was some culture shock, as he came from a more modest background," she says to me.

Boyfriend, too, comes from a more modest life, which I really believe is situational, as he led me to believe it was. He spent thousands of dollars to furnish an entire house after he moved out. Plus, his contentious divorce is still ongoing, so he and his bank account have taken a huge financial hit dealing with lawyers and court dates and what he perceives as an unreasonable ex. Besides, Boyfriend makes a pretty good case that if I moved in with him and I couldn't afford to live where he lived, he wouldn't make me pay any rent. I completely believe him. For richer or for poorer, right?

Like my friend's husband, Boyfriend really can't afford to live in my area. The property taxes alone, which I pay for, are outrageous. I need a weekly gardener, for example, because, while my house is not huge, the property is. I also have a nanny, another cost that is new to him. Should he start chipping in for the nanny, who takes care of Rowan but now will be making dinners for Boyfriend, as well as his daughters when they stay with us, and doing their laundry and cleaning up their messes around the house?

And, like my friend, travelling for me is a necessity, not a luxury, unlike for Boyfriend and his children. The truth is, I really have no idea what he earns, and I don't ask, and he doesn't share it with me. (I assume Boyfriend's ego won't allow him to tell me.) I know he has a job, which I can't describe, with employees. I know he makes money. But his lawyer bills are growing as quickly as weeds and putting him into debt. But don't all couples, blended or not, have to negotiate money and contributions based on their individual situations? We're not *that* unique.

"Ugh. I hear you. I think the biggest blended family money argument we've had was over paying for the lawyer's fees when he went to court with his ex-wife over their son's schooling," a friend tells me much later about her husband. "His ex-wife wanted their son to go private — her parents were paying the fees — and my husband, who is a deeply principled social democrat, went to court to try to put him in the state system. He ended up spending a year's worth of private school fees trying to keep his son out of private school — and lost! From then on, I told him if he wanted to take his ex-wife to court, he could defend himself. I don't want our household income being spent on court battles."

And neither do I. So I loan Boyfriend $20,000 to help him pay off his lawyer's fees, which will also later bring up a lot of resentment on my part. But not yet.

I truly believe Boyfriend. If my daughter and I had moved into his house, he wouldn't ask me to pay for anything. I truly believe that if I were the one who needed money for my lawyer's bills, he would help me if he could. Why wouldn't I believe him? We're in love! Love is blind. Love also makes us completely foolish. But, again, like my girlfriend, I think of Boyfriend moving in as a small investment that will yield a lot of interest, just in other ways that don't have anything to do with money directly. He could help with driving my daughter to school and her activities. He could take over the snow shovelling. He could make dinners, since he enjoys cooking and I enjoy eating. I expect this particular bonus to pay off with dividends, especially now that I'm pregnant with his child.

This baby, after all, will free us from all potential conflicts about "mine" and "his" because we are going to share a human, so who cares, at this moment, who is going to pay for what or what is fair? Mostly, I give Boyfriend a free pass on chipping in with the mortgage, because talking about money is such a downer and I'm sure we'll just figure it out later, as we go along, as we have done throughout our entire relationship. Contrary to what experts say about planning and discussing money matters before blending households — *Create a dual budget! Joint accounts or separate accounts? Will you make all future financial decisions together?* — having no plans in place actually works for us. We had no plans to date, for example, and look at us now!

I also just feel kind of guilty, to be honest, that his life and his children's lives are changing far more drastically than mine and my daughter's. Boyfriend now has to drop off and pick up his two children numerous times a week at their mother's house, outside the city. This means that Boyfriend will spend hours in his car, including having to get out of the house at 6 a.m. on school days, because they go to school near their mother's house. It's no picnic for him. His old back problems flare up from sitting in a car for so many hours every week.

I may have given up my closet space and opened my doors, but he's given up a lot, too, by moving into my house. So have his girls. They now not only have to share a room when they stay with us, unlike at their mother's home, where they each have their own room, and unlike my daughter, who has her own room, but they also don't have any friends in this new neighbourhood they'll be living in part-time. Plus, they have to wrap their heads around the fact that their own father will be seeing my daughter and me every day, and they now have another sister. And they'll soon have the sibling currently baking in my belly. It's a lot of change for me. But it's a lot of change for everyone. The one room that remains the same is my daughter's bedroom, but that doesn't mean she, too, isn't affected by Boyfriend moving in.

"Don't you remember, Mommy?" my daughter asks me, years later, when I ask her if she remembers how she felt when Boyfriend moved in. "You bought one of those pill cases that have the days on them, the ones old people use to organize their medicine every day? You would put brown M&M's in the days that I still got to sleep with you and red M&M's in the days I couldn't sleep with you, so I knew what days I could still sleep with you."

Kids remember things like their fourth-favourite reptile, but also when they realized they could no longer sleep with you every night because the bed you shared would now be occupied by someone else, someone Mommy loves, too.

For years, my daughter and I have slept together, so the biggest change for her is not being able to sleep with me every night.

Boyfriend will learn immediately after he moves in that I still will want to sleep with my daughter, now climbing into her bed, instead of her sleeping in what was just my bed, a couple of times a week, on brown M&M days. Boyfriend knows my daughter and I are super tight thanks to living together, just us two, for years. I don't waver on this, even though Boyfriend thinks she's way too old to still be sleeping with me. I tell him that she doesn't *have* to sleep with me — she goes on sleepovers and to overnight camp — but that we *both* like to sleep together.

"It's not like she's going to still want to sleep with me when she's eighteen," I tell Boyfriend. "Plus, it's just a couple times a week." Without realizing it, in a way, I choose my daughter over him, right from the start.

Change is scary. What's even scarier is regret, and I don't want to regret him moving in or for my daughter to regret my decision for us to live together, so, yes, I continue to sleep with my daughter a couple of times a week. I cherish brown M&M days. Even if Boyfriend doesn't get it.

Money talk? Whatever. Sleeping with my daughter, occasionally, after Boyfriend moves in? Whatever. What can I say? Being pregnant kind of stops every cognitive function, other than joy.

. . . . .

It takes eight hours to unload all of Boyfriend's stuff. It takes us three weeks to unpack and find room for all of it. But, now, finally, it's done. Our — OMG, *our* — house is now an eclectic mixture of my modern furnishings mashed in with his bachelor-pad furnishings. I'd describe the new decor as "flea market." The only other room, aside from my daughter's bedroom, that looks mostly like its previous self is my master bedroom. The rest of my house has very, very visibly become ours. I'm so deeply in love with Boyfriend that I don't even fight about the fugly leather chair. I let him keep it. This is what happens, I assume, when you first blend households. You compromise. He hates my fabulous modern but totally uncomfortable couch. I hate that fucking leather chair. I'm adamant the couch stays. He's adamant the chair stays. So we all win! And lose.

Bonus Children's beds and dressers are now in the large finished basement. I wonder if they think it is unfair that Rowan gets to keep her solitary space. But Bonus Children also have a steam shower down there, which is nicer than the washroom Boyfriend and I will share. I call it a wash. We are now all living together in one quasi-organized household. The U-Haul has long since left the driveway, the useless bottle of Ativan has been tucked safely away, and my heart rate has returned to normal. Everything is blissful and wonderful, and we are finally one big, happy blended family. Everything feels perfect.

The baby, too, baking in my belly will also essentially bond not just Boyfriend and me together for infinity, but our children as well. We really are for better or for blended. Meanwhile, the cohabitation agreement is still in my purse, not touched and not signed. Stupid, glorious love!

· THREE ·

Boyfriend's reverse vasectomy cost $5,000. I paid for it with a credit card. Even I was surprised when I saw the word "Approved" light up on the machine. This is, by far, the strangest and largest "item" that I've paid for with a credit card.

Baby Holt joins our blended family a few months after we all start to settle in. He is the blessing that we decided to add to the mix pretty much right away, because of course we couldn't wait to solidify our family bond with a relationship we all share.

The beginning of my relationship with Boyfriend coincided with my uterus crying out and my ovaries being all, "We're still here, doing our thing. Just saying!" I would pass pregnant women on the street and think, "Need another. Need another." I was like a feral cat, and whenever Boyfriend would cum in me, I couldn't help but feel disappointed. I knew there was no way I was going to get pregnant. He'd had a vasectomy after his second child and was sure he was done.

But then we met and fell in love. Maybe we were lured into a false sense of security. Whatever the reason, Boyfriend and I, in our infinite wisdom, thought, Hey, you know what we need? A baby!

It was really *my* genius idea. I blame the weeping ovaries. Things could only get better with the addition of another character in our sitcom, right? The more the merrier! Rowan exits the scene from time to time to visit her dad. Boyfriend's girls are with their mother half of the time. But Baby Holt? He would be the constant. Holt wouldn't leave. Holt wouldn't have *other people*. Boyfriend and I would be it. Holt would be the one and only entity in the walls of the house that was both of ours equally.

· · · · ·

Yes, having a baby was my idea. In fact, when Boyfriend and I were falling in love — the sweet spot of any relationship — I gave him an ultimatum. After only about three months of dating, I told him that I wanted another baby and that I *would* be having another baby, with or without him. I remember when I told him, early one morning, after he slept over. The kids were with their other parents, so we were alone, and I think I startled him with the idea of having a baby. I thought two things. First, I thought he'd spew out the coffee I had made him. Second, I didn't think I'd ever see him again. I truly didn't. Yet even after I told him what I wanted and gave him, for lack of a better word, a "deadline," he didn't immediately race out of my house, making up an excuse to leave as quickly as humanly possible. He finished his coffee and went to work. I don't even remember him saying, "I'll think about it," but he must have said something.

Still, I bit my lip the entire day, wondering if I'd ever hear from him again, let alone see him. But he did call again. He didn't ghost me. We were still dating exclusively. As I had told him, I wouldn't bring it up, and I didn't, somehow finding the strength and willpower to not ask him if he'd thought about it. His answer, I knew, would be up to him, and he knew what I wanted.

"I'll give you nine months to think about it," I'd said. "And I promise to not bring it up again until you make a decision either way." And I didn't, not once mentioning, "So … about that baby?"

I don't like using the word "ultimatum" because it sounds threatening or like some pushy demand and makes me seem like a batshit wacko. It wasn't like that at all. I was just stating the facts. And the fact was, I wanted another baby, and, therefore, I should be dating someone who would be open to having a child with me. There's nothing wrong with a girl who knows what she wants. Many women are having children on their own. Why couldn't I? I was upfront and honest about what I wanted. I didn't want to waste my time on the wrong person for what I wanted for my future. What is it the young people say? *There's no shame to my game.*

But it's not just women who are giving their men an ultimatum to have another baby, when it comes to blending families. These days, it's also men.

One of my friends who blended and already had three biological children married a very nice man with two children, so between them, they had five children. Even though my friend swore she would *never* have another baby ever again, she was on the receiving end of someone peppering her with baby talk. Her husband was the one pressing my friend to have a child with him, and he was even more adamant about it than me, or at least equally as adamant.

"From the start, he wanted to have a son together. How did he know it would be a son? Anyway, I was adamantly against it, to the extent that I had a calendar reminder for myself to send a weekly text to him begging him to have a vasectomy," she tells me when I ask why, or what, changed her mind. "He'd always say to me, 'No, I'm not going in for that appointment, because I still think you will give me a son. As soon as you do, I will.'"

She tells me that her husband would bring up having another baby every six months or so, and she kept saying no.

"My husband is an amazing father, like one in a billion, and for years I wanted to do it for him, but I kept saying I couldn't do it unless I wanted it too."

So what eventually changed her mind? Well, first, she came with demands and negotiated. "Things were more calm," she tells me. "I said, 'Let's try,' provided we had a baby nurse until the baby slept through the night. And I guess I liked the idea of creating a baby with someone I love so much." So, with the promise of a night nurse, and because she loved him and knew he wanted a baby, and because it seemed like all the kids had settled into their blended lives, she folded. She, too, was lured in by a sense of security. It took two years to convince her, but they now have six children between the two of them.

.   .   .   .

Flash forward three months, and I am enjoying reading a book, lying by the pool on a Jamaican vacation, when Boyfriend comes back from a round of golf, super sweaty, with a mischievous grin and a twinkle in his beautiful blue eyes. I wonder, Did he just get a hole in one? Nope. Did he smoke some ganja? Nope.

"I want to have a baby. I'm in. I'm all in," he announces.

"What?" I say, tossing my book aside. I can't believe what I am hearing. "You want to have another baby? What made you come to that decision?" My heart starts pounding, like I think an Oscar nominee's heart would beat in those couple of seconds before they announce the winner.

The truth is, it isn't *me* who convinces Boyfriend to have another baby so we could have a child together, one who shared both our DNA.

One of the men he was paired up to golf with had remarried after divorce and had a reverse vasectomy to have a baby with his second wife. Incredibly, this random golfer was also a urologist. What are the fucking odds that Boyfriend would be paired up to golf with a divorced urologist, who spent his days looking at and operating on other men's penises, who had also had a reverse vasectomy to have a baby with his second wife? Thank you, universe! (In case you were wondering, the chance of an average golfer making a hole in one is approximately 12,500 to 1.)

"Having a baby with my second wife was the best decision I ever made," I would learn this random urologist told Boyfriend, who obviously had been chatting about us and our relationship as they golfed.

Right there and then, as we lie in a cabana, Boyfriend in his colourful and sweaty golf attire, he begins to tell me all about all the different, modern procedures he discussed with the golfing urologist to get the sperm out of him and into me. It is as if Boyfriend had suddenly become an expert on fertility. I listen as Boyfriend tells me about these state-of-the-art procedures, which all sound painful, expensive, time-consuming, and definitely *not* the Theory of Least Effort when it comes to making a baby. Much as I was all about the Theory of Least Effort back when I first hooked up with Boyfriend, I am also about the Theory of Least Effort when it comes to getting pregnant. Looking back, we may both have been suffering from heat stroke, because the easiest and quickest way — duh! — for us to get pregnant didn't come to us immediately.

"What if you just got a reverse vasectomy and we could just try making a baby, you know, the old-fashioned way?" I suggest, seemingly hours after we have discussed all other potential ways for me to get pregnant.

"Yeah, I mean, that really does sound like the easiest way," he says. Of course there is no thought about how a bio child for Boyfriend and me would integrate into our existing precious, messed-up, fuzzy blended family dynamic. I do, however, think a lot about how cute our baby would be. Would the baby look like Boyfriend, who has fair skin and gorgeous blue eyes, and who had blond hair before he went bald? Or would our baby look like my daughter and me, with our olive skin and dark hair?

"So we're really doing this?" I ask, holding myself back from getting up and screaming at the top of my lungs, "We're having a baby!" while doing a happy dance, feeling even more in love with him.

Just weeks later, after an initial consultation, I have set up a second appointment with a urologist I know from my gym for Boyfriend to have a reverse vasectomy, a procedure that takes almost five hours. His poor penis. While Boyfriend is knocked out and getting the procedure done, I sit in the waiting area, thinking of all the ways I can be a sexy nurse as he recovers. It's the least I can do.

While Boyfriend is in the recovery room, the urologist comes out to talk to me. He takes a seat beside me.

"It went well. But the majority of couples I see who want a vasectomy reversal are trying to have their first baby together after a remarriage with a younger woman who has not had children," he says. Wait, was he calling me *old*? He *was* calling me old. But it's not *not* true. I'm closer to forty than I am to thirty, so I'm well aware that getting pregnant may not happen so quickly.

"I have to warn you," the urologist continues. "It all looks good, but because of your age, coupled with the fact that he had a vasectomy twelve years ago, it could take up to a year for you to get pregnant." This is not something I want to hear. Urologist sounds so negative, and I'm in such a positive mood!

Boyfriend is not pleased either when he hears about the follow-up instructions to heal from the procedure. Rule number one? No sex for a few weeks. Boyfriend and I have a lot of sex. Boyfriend needs sex. In Boyfriend's opinion, what makes a relationship great is "to be kind and to have a lot of sex."

He lasts an entire two days before initiating intercourse.

"Isn't it going to hurt? Are you sure?" I ask. It was maybe three minutes ago that he was groaning in pain with an ice pack on his package as he walked from the washroom back to the bed at the pace of a snail.

"I'll just put the tip in," he says. But the tip turns into full-blown sex. Apparently, not even a five-hour operation on his penis will hold him back, and now that he has fresh, working sperm, not only is sex fun, but there's motivation to have a lot of it. After we have sex, I lie with my legs up in the air, praying those little swimmers do their thing. Let the strongest and fastest sperm win!

Three months later, Boyfriend and I are pregnant. I will later refer, jokingly, to our baby as my Mid-Life Crisis Baby, especially when we argue and he says, "Having a baby was your idea!" Aside from moving in together and blending households and our children's lives, having a baby together will be our first co-venture at being equal parents to one of our children. Or one-quarter of our children.

. . . . .

Boyfriend tears up at the gender-reveal ultrasound appointment, when he finds out we're having a boy. He's always wanted a son. He has been nothing but supportive of my pregnancy, coming to every appointment and going out to buy me my cravings (chocolate croissants). I've turned into a human garbage chute. One morning, we are at a diner eating breakfast. I order the Truck

Driver Special. It's enough food for maybe four people. Momma is hungry. The server starts to walk away. "Excuse me," Boyfriend calls out to her. "That was just *her* order."

The pregnancy hasn't just changed my appetite; it's changed the mood of everyone in the family. Everyone is so fucking excited it's like we're waiting for our first flight to Disney World, but this is a ride we get to stay on together, forever. Woo-hoo!

Boyfriend's mother is beyond excited to have another newborn in her family, especially since it will be a boy, who will remind her of her son. She's psyched to have another grandson. Nana was a stay-at-home mother her entire life, and she lives and breathes for her children and grandchildren. This new baby growing in my belly has given her a new lease on life, and for a while, I feel like the ideal daughter-in-law. I'm giving her baby boy a baby boy! She likes to say to her friends, and anyone who will listen, "I'm going to have one grandchild in diapers and one graduating university!"

My parents are excited, too, but I can tell they haven't quite grasped their role in my blended household yet. Unlike Boyfriend's parents, who split up after forty years of marriage, my parents have been happily married for more than fifty years. Both Boyfriend's mother and father have found new partners, so Boyfriend himself is from a blended family. He never had to share a house with his stepfamily, though — one silver lining of having been an adult when his parents divorced and found new partners. My parents have only one friend who has been divorced, so they don't really understand divorce, let alone what happens in second-chance relationships and blended families.

Boyfriend's girls don't completely get it all, either.

"So how is this baby going to be related to me?" one of his daughters asks.

"He's going to be your brother," Boyfriend tells her. "I'm going to be his father and Rebecca is going to be his mother."

While I don't worry about how Boyfriend's daughters will take all this in — they are older and have each other and are extremely close — I mostly worry about my own daughter, not just because she's my biological child (although, admittedly, that's a large part), but also because her place in our blended family will shift the most.

Boyfriend's children may have been affected the most by the move into our home, but my daughter will now have a full-time blood sibling, something her stepsisters have always known and she never has. Rowan is, essentially, going from being an only child to being one of four. She also went from being the only girl to one of three girls. She will no longer be the youngest of our brood, nor the eldest, either. The new baby will make her a middle child. No one wants to be the middle child. Nothing personal, middle children. But you know it's true. I can say this because I am a middle child.

I go out of my way to make sure she's happy about this new baby. When I first missed my period and went out to buy a pregnancy test, Rowan came with me. I also took the test in front of my daughter. We jumped for joy when we saw those two lines. I happily obliged when she asked if she could pee on the second unused test that came in the box for fun. I figured, at age eight, I didn't really have to be stressed that it might, unexpectedly, come back positive.

We choose the name Holt for this new addition. The baby will be named in honour of my late grandparents. My grandfather came to Canada from Poland with the last name Burnholtz. Like many immigrants during that time, he found his last name was a determent to finding a job, so he shortened it to Burns. I wanted to honour him by bringing back his last name, and also honour my grandmother, Helen, by having the baby's name start with an "H." And so, Holt!

It wasn't my first choice of names, although I do love it. I wanted to name the baby Rocco so I would have two children sharing the first letter of my name. But Rowan, who had named one of her baby dolls Rocco, refused to let me use the name. I wanted so badly for Rowan not just to be onboard with this baby, but also to feel like she was a part of the entire pregnancy. So I let my daughter keep the name Rocco for her future child.

The day Holt is born, everything in our house changes. So, let's lay this all out: Boyfriend's children gain a brother from another mother. Rowan has a brother from another mister. Boyfriend is now the biological father of three children, and I'm the biological mother of two. (I'll give you a second to figure that one out.) Just your average, everyday modern family!

Oddly, I almost feel sorry for Holt, for having two parents who are in love and live in the same house. As he gets older, he will realize that he's the only one who stays put as two of his sisters go back and forth to their mother's home, while his other sister goes off with her father for weekends or vacations. He will probably feel that his sisters get to go off and have these separate lives and all of these great adventures, while he's stuck at home with us. When did it become normal to feel sorry for the child who has parents *who are together and love each other*? But it has become the norm as more and more people blend families, with so many different variations of "family."

"I try to be mindful of the fact that my stepson has got a more difficult situation than his brothers," one of my friends tells me. She became a stepmom first, before she and her husband went on to have two more children of their own. "He also has a stepfather and a six-year-old brother at his mom's house, so he's the only one of four brothers who has to move back and forth between houses. He doesn't complain about this, but sometimes when he is angry or upset, I think it must be related."

Even so, not only do we worry about our kids who have to split their time between houses and parents, we also feel bad for the ones who *don't* have to split time between houses and parents. *Sorry your dad and I are happily together!*

It's. Fucked. Up.

· · · · ·

Holt's sisters are enamoured with him the second he comes home from the hospital. They all want to spend as much time holding their new baby brother as possible. There is almost a decade age difference between the baby and my daughter, and a fourteen-year age difference between the baby and Boyfriend's eldest daughter. We have to monitor and referee, down to the minute, the amount of time our children get to hold him.

"You've been holding him forever! It's my turn!" the children bicker, the only time they argue.

"But I've only been holding him for seven minutes!"

At one point, we even use an egg timer to make holding the baby equal for all his sisters. We are all blissfully happy about this baby who, because his sisters are so much older, has four mother-figures. They change his diapers. They love to give him baths. They love to dress him up and take selfies with him. He's their doll and they love him. We love him. We all love each other!

Everything is awesome.

· · · · ·

As it turns out, you don't get a discount for having a reverse vasectomy and then another vasectomy. Trust me. I asked. Baby Holt, amusingly, shares the same birthday as the urologist who did Boyfriend's vasectomy reversal. We learn this on the day Boyfriend goes in to get another — his second — vasectomy, a couple of months after Holt is born.

We are idiots, of course, to think that having a baby so soon after blending households will go as smoothly as Holt's conception did. After the novelty of having a newborn wears off, cracks in our once blissfully blended family start to appear. Like any new parents, we are beyond exhausted, and this time, we are older — *read: mature* — parents, so we are extra fucking tired. Not only that, but as I did after giving birth to Rowan, I am suffering from the Baby Blues, which has shown Boyfriend a new side to me, one that is overly sensitive and cries for no reason. The Baby Blues are no joke, and I'm not laughing.

"This was your idea," Boyfriend will throw out every time we bicker over something, mostly due to our exhaustion. When Baby Holt was born, Boyfriend had been out of practice of raising a baby for twelve years. I was out of practice with a newborn for nearly ten years.

"I didn't hold a gun to your head when you went to get a vasectomy reversal, did I? I didn't put a gun to your head when you came in me, did I?" is my usual retort.

I am not myself, and we start to quarrel for the first time in our relationship. "My heart is with you and it is you that I want to be with," Boyfriend sends me in an email after one fight. "Getting a reverse vasectomy should prove just how much I love you and what I would do for you. Holt is getting easier, and although we never admit it, he has changed our lives and we are learning what life is like with another baby while we are raising other children." We most certainly are. We're just tired and snippy. This, too, shall pass.

Boyfriend was a package deal. He didn't just bring his girls, his clown-car of a U-Haul, and that fucking nasty chair the day he moved in. He also brought Toby, his dog. And when Holt joins our family, that dog loses his shit. Literally.

Toby takes to shitting in Baby Holt's bedroom, on his Superman rug, multiple times a day. The dog has become so brazen, he will literally take a crap in our newborn's bedroom even if we are *right there*, changing the baby's diaper. I am already having issues with this four-legged animal who eats underwear, the crotches of our pants, bras, hand towels, and toilet paper. He also jumps on the kitchen table and has scratched the paint on both the inside and outside of the door to our backyard. Toby shits and pees inside, not just in the Baby's room, but in my daughter's room as well. He was already a pain in the ass, and he has gotten exponentially worse since the baby was born. Like, he'll look us square in the eyes, squat, and take a shit right there in the middle of our baby's room, eerily looking at us the whole time. It's like a "Fuck you for doing this to me, humans. Fuck. You." A small part of me wonders if this dog is a prophet for what's to come.

I love animals, I really do. But I don't like that I was forced into keeping this dog, and I'm reminded of that every time Toby acts like a dick. I yell at Boyfriend that his dog needs to be trained. We have to keep every single door in our house closed because of the dog, which pisses me off. Boyfriend promises to get a trainer, but he never follows through.

The first time I went to Boyfriend's house, Toby happily wagged his tail at me. Boyfriend says he "knew" I was The One because Toby never barked at me. And he barks at everyone. So I guess that automatically meant I'd love to share my house with him. When Boyfriend separated from his wife, they had a deal that the dog would go wherever the children were, essentially a custody schedule for their dog. When the children were at their mother's, the dog would go with them.

When they were staying at their father's, the dog would go there. Then, one day, just weeks into us blending households, Boyfriend's ex-wife announced that the dog was too much for her and said, "Either Rebecca takes him full-time or I'm going to get rid of him."

Thanks, ex! No pressure. What was I supposed to do, backed into a corner like that, at such a critical time in blending, when I wanted Boyfriend's children to like me and feel at home? Boyfriend and his children love Toby. They picked that dog out of a litter. They bonded with him from the beginning. I, however, am not his greatest fan. I told Boyfriend that if I had wanted a dog, I would have already had one. After all, Rowan was seven when we started dating. What do all seven-year-old girls ask for? A dog, that's what. Rowan had been begging for a dog for years, and I'd always said no. And didn't we already have enough on our plate, with our three, soon-to-be four, children? But, if I was the reason those girls lost their beloved pet, I'd be the bitch who made them lose their dog. Not their mother, who gave the ultimatum. Me.

So, I was really between a rock and a hard place. I said I'd take the dog permanently, but I had demands. "I will not be responsible for this dog," I warned him. "I will not be expected to feed him, walk him, pick up his shit. If we go away or you have to go away for business, you'll have to make other arrangements," I said. "The dog will remain your and your kids' responsibility." I got no praise, no thank-you, no nothing after agreeing to take on the dog. And neither did Rowan, who would end up spending the most time with Toby, happily playing with him, taking him for walks, and making sure he had water in his bowl.

I, too, would end up cleaning up shit in the house. I would end up feeding the dog when Boyfriend is on a business trip. Toby would continue to eat our underwear, the crotches of our jeans, and the toilet paper, and would scratch the paint off the door when he wanted to come inside or be let out.

Still, shitty as that nutty dog is, shitting and peeing on my carpets, shitting and peeing in the baby's room, shitting on our bliss, the humans in the house are loving every second of this precious new addition that is Baby Holt.

· FOUR ·

It actually took a surprisingly decent amount of time for the first bump to plant itself right in the middle of our love highway. The early days of our new blended life were oh-so blissful. Look at us, all blended and perfect! Baby Holt has worked his adorable way into our lives. Boyfriend and I have settled into this co-parenting thing really well. The girls love their brother. We are all getting along so well. Until we aren't. And it isn't adjusting to the baby that does it. You'd think that would be a huge deal, but nope. Baby Holt joining our family was a breeze.

It starts, as many fights do, over something seemingly really inane. And we were all on such a blissful role, damn it! Like I've said, the early days of blending are both surprisingly and fortunately not bad at all. It feels like we are doing a fun experiment to see what happens when you throw a bunch of random people in a house together. It's like our own reality television show: *Real World: Blended Family*. Boyfriend and my daughter get along. Boyfriend's kids seem happy. They seem to feel comfortable around me, and I feel comfortable around them. Blending households is still a novelty for all of us. We have a superb cast, but as in any good thriller, we didn't see this plot twist coming. I certainly didn't.

We all are usually in good moods around each other, as we mostly go about our business and slowly adjust to our new reality. We all eat together when the kids are with us. We all enjoy our movie nights. I guess it makes sense, then, that our first battle isn't over some massive misstep or overstep. Just when we thought we were getting used to this whole blended family thing and getting pretty damn good at it — *boom!* — a battle has emerged. It's a ridiculous fight. Like, seriously cuckoo. Like a bear-combing-his-hair or a cat-wearing-a-hat ridiculous.

I start calling it the Hi/Bye Fight, because that's exactly what it is. The debate is over who should say "Hi" first when Boyfriend's children are staying with us, when they walk in the door, and who should get up to say "Bye" when they leave. Here I thought everything was going along swimmingly, when Boyfriend's kids tattled on me for something I didn't even know I was doing — or, rather, not doing.

"They told me you didn't say hi to them when they walked in this afternoon," Boyfriend says to me after the girls have headed to their bedroom to sleep. One of the many joys of being in a blended family is that there is, by virtue of our dynamic, a lot of tattling. When Boyfriend tells me what his girls said to him, I feel like I have been called down to the principal's office or that Boyfriend has just told me his children have filed a complaint against me with Human Resources. I'm such a monster!

I'm not going to lie. I'm not rushing to apologize for this perceived slight. Were they even serious? Is he serious? I do have flaws, of course, but I'm the first to concede (and apologize!) when I am wrong or have upset someone. But now I'm pissed off. He's fucking with me, right? Boyfriend surely is about to follow up with a comment like, "Can you believe that?" We're not actually going to have a discussion about the fact his girls complained that I didn't say hi to them first, are we?

But he is completely serious. His children were completely serious. What the actual fuck? First, I didn't actively ignore his kids, because I'm not an asshole. Second, why is this popping up only now? They've walked through my doors hundreds of times. It's actually been two years since moving day, and things, quite frankly, have been lovely. There has been nothing to indicate a disruption in the force. I guess the honeymoon phase is over.

One of two things must have actually happened: either I was so engrossed in what I was working on that I didn't even hear them come in, or I said hi and they just didn't hear me. How either option leads to me being "in trouble" is beyond me.

It doesn't really matter how silly I think this is. Boyfriend's children feel insulted and now I'm in trouble and I have to make it right because I'm the adult and I can't believe this has turned into a *thing*. From their perspective, they truly believe I didn't say hi, an apparently egregious offence in a blended family, and so they told on me. Even if it is true (which it is not!), why is this such a big deal? Is our first big riff really going to be over greetings and salutations? This is bullshit.

Why the fuck didn't anyone warn me? If I knew this would eventually turn out to be a years-long standoff, you bet your ass I would have rolled out a red carpet for them every time they arrived, just so I wouldn't have to deal with this bullshit of who should say hi first.

"That was my biggest pet peeve," one friend tells me when I ask her if this fight happened in her blended household, during a bitch-fest. "I would walk in the kitchen after a long day at work, see empty pizza boxes everywhere, and my husband's children wouldn't look up from whatever they were watching on television to say a simple 'hello' to me. I felt so disrespected." Like me, she too thinks the children should say hi first when walking in the door. Her (now) ex-husband, she says, refused to get involved in their hi/bye standoff. Even when my friend would say "H-e-l-l-o!" to them, somewhat sarcastically, so they knew she was home, they still barely looked up. She would barely get a caveman-like grunt as an acknowledgment that she was home.

Blended families necessitate tattling. Kids tell their bio parents if they're pissed about something so that they have an advocate in whatever battle they want to fight. Battles in our household are a mixture of monkey-in-the-middle meets broken telephone. It's about as mature a scenario as it sounds.

"I don't think that's true that I didn't say hi," I tell Boyfriend. "Do you really think I wouldn't say hi if they said hi to me? That doesn't sound like me. I mean, I say hi to perfect strangers in elevators!"

"Well, they think you just ignored them," Boyfriend says, leading me to ask myself, *Was I so immersed in what I was reading on my computer that I didn't hear them say hi to me?* I suppose it could be possible.

"Well, they don't say bye to me when they leave," I tell him, like a petulant child. I know in my gut that Boyfriend is about to tell me I have to be the Bigger Person, because I'm the adult, and because I see that Boyfriend is also suffering from Guilty Father Syndrome, where he's both an ATM machine and, now, a mediator.

"You have to be the bigger person," Boyfriend says. Inwardly, I snort. Outwardly, I let out a huge sigh. *I called it.*

To me, especially since they moved into my house, it's a simple matter of respect. In non-blended families, a parent may get angry if they walk in and their kids don't say hi first. But when you're in a blended household and two out of the four children aren't biologically your own, respect isn't automatic. It has to be earned. Clearly, we had some work to do in the respect-earning department. But I have always tried to be respectful to his children.

"So, I'm supposed to say hi to your kids first, even if they are already home when I walk in?" I press. I want to make sure we're on the same page here so that I'm tiptoeing over this eggshell correctly. Heaven forbid I misstep. Boyfriend's answer, of course, is yes. Yes, I should be the Bigger Person and say hi first, because I'm the adult and they are just children and this is a really stupid thing to fight over, so what's the big deal if I say hi first? Honestly.

I don't think Boyfriend realizes that his children are old enough to also be Bigger People. They're not toddlers. Shouldn't the respect be bottom up?

Ultimately, I choose to not let this be a hill I'm willing to die on. Maybe it's popping up only now because they are pre-teens and hypersensitive. Still, I'll make sure my hi's and bye's are loud and emphatic and full of syrupy sweetness so as to leave no doubt that I'm acknowledging them.

I'll do it. But now it feels forced. And I'm not a very good actor.

·   ·   ·   ·

I can't help but think of my friend who married a man with two children and later went on to have a child with him. They couldn't make blended splendid. She is single now, and I'm pretty sure she has "I will never blend again" scrawled on her bathroom mirror in red lipstick. If it's not tattooed on her forehead yet, I'm confident it will be soon. She's pretty fucking emphatic about it. Turns out, while it wasn't the only issue that resulted in the demise of her blended family, the stupid fucking Hi/Bye Fight was right up there with all of the other more normal shit couples fight about.

"There were so, so many issues, but the one I can remember best is that whenever his children stayed with us, they barely even grunted a greeting to me. Wait, sometimes they would grunt, but I would never get a proper hello," she says.

Out of all their fights over their four years of marriage and blending, this Hi/Bye Fight is the one that sticks out for her the most. Probably because it was so fucking stupid and seemed like such a non-issue, and yet it was one of the biggest issues of all.

Bonus Daughters really opened the flood gates by telling on me. I feel duly chastised. And it does make me wonder whether this would be an issue at all if we had purchased or rented a new house. One of my friends, who was contemplating blending houses by moving into his girlfriend's house with her two children and his two children, came up with a pretty brilliant way of making sure all the kids felt equal, even if they were going to move into her place. He proposed they would all get to pick their own bedrooms.

"I told my girlfriend that the only way I'd move myself and my children into her house is if we started from scratch, and that meant even the bedrooms that were her children's. I thought the only way it would be fair was if we chose sticks, so that each child would feel that it was all of their homes." His girlfriend refused, just like I never once entertained the thought of Rowan having to move her bedroom. In fact, Boyfriend feels bad that, unlike at their mom's house, his girls have to share a bedroom. However, there are only so many bedrooms in the house. And their bedroom — the finished basement — is massive, so it's not like they are crammed into a small space.

"But so many kids share bedrooms," I tell Boyfriend. "What's the big deal? They have the largest room in the house. They have a fireplace! We built them a walk-in closet!" It's true that in traditional families, many siblings share rooms. It's far from the end of the world. In fact, from what I've seen, it can actually bring children closer. And, no, there was no way I was taking my chances on picking straws. What if Rowan had ended up with a short straw and had to not only share her space, but also move rooms and share a room with someone she had practically just met? That was one upheaval I wouldn't ever entertain.

But, maybe, Boyfriend's children never entirely felt quite at home when they stayed with us — and thus the reason for the Hi/Bye Fight popping up. Maybe they became a little resentful over the years, knowing my daughter had her own room and their brother had his own room. Not only did Boyfriend's children never get a chance to pick their rooms, but when I think about it, they didn't even get to pick where they sat at the dinner table, with Rowan always eating in her chair and me always eating in mine.

. . . . .

Because of the Hi/Bye Fight, lines have been drawn, and over something seemingly frivolous. All residents of this house can be extremely stubborn. The fact I make their dad happy and they are in my house (fine, "our" house) seems to matter to them not at all, not to the girls and not to Boyfriend. I think this battle has resulted in the rose-coloured glasses officially coming off.

I keep reminding myself, *Rebecca, you are the adult. Why do you care so much about this? They're just kids. Kids can act like jerks, whether they are related by blood or not.*

But this fight screams to me that it's not *really* about saying a simple word, like "hello" or "goodbye." It's about so much more. It's about what we say when we walk into each other's world. It's about the respect we feel the other is due. It's about the overall importance of recognizing the other people in our lives.

We are a part of each other's lives, not me a part of theirs and they a part of mine. Isn't that what being a family is all about? Aren't we supposed to be pieces of a puzzle, rather than a square peg in a round hole? Apparently, we're not so much blending as we are playing an aggressive game of bumper cars. I've already owned up to the fact that Boyfriend and I basically discussed, um, nothing before we moved in together, so I guess it's no surprise that we never worked out how we'd deal with inter-family drama.

"We discussed everything before we got married. And I was only twenty-five years old," a new friend told me recently at a cocktail party. She married a man with two children, and they would go on to have one of their own. "All my friends were like, 'Why are you talking about such serious issues?' But we discussed everything, from how much I would chip in for rent, to how many kids we wanted, to how to deal with the exes, to how to discipline the kids." She's happily married. Even a twenty-five-year-old had the wherewithal to discuss practically every issue that could arise, which obviously makes me feel like Boyfriend and I were complete twits when we blended.

Still, the next time Boyfriend's daughters walk into the house, I stand at attention like a fucking Navy SEAL, such is the pressure to not offend now. The incredible amount of stress that comes with this whole stupid hi/bye standoff is ludicrous. I will, henceforth, force myself to give them a warm welcome — the warmest — every time I walk into the room. Let there be no doubt I know they're here, am happy they're here, and have acknowledged their presence.

Once they descend to the basement, only now do I start to wonder if Boyfriend and I should have just sold this place and bought a new one together. Old habits die hard, and I fully admit that I can't help but think of this as my house still. And maybe that's the vibe I give off. Or maybe Bonus Daughters feel it simply by virtue of the fact they are well aware they moved into my space. Though they certainly don't act like it's not their place, with their homework spread out on the kitchen table, their drawers overflowing with clothes, as they sprawl out on the couch to watch a movie, and when the nanny makes their beds. I think they make themselves quite at home when they're here, as they should.

We've gone out of our way to make our house their home, but I'm pretty sure they just see my house as a place they have to come visit in order to see their dad and their brother, rather than a home they share with me and Rowan. The house is more like a hotel to them where they can check in or check out when they want to.

There is something so real and so visceral about this stupid fight. It sounds insane — I know it does. For me and for a lot of people embarking on, or in, blending families, I think this battle is a common trigger that ends the honeymoon phase. Not only that, but it's an ongoing battle. I went from blissful ignorance that we were all happy in our new life together to feeling like a guest in my own home, like I was the one who had to please the host and be on my best behaviour. Sure, we might not be yelling in each other's faces or throwing tables through windows, but the spite is real. It's a perpetual merry-go-round from hell.

The Hi/Bye Fight will linger, like a bad aftertaste, like when you went to sleep after a drunken night and midnight pizza without brushing your teeth. I realize I make it sound like we're starting to not like each other. The truth is so much more complicated. There is love in our house. A lot of love. But I'm realizing we are a constant work in progress. We aren't the well-oiled machine I thought we were.

Some experts say it can take up to five years for everyone to be comfortable in a blended family, but now I'm beginning to wonder if there is even such a thing as an expert in blended families, because the hi/bye war is real and I've never read of it in any book or article. No one warns you that you can go from blissful to bullshit years after you blend, completely out of the blue. I never saw this coming, and this, this right here is bullshit, and it's hit like a manure truck. The only person in the house who seems immune is Baby Holt, mostly because he can't speak. The baby is the strongest and most durable glue that makes our blended family work. Baby Holt doesn't give a shit about who says hi or bye first, because he's just happy to find his belly button.

· FIVE ·

Ah, family dinners. Such a lovely opportunity to get together and enjoy a home-cooked (or catered) meal, touching base with grandparents and uncles and aunts and cousins, shooting the shit and catching up on our lives. Good times. Until, that is, someone in the family says something that makes you do a double take.

"It's just not the same," Nana says. Those five words will be imprinted in my brain for eternity. The sentence hits me square in the gut. What fresh bullshit is this?

We're sitting at dinner, talking about all of the amazing grandchildren she has … *but.* Yes, there's a "but."

Rowan is with her father and her grandparents tonight. Nana — Boyfriend's mother — and I are discussing my daughter's father. I'm not sure how we got on the topic of my ex procreating. Is this something people typically talk about with their mother-in-law from their second marriage? But here we are, two voices among a table filled with Boyfriend's blood relatives, Nana curious about my ex's family planning, me wondering why she's so interested.

"I don't think Rowan's dad will have more children," Nana postulates. "So Rowan will be his parents' only grandchild. Let her grandparents spoil her rotten!"

I stare blankly at her, not really sure where she is going with this. For whatever reason, I feel the strange need to defend the possibility of my ex growing his family.

"Well, he *could* meet and marry someone with children, and then Rowan's grandparents will have more grandchildren in their lives," I respond, a tad defensively. I mean, that's what happened to both Boyfriend's parents and my parents when Boyfriend and I blended families and households. Suddenly my parents had two new children growing up with their granddaughter. And Boyfriend's parents suddenly had my daughter in their lives, growing up alongside their biological grandchildren. How has this slipped Nana's mind?

"It's not the same when they're not your own," Nana responds.

I only have a small window of opportunity to respond to her slip or admission, or whatever the fuck it is, that Nana loves her biological grandson *not the same* as my daughter, who is his sister, for fuck's sake. I'm in shock, yes. How could I not take this to mean she doesn't love my daughter *as much*? That's what she's saying, let's be real. How could she admit this out loud? Why didn't she think before she spoke? It's like the first lesson we learn in life, isn't it?

"So what you're really saying is that you don't love Rowan as much as you do Holt," I say, clearly miffed. Mama Bear has been poked. I suddenly feel far from a doting daughter-in-law. I'm guarded now, ready to battle on behalf of my daughter, who, frankly, I've known longer than both Nana and Boyfriend. I think Nana knows that she has fucked up instantly, upon hearing my straight-to-the-point question, or maybe my response sounds like more of an accusation. I know that she has fucked up. She knows that I know that she fucked up. And I know that she knows that she fucked up. Everything at the moment is really fucked up.

It's not the same when they're not your own? It's not just a slip of the tongue. It's a *colossal* slip of the tongue. Nana knows I'm beyond fiercely protective of my daughter and her well-being.

Apparently, love in this family is conditional. This is news to me. She may love Rowan, but she loves Holt more because, though they both came from my womb, Holt is her biological grandchild, and that, it seems, makes all the difference. The fact that she's known my daughter longer than she has known my son doesn't seem to matter. Apparently, the DNA she doesn't share with my daughter, but that she does share with my son, tips the scales in her heart.

At our family gatherings, it's not alcohol that is the truth serum. It's cake. There is always a fucking cake. I wonder if Nana, sweet Nana, has had too much cake this evening and, like a child, has spit out this admission due to an uncontrollable sugar high. How could she admit such a thing, especially to me, the mother of both these children? I'd always — stupidly, I guess — operated under the assumption that she now considered Rowan one of her own. Maybe that was foolish. Maybe I should have known. But I didn't. My heart hurts.

Thankfully, everyone else at the table is immersed in their own conversations, or this could have potentially deteriorated into a bitter family feud. I feel a knee-jerk reaction to stand up and lose my ever-loving mind on Nana, defending my daughter's right to equal love. My brain is reeling. I can't let this go. I need to say something without being overly snide, since, honestly, Nana has a kind heart and would do anything for her loved ones, who I *thought* included my daughter. Had I been fooled all these years? Or am I being too harsh, considering old people often say stupid things. Was this a brain fart?

Maybe I shouldn't question her. Maybe I should let this go. Maybe, like normal, nuclear families, I should pretend she hasn't said anything and shove some cake in my mouth.

It *is* painful to see Nana trying to stutter her way out of … what? Her *truth*?

"Well, it's different. I mean, I mean, I've known Rowan for years," she says, her face now a blotchy red, and this time it isn't the result of a menopausal hot flash. She's clearly embarrassed. As I think she should be.

Yes, she's known my daughter for two years longer than Holt, in fact. But who's counting. Oh, right. I am.

Will I ever look at Nana the same, knowing she doesn't have the same sort of love for both my children? It may have been a slip of the tongue, but her words aren't just out there in the dining room. They are out there in the universe. Worse, they are stuck in my brain. Contrary to what I thought, family isn't family, exclusive of when you come into each other's lives. At the very least, love isn't equal when it comes to the family you gain along the way while blending.

Maybe deep down a part of me always has wondered about this. Maybe there has always been a part of me that didn't want to acknowledge that this amazing, wonderful woman didn't consider herself to have the same role in Rowan's life that I thought she did. Maybe it's always been an unconscious fear that the lines between biological and non-biological weren't as blurred as I hoped and prayed they should be or actually are. Those words, "It's just not the same," expose Nana's bias. They also expose a wound that maybe I haven't done a good enough job protecting. Her admission forces me to think, and question, what love really means in a blended family. Do I love Boyfriend's children as much as the two who came out of me? Do I love my biological daughter differently than I love

Boyfriend? Love is confusing at best in blended families. Love isn't equal.

Nana was just the first to come out and say it out loud.

．　．　．　．　．

So maybe love isn't *the same*. Even if Boyfriend and I make it to our tenth anniversary, it won't be before I celebrate my daughter's seventeenth birthday. Unlike traditional families — first comes love, then comes marriage, then comes the baby carriage — when you're in a blended family and there are children involved, you'll always have known your biological children longer than you've known your partner. In a blended family, you've met your children first. You have loved your children first. You have raised them, your way, first. You have bonded with your children first.

Many of my adult friends are children of divorce and grew up in blended families, with non-biological parental figures and non-biological siblings. They are the first to say that they know they were treated differently by non-biological family members. They may use the word "treated," but I wonder if they really mean "loved."

"*Of course* she loves her biological grandson more," my friend says to me later when I'm crying into the phone with rage and sadness. "It's completely different with stepchildren, and even more so when you're the mother or father. I personally feel that to pretend differently only causes bigger problems. I love my stepson, but I don't love him like a mother, because he has a mother and I'm very aware of that. Just like my mom doesn't love my husband's child from his first marriage like she loves the ones who came out of me."

My friend married a man with a three-year-old and then went on to have two more children with him, so she's not without a form of reference for what I dealt with tonight, but I'm surprised that she isn't taking my side here, as friends usually do, whether they agree with you or not. But my friend may be right. Maybe pretending that love *is* equal causes bigger problems. Actually, make that a yes. Pretending that love is equal does cause bigger problems, when I look back at some of the issues Boyfriend and I have dealt with while blending and the feelings I'm having.

My friend's parents, after all, split up when she was a pre-teen, so she has had step-parents for most of her life. Plus, she's *in* a blended family, so she sees the question of love from both sides. But I'm glad that she sets me straight by being truthful, because that's also being a good girlfriend, the kind of girlfriend who will tell you that your boobs look lopsided in the dress you are wearing.

But I'm still stung by Nana's words and I wish that my friend had at least said that I had a right to feel how I feel. Had I really wanted to hear the truth? Maybe Nana had just finally broke and this was her way of saying, "Let's not pretend."

But we were doing so well pretending! A lot of people pretend!

"The hardest part of blending, for me, is for sure treating all the children the same," another friend admits to me. I call a lot of friends to commiserate. Sometimes you just want a bunch of perspectives, hoping at least one friend is all, "Yeah, man. I'm totally with you!"

"I find it very hard to love non-biological ones. I am a fierce mama, and when his kids are being mean to mine, or I perceive him as favouring his kids in a fight they are having, I suddenly become full of rage," my friend continues. She has witnessed her husband's kids picking on hers and took it out on her husband. I totally do the same with Boyfriend when I feel he doesn't treat Rowan the same as he does his own children, though, fortunately, our children never pick on each other. Boyfriend will never admit to not treating Rowan the same as he does his own children, which leaves me to solo-parent Rowan even after he moves in and sees all I have to do for her. On a day-to-day basis, responsibility for her falls on me and me alone.

Another one of my friends also grew up in a blended household. Her father died when she was only twelve years old, and her mother got remarried a little while later, to a man who had a child. She's always described her mother's new husband as a loving parental figure who was caring and generous. When I spoke to her recently about what Nana said, she kind of laughed. But not a "ha ha" laugh. More like a "Fuck, man, I know where's she's coming from" laugh.

"My mom's husband did for us what he did for his own kid. He sent us to camp and paid for university. Not many men his age, forty, would take on a woman and her two kids and dog, especially in the early eighties, when this was not the norm," she says. Although she had a fabulous relationship with him, she says she did feel like she was treated differently.

"My mother would say she felt bad for her husband's son, because his parents were divorced. According to her, divorce was worse than the sudden death of a parent. I disagree, if you can imagine! I felt jealous that he still had a parent to *go to* and get away from the dynamics of the blended family."

Mostly she felt jealous, and rightly so, that he got to go to his other parent, because he *had* another parent. "But then he lived with us full-time, and I felt annoyed because we were the same age and in the same grade and he was strange and I hated having a new brother," she admits.

No one expects people to automatically love their in-laws once they marry, and the popularity of mother-in-law memes is proof of this. *Dear Mother-in-law, please do not tell me how to raise my kids. I'm married to one of yours and he still needs some work.* Or, *I can't wait to spend the rest of my life being judged by your mother.*

I guess, if I'm being honest, the question of unconditional love was always on my mind, especially when we started introducing our kids to each other. It only amplified as our extended family met our respective children, to whom they were now related by common-law marriage but not by blood. Is blood really thicker than water? If blending families is any indication, the answer is a resounding "Yes."

My parents, even if it's our weekend with Boyfriend's children, will often invite just my daughter to go out with them on some fun all-day excursion. My parents love spending one-on-one time with Rowan because she is, by far, their easiest and most outgoing grandchild. She is always up for everything and never complains about anything. She's a people pleaser.

My parents are friendly to Boyfriend — my mother will bring him her famous homemade pea soup Boyfriend loves so much — but I can see that they still aren't sure how to act around him. Sure, they are friendly to him, but I wish they would put more effort into getting to know him. My dad loves golf. What I wouldn't give to have him suggest they hit the green together. My heart would burst (and my head explode from shock) if my mother invited Boyfriend's children to go along on their excursions with Rowan. No, my parents aren't heartless jerks. I think it just doesn't occur to them that Boyfriend and his children are a part of my family now. Frankly, I also don't think they've quite gotten over my split with Rowan's father, even after a decade. Maybe they are simply gun-shy to get to know Boyfriend's family. Once bitten, twice shy! Still, they never forget Boyfriend's children's birthdays or graduations and they give them presents. They ask about his children when we talk on the phone. My parents care. But do they love?

Turns out, as much as Nana's words sting, my parents feel the same way about Boyfriend's children. If it isn't already clear from the lack of socializing, an almost terrifying car crash brings it to the fore.

·　·　·　·　·　·

It is a cold as fuck January morning and my snowbird parents are driving to Florida, where they will spend the next four months in the warmth, away from the brutal Canadian winter. Less than twenty-four hours after they leave, a text pops up on my phone.

"Our car skidded onto a slippery off-ramp, and now we're stuck in Detroit while waiting for new parts. Just our luck!" my mom writes in a group chat to me and my three brothers. Luckily, they weren't hurt. I wish that was the end of their miserable texts, but as the day wears on, I am progressively more annoyed as the texts continue to pour in, giving updates every hour, it seems, complaining about the shitty hotel they have to stay in and how they'll have to wait another two days for new parts for their car. I want to stab myself in the eyes.

I call them — my mother now has her own iPhone — because I'm worried, but also to yell at her.

"What the fuck are you complaining about?" I shout at my mother when she picks up the phone.

I am, by far, the most emotional, most impatient, and most sensitive of their children, and, unlike my brothers, I have no trouble letting them know how I really feel. They are well aware of my flare-ups when things don't go my way or even if someone says something stupid at our family gatherings. The fact I have no patience for this shit is hardly news.

"You are lucky to be alive! It could have been much, much worse. You could have been killed!" I scream at my mother. "Do you realize that?" Like honestly, they slipped on a goddamn icy off-ramp on a highway. So sorry that means you need new car parts. Better than needing a new liver!

"You're right," my mother responds, somewhat defeatedly, even though I'm trying to both give her a pep talk and remind her to be grateful that they weren't hurt or, worse, killed. Waiting for car parts and having to stay in a shitty hotel are pretty much hash-tag-first-world-problems. For real.

"You could have died and then you wouldn't see your grandchildren grow up!" I continue, driving the point home. I'm on a roll. "So stop complaining about your fucking shitty hotel and just be thankful you are alive!" I think my mother needs a fucking reality check, and I'm way too happy to provide one. I yell at her like I yell at my children if they start to cross the street without looking both ways. I sound harsh and angry, but it comes from a place of love.

"You're right. I have five wonderful grandchildren," my mother responds.

Oh Jesus! You too?

My mother seems to have forgotten about Boyfriend's children, which would make her a grandmother of seven, not five.

What is *wrong* with everyone's memory? Maybe I should suggest to all of Holt's grandparents that they invest in some ginkgo biloba. I'll even buy it for them! Last time I checked, my family expanded when Boyfriend and I joined each other's lives. Why is it I'm the only one who seems to think so?

Since I know my parents are shaken from their car accident, I don't have it in me to say, "You actually have seven grandchildren," which would make her feel worse. I've already made my mother cry. I've already made Nana feel guilty. I may as well yell at myself too at this point, because, upon being forced to think about it, I do not love all the children equally. Well, maybe I do love them equally, but I'm way more protective, supportive, and fiercely loyal of the two who came out of me — which means I must treat Boyfriend's children and my children differently, or *not the same*, no?

Maybe I'm a big hypocrite. Maybe I'm so mad at Nana and at my mother because they seem to readily admit what I have been forcing myself to feel is not the case. They are forcing me to accept what is real and true.

It *is* different. *It's just not the same.*

I hang up the phone after ripping my mother a new one, and forgiveness washes over me like a warm shower. I no longer am angry over what Nana said. It would be entirely hypocritical of me to remain mad at Nana for saying pretty much how all the grandparents in our blended family feel. They are all old-ish, and sometimes you can't teach an old dog new tricks; you need to give them a free pass and just eat that fucking cake.

· · · · ·

No one asks parents who share biological kids if they love their kids equally. This is not an issue in first-time families. But let's be real: parents totally have favourite kids, at any given time, although they would never admit it. It's easier to bond with a kid with whom you share interests. It just is. But when you couple with someone who already has children, people have no qualms about asking you if you love all of the kids in the house equally. They seem to give no fucks that you might consider it an insanely personal question. People can be very brave. Or very curious. Or just plain nosey. But no one ever asks outright. No, no. They buffer the hyper-personal question with a lead-in to soften the blow.

It usually starts with, "I have a *friend* who is now in a blended family and she says she doesn't love her partner's children as much as their own. You're in a blended family. What do you think?"

First, what I think is that there are a lot of people out there who have *friends* who want to know the truth about loving someone else's children. The people who have asked me, and still ask me, about what family and love mean when you blend at least have the sense to know that it is an intimate question. They always seem to ask in a hushed tone, as if we were in a monastery or they were in need of a tampon and wanted to know if I happened to have an extra one in my purse. It's like they acknowledge it's a question we might not want the world to know the answer to. It's not that I find this question about love inappropriate. I know a lot of people have and will and do struggle with this question, including me. Everyone wants to know if, in a blended family, you can really love all of the kids equally. Every house is different. I can only speak about my own.

Holt was a real eye-opener for me. So was that conversation with my mom. I don't think Boyfriend loves our son and his biological daughters more than he loves my daughter, but like Nana said, I'm sure it's not the same kind of love. And now I'm wondering if that's really *that* big of a deal. It's not like there's only one kind of love. I mean, I, too, have obviously been guilty of not loving all the children equally. I don't take Boyfriend's children on one-on-one holidays, like I do with my daughter. Boyfriend would never say that the love he has for our son is different than the love he has for Rowan, because he knows … *better*. But I'm not an idiot. If I hooked Boyfriend up to a lie detector and asked him if he loves our son and my daughter equally, with the same kind of fierce and unconditional loyalty and support, I'm pretty sure that if he said yes, the dial would fly off the spring and his pants would immediately catch on fire. Yes, he's known Rowan longer, by virtue of the fact she existed before we even met. But if I put him up on the stand, as if he were on trial, he'd plead the fifth. He values his life. I don't ask Boyfriend if he loves my daughter as much as he loves his biological girls. And I would hate it if he asked me the very same question. He knows what my answer would be. Because I can't pretend.

Fuck, I was so mad at Nana. But Nana isn't exactly wrong.

· · · · ·

It's not the same kind of love when they're not your own. It's not a lesser love. But it is a different one. It's a kind of love that can often feel delicious, like a ripe peach. We are a family comprising people who love each other. We do. There is love among us all. Is it all the same love? Does it really matter? Is that even a realistic thing to expect? When we're all watching a romantic comedy together, the six of us curled up on one couch, it feels like we are just another family.

But then there are the other times, when it can feel nothing short of yucky, like a nasty rotten peach you find when you excavate the fruit bin in your fridge. You know the one. It's bruised and unrecognizable as a fruit. When Boyfriend's girls, for example, one year forget to wish me a happy birthday, I am that peach.

The best way I can describe loving someone else's children is like being friends with someone and suddenly you both realize your feelings toward one another are stronger than "just friends." Often those turn out to be the best kinds of relationships. Just like in a rom-com, where two characters are best friends, but they get along so well that they never even notice the right person for them has been there all along, just waiting to be discovered. Maybe I will eventually discover that I love Boyfriend's children as much as the two who came out of me. Likewise, maybe Boyfriend's children will discover that yes, they love their brother, but they also love my daughter. Or me. Love is also about respect, which, in a blended family always has to be earned.

Sadly, the truth is, we've been doing this blended family thing for years, and our children still haven't bonded in the way I hoped or once imagined. Rowan doesn't seem important to Boyfriend's children. Boyfriend's children don't seem all that important to Rowan. Pretty much, to tell you the honest truth, at some point we all just stopped trying to get to know each other. We've long since settled into never going out of our way to know what's going on in each other's lives. I stopped trying as hard with Boyfriend's children. He stopped trying as hard with my daughter. When relationships stall, it's pretty much the same as going backwards. Momentum, after all, is everything.

· SIX ·

Sometimes a picture really does say a thousand words. Boyfriend and I are lying in bed, and I catch a glimpse of his screensaver on his phone out of the corner of my eye. It's a new photo, one that I haven't seen before. His screensaver features three beautiful, beaming children. His two girls are wrapping their arms around Baby Holt, their brother from another mother (me!). I'm immediately agitated, because it only features Boyfriend's biological children. Noticeably absent, especially to me, is my biological daughter, Rowan. What photograph Boyfriend chooses to use on his phone screensaver may not seem like it should be an issue at all. Maybe I am overly sensitive, or maybe I'm about to get my period, but, I admit, I'm a little stung by the photo he chose. After all, it's a photo he sees every single time he uses his phone.

I know, rationally, that even in non-blended families, not all children are always featured on a parent's screensaver. However, it may seem like just a photo, but when you leave one kid out when you're in a blended family, it could potentially be the spark that ignites a battle. The Hi/Bye Fight is all the proof you need that conflicts in blended households don't always come from a place of legitimate wrong.

This feels different, though. And so I take this screensaver photo personally, even if there's no malice behind his choice.

"Why does your screensaver only feature your kids? What about Rowan?" I ask, also wondering, *And me?* At one point, I was Boyfriend's screensaver.

"I don't know," Boyfriend says. "I just liked this photo."

Am I acting like a brat? I mean, who cares? It's just a screensaver. So why am I looking at it as if there's some deeper meaning? Boyfriend has said he just likes the photo — it is, indeed, a nice photo — and so he probably chose it without a second thought. Or maybe he subconsciously forgot my daughter, the only one not related to him by blood. My brain has been working overtime, ever since we blended, to make sure everyone feels equal to us and to each other. So, yes, I wonder if perhaps it was a subconscious move on Boyfriend's part to choose that one photo over one in which all the children are featured or one that featured us. Is that image trying to send a subliminal message to his children? Like, "You're still my favourite. Don't worry!"

I can't help but inwardly question if he picked the picture with his biological children because they hold the most special place in his heart. If he indeed just chose it without a second thought, that means that my daughter and I weren't first thoughts, or thoughts at all. Which stings.

Behind the closed doors of a blended family, there's a high probability that feelings do get hurt over something as silly to the outside world as being left out of a screensaver. At this point in our relationship, the novelty of blending is fading slowly, like a piece of artwork the sun beams on, making the colours fade. Obviously. But my daughter being left out makes me feel left out on her behalf. I feel like Rowan and I are interlopers or failed a test. I hurt even more for Rowan.

As always, I call a friend to vet my level of crazy.

"I don't think you should take it personally," she says. "My mother-in-law asked me why I never post pictures of her son's children on social media. So I asked her, 'Why don't you ask your own son why he doesn't post pictures of them? He is their father.' Then my mother-in-law said to me, 'You are his wife, so that makes them yours as well.' I pretty much hung up on her. Not my proudest moment."

"See, you took it personally!" I shoot back. "Why can't I?"

"Fine, yeah. I overreacted for sure. I actually de-friended her after that," she laughs.

"You did not!" I say, because in this day and age, de-friending someone on social media is akin to, well, basically telling them to go to hell. She pretty much flipped her mother-in-law the bird over social media photographs regarding their blended family.

It's another evening-time fight. Boyfriend and I retreat to the yard — the location where we film our fight scenes so the kids can't hear us.

"You only have a photo of Rowan on your screensaver," Boyfriend says to me. He's not wrong. In fact, he's entirely right. The screensaver on my phone features a photo of just Rowan, beaming in a red ski-racing one-piece.

"It's been my screensaver for years, mostly because I'm too lazy to change it," I say to Boyfriend. Yes, yes. Hypocritical for sure. But I'm leaving out three kids in a family with four.

Ever since we blended families, there has been an unspoken, but playful, war over who is featured on Boyfriend's phone. At first, it really was entertaining. Back before phones had finger-print or eyeball recognition, and back when I knew Boyfriend's password, as did his two daughters, it was sort of amusing screwing with his phone and his screensaver. At least in the early days, before jealousies and loyalties reared their ugly head. It didn't seem so divided when I would pick up his phone while he was in the shower and playfully change his screensaver to a photo of me. The photo of me never lasted for more than a week, because Boyfriend's children, too, were in on this game and would hack into their father's phone to change the screensaver photo back to one of them. Honestly, it really was playful for all of us. Even Boyfriend thought it was pretty entertaining, rolling his eyes after seeing a new photo when he picked up his phone. He never knew, from one day to the next, what or who would be featured on his screensaver.

None of this was done with any malice. Boyfriend seemed to get a kick out of seeing a new photo on his phone, shaking his head over our silly antics.

But I wonder if we were all, essentially, fighting for his attention. His daughters and I were joking around, trying to put our faces front and centre. We all laughed about changing his photos until it no longer seemed like a laughing matter, especially after we had our son.

"It's just sort of weird that you only want to show off your biological children and leave Rowan out," I tell him. I'm not exactly mad about the fact he chose to feature only his biological children, but I'm not *not* mad either. Mostly, I'm annoyed and a little bit hurt. Since his phone now requires fingerprint recognition to gain access, I can no longer hack into it to change the photo.

Somewhere along the way, and I'm not exactly sure when or why it happened, we stopped sharing passwords. Sharing passwords in this day and age really is a sign of true trust and transparency in a healthy relationship. So why, as our relationship has grown, has our access to each other's digital worlds shrunk?

"I would change it to a photo of all the kiddos, but I don't have a photo of all of them," Boyfriend says. This is not altogether true. Just months after our son was born, I hired a professional photographer to take group shots of all four children together, each child on their own, and each child holding their new baby brother. The shoot took hours, as if we were posing for a Calvin Klein spread for *Vogue*, but the results were fantastic. I spent a small fortune to blow up one of the photos on a large canvas that hangs in our kitchen, the three girls surrounding the baby. It's the first thing everyone sees when they walk into the kitchen. Here we are! Our four beautiful and happy children!

The massive canvas of all our children not only shows that there are four children in our blended family, but, also that Boyfriend and I are proud parents — just like any other family — eager to show off our offspring to anyone who visits.

In our television room, there's another photo of just the girls hanging on the wall, before we had Holt, taken when we first blended and we all took a vacation to Jamaica together. When I look at that photo, Boyfriend's children and my daughter look like true sisters, smiling in another blissful blended family moment, even if they look nothing alike.

We have just one or two photos of the six of us. One was taken when our son was two, which was featured in a magazine, to go along with a story on blended families. Looking back at the answers I gave the magazine, I can see why people don't understand what really happens in a blended family. Because anyone who has been interviewed about blended families, including me, avoids admitting to the outside world (but maybe to ourselves, also) the real truth. It took six weeks for all of our schedules to match so we could do this photo shoot, for one.

When asked by the interviewer to explain the bonuses of being blended, I answered, "I do call them 'bonus children,' because they are a bonus! ... I actually love the mayhem that comes along with it, though it took some getting used to. When I hear all of them getting along and laughing, I almost want to cry. It's so nice to see and hear!" I said at the time, when interviewed for the magazine, called *InBetween*. "It feels more like I'm living with fun roommates. One of his daughters will do my hair. The other will do my makeup. And both of them will give Rowan advice on friendships or other things."

Holy shit, how much fun did I make my life and blending sound? Everyone is going to want to run out, get divorced, and remarry with a partner who has kids. *Join the fun, people. Blending is where it's at!* But, alas, looking back, I can see that my answers were bullshit, as if I were trying to convince myself that all was perfect.

First off, I really don't "love" the mayhem that comes along with it and, no, I've never gotten used to it. Sure, yes, when I hear all of the kids getting along and laughing, it does warm my heart. And maybe once or twice his daughters have been my glam squad, but it isn't a regular occurrence, as I made it seem. Maybe a couple of times they've given my daughter advice on friendships and life shit, but that too isn't a regular occurrence. So, yes, anyone who read that article would think I am having the time of my life blending, even though, in reality, we have started to argue over everything.

I do feel guilty for leading people, or at least the magazine readers, to believe that blending is the Best Thing Ever because I wanted the outside world to think that all was good and that my life was … maybe not perfect, but almost perfect. Not only did I think that people didn't want to hear the truth, but I probably didn't want to face it, let alone have strangers know my truth.

Also, if you look closely, as I do often, at this photograph, you can see that we are divided, even if we are all in the same picture. Boyfriend and I are in the middle with Baby Holt on his lap. On my left is Rowan. On Boyfriend's right side are his two children. It wasn't the photographer who had us pose like that. But when the photographer asked us to "squeeze in tighter," Rowan immediately nuzzled up to me and Boyfriend's girls squeezed in with him. It happened as if we were all on autopilot, obeying an unspoken rule of loyalties. Still, it's a nice photo, one that I will cherish because it features all of us.

When it comes to other photographs, it's also clear that loyalties are and have always been divided. In my daughter's bedroom, there are framed photographs of her and me, many of her with her father, and many more of her and her friends. There are no photographs of Boyfriend or his two children, but there is one of her holding her baby brother shortly after he was born. In the room Boyfriend's girls share, they have put up numerous adorable photographs of themselves when they were just toddlers — a time before I entered their lives, when their parents were still together, before they had a brother from another mother, before they lived part-time with my daughter. Basically, all the moments featured are from before we blended.

"I give up," Boyfriend says, after I continue to pester him over his choice of screensaver photo. I've gone off on tangents about how I don't feel I'm a priority. The screensaver is a trigger for all the other times I've felt left out.

Boyfriend changes his screensaver to a photograph of a beautiful, peaceful sandy white beach, effectively ending the screensaver jealousy feud forever. A beach, after all, is neutral, like a sunset. Not one of us can get upset over a screensaver of a beach, right?

The beach is not just a stock photo, though. I have bought a condo in Mexico, for all of us, in hopes that we will have many happy family vacations together for years to come. It was a large investment, for sure, but one that I also hope will yield great returns by way of making unforgettable memories, getting our children to bond, and providing a place for Boyfriend and me to end up in our old age.

Even though I alone paid for it, I truly did buy it for our entire blended family. Boyfriend takes care of the renters, who help pay for the condo fees. Boyfriend and I sometimes vacation there, without the children, too. When we do, we go for massages and then have sex on the table afterwards. On these vacations, we reconnect and go for walks on the beach, holding hands. We are still very much in love ... when we are in Mexico. But once our vacation ends, we are right back to reality and blended-family bullshit.

Now I own two places that Boyfriend doesn't chip in for, at least not equally. I'm the queen of two castles, and as I said, you can never be the king or queen of someone else's castle. I'm starting to think that his money woes are no longer situational, which makes me feel like he simply assumes that I have the money to take care of two homes. It's this assumption that pisses me off, because I don't think Boyfriend quite understands that I worked very hard to be able to buy the Mexico pad, paid for in cash. It also makes me feel like he has no respect for my career, which has helped buy this place in Mexico and keep up with the bills at home. Yes, he pays half the bills, aside from the cable and internet. Yes, he pays for half of the nanny, and he pays for the groceries and household supplies. But that's about it. Just the thought that he doesn't respect how hard I work, and that he expects I'll just take care of the big-ticket items — property taxes, condo fees, the gardener — starts to grate on me.

I hate to admit it, but I detest that he simply assumes that these places are his just as much as they are mine. It feels — to me, anyway — as if he's starting to act entitled. He likes the idea that we have a place in Mexico. He likes the fact we live in a fancy area. He likes to drive the motorcycle I bought him for his birthday one year. It gets to the point, sometimes, when we're arguing over who paid for what, that I want to say, "It's not yours unless I tell you it's yours!" much like telling a kid not to touch someone else's toys unless they ask first. When you start to feel that things are unbalanced, you forget that daycare motto: Sharing is caring.

·   ·   ·   ·   ·

Years later, photos will pain me again. But since I've toned down my expectations when it comes to blending, I'm not as upset as I once was, at least on this day.

Boyfriend's eldest child has just moved into residence at a fabulous university. We are all so insanely excited and happy for her. I watched as she busted her ass to earn the grades she needed to get in, and Boyfriend and I are giddy on the long drive to visit and check out the campus and her room.

Boyfriend and Bonus Daughter's mom helped her move into residence just before the start of school, a few weeks earlier. I wasn't invited to come along when she moved in. I was fine with it. It would have been awkward for everyone, and on such a milestone day I wasn't going to chance ruining it by making an appearance. But on this day, I am wearing a T-shirt with her university's name scrawled across it. I remember feeling so proud of her when she found out she was accepted. I wonder if she knows how proud of her I am. This is what love must be. Love is really giving a shit. Love is wearing your Bonus Child's university colours.

It's a typical dorm room. Boyfriend's daughter has decorated the walls around her bed with numerous photos dangling off a long string, like Christmas lights. There are photographs of her many friends, both old and new. There are photographs of Boyfriend and her. There are many photographs with her biological sister and Baby Holt and her boyfriend. And, of course, there are photographs of her with her mother.

There is not one photograph of me. There is not one photograph of Rowan. Despite giving her a $500 cheque as a graduation present, and despite my history of feeling slighted by pictures (or lack thereof), this really doesn't bother me as much as it would have a few years ago. The truth is, I've long since lowered my expectations and realized that just because we're not shown in pictures doesn't mean we are non-issues in the girls' lives. I've learned to realize that my perception of what it means is different from theirs. To me, I'm left out. To me, my daughter is left out. To them, I just wasn't included in this particular photo montage.

Still … if a tree falls in a forest and nobody hears it, how are we supposed to know it fell? Does it even matter if it did? If there isn't a photograph of me and my daughter in Boyfriend's daughter's dorm room, does that mean Rowan and I simply weren't there all these years? I know it would be fruitless to say anything to Boyfriend. Nor do I want to ruin this special day, and his daughter is practically an adult. I meet Boyfriend's daughter's friends, see the campus, and we enjoy a nice meal together, as a family. When Boyfriend and I are leaving, I hug her goodbye. I'm tired but I'm happy. I'm glad and relieved that she's having fun and has met great new friends. I give a shit, apparently. Genuinely.

Like I've said, Boyfriend's daughters and my daughter didn't exactly gel as much as I had hoped they would, as they grew older alongside each other. Although their periods have synced, their schedules have not. Maybe it was just plain bad luck that, as the children got older, aside from spending a week vacationing together, Rowan and Boyfriend's daughters have been ships passing in the night. Rowan's social life and family life keep her travelling locally and internationally with her father, often. And Boyfriend's girls have friends, boyfriends, and part-time jobs near their mother's place, so it's easier for them to stay with her, and that is where they, as they get older, prefer, or need, to be.

Boyfriend doesn't think the lack of bonding is because they're rarely around each other. He blames age difference. When Boyfriend's daughters were starting to get into fashion and boys, my daughter was happy still playing with her stuffed animals, which she believed were real, or at least she liked to pretend they were.

Our first blended family vacation, before Baby Holt was born, showed that the age difference did actually matter. Not so much as gender, though, which I know affects the families of many of my friends who have blended and have kids of different genders.

"Every fucking weekend, it's the same. My boyfriend has two boys and I have one boy and one girl, so my daughter always feels left out. The boys are rowdy and into sports and video games, and there's no way they want to do what my daughter likes to do, which is reading or shopping, and more often than not we end up doing what they want to do, simply because we are outnumbered by males," says one of my friends. "I have to pay extra attention and do things alone with my daughter so she doesn't feel left out. But she does. I know she does. And it breaks my heart. It feels like I'm choosing everyone over her, but I'm just trying to make everyone happy. That's fucking impossible, I've learned. I keep trying anyway."

· · · · ·

Even though I have a hard time remembering what I ate for breakfast, I have an amazing ability to remember the numerous code words my daughter and I came up with when Boyfriend and I were dating, and after we all had met and hung out, for how she's feeling when we are all together. It's easier for her to have code words for her emotions, which she only shares with me:

Mango = *Feeling left out.*
Apple = *I just want to be with you.*
Banana = *I'm just sad and I don't know why.*
Pineapple = *They are making fun of me.*
Pear = *I'm feeling jealous.*

My daughter manages to work these code words seamlessly into our conversations when our blended family is together. "I just feel like some mango," she will say, for example, at the dinner table, to which I'll respond to everyone, "I just have to talk to Rowan alone for a second," before I whisk her away from the rest of our family so we can chat and deal with how she's feeling. Often, she just needs a pep talk, a reminder that I love her and that even after we've blended, it's still me and her, and will always be me and her, first and foremost. I'm unapologetic about this, even though it will and does cause friction between me and Boyfriend.

Basically, I have been telling my daughter, without actually saying it, that it is *us* … against the world, which, yes, includes the rest of the family.

There's no shame to my game when I say my daughter will always come first. I give precisely no fucks if everyone in my blended family knows that my daughter is the light of my life and can do no wrong in my eyes.

"Everyone sees how you treat Rowan," Boyfriend says when I find myself defending my daughter for forgetting to clear her plate or shut off her washroom light or say "thank you" after Boyfriend makes a meal, or for allowing her to come into our bedroom and sneak into our bed. Of course I do tell her, after Boyfriend complains, to say "thank you" and to put her dishes in the dishwasher and to turn off the lights, but I still allow her to come say goodnight and walk into our bedroom, numerous times every night, as Boyfriend and I try to watch a series on Netflix.

"Rowan," Boyfriend will say, after I ask him to press "pause" when she walks into our bedroom. "You've already come in here three times to say goodnight. *It's enough.*"

I'll jump in and say, "She's just here for one more hug." Then my daughter will crawl into bed, on my side, to cuddle with me. Boyfriend will get annoyed, because this is not a one-off. It happens almost nightly.

"You can cuddle for two more minutes," I tell my daughter, trying to placate Boyfriend while also trying to placate my daughter. It's a tightrope walk from hell, trying to make everyone happy while I'm stretching myself paper thin in the process.

What I really want to say to Boyfriend is, "She was here first. You're the one who actually took *her* spot in the bed. So cut her some slack." This is an ongoing source of tension for me and Boyfriend, who thinks that I baby my daughter too much, which is ironic, because I think he babies his children too much. Still, apparently, it's obvious to *everyone* just how much I adore my daughter and how little I try to hide it.

"It's so obvious to everyone that you favour Rowan," Boyfriend tells me.

"Who is everyone?" I press, my back up, feisty and ready to fight.

"Just everyone," Boyfriend says.

"Who is everyone? Give me names," I demand. I'm not being bitchy. I just want facts.

"*Everyone!*" he says, sighing in exasperation. But I'm just as exasperated. I want to know names, and Boyfriend is either refusing to name names or is lying about *everyone* seeing that I "favour" my daughter. Either way, I don't like the fact that I feel totally gossiped about, and apparently Boyfriend and his family talk about me and my daughter's relationship behind our backs.

"Well, *everyone* can just fuck right off," I say sarcastically. "She's my daughter and I'll raise her as I please. And remember, she's younger than your children, so cut her some slack."

Boyfriend may *think* that I'm the only one who doesn't notice that I treat my daughter like my best friend, or that I'm oblivious to how I'll do anything for her, but that's not the case. Of course I know what I'm doing. I'm not a fucking idiot. I'm aware of the fact that I put my daughter's feelings before anyone else's. They don't know what it's like to be a single mother for years, and they don't understand the unbreakable bond my daughter and I formed during the many years we lived on our own. So, yes, everyone can just fuck right off if they have an issue with how close I am with my daughter — that is, whoever "everyone" is.

· · · · ·

The code words come in especially handy on our first blended family vacation, before Holt is born. Rowan is seven and still obsessed with her stuffed animals, so of course her carry-on is just a bag, busting at the seams, filled with nine of her favourites. It was a battle to get her to narrow it down from the fifteen she regularly sleeps with in her bed. Rowan treats her stuffed animals as if they are real. I don't tell her otherwise. Of course, I tell her, they are real. Of course, I tell her, they have feelings. Just look into their eyes, I tell her! (If you do actually ever stare straight into the eyes of a stuffed animal, it's kind of creepy that they do look as if they have a soul!)

On this trip, like all other trips I've taken with my daughter, Ellie the Elephant is one of the "chosen" stuffed animals that comes along.

For the longest time, Boyfriend couldn't believe that I refused to tell my daughter the "truth" about her stuffed animals, namely that they aren't real and thus have no feelings. That being said, let's be real: my daughter has always known her stuffed animals, or her stuffies, as we call them, aren't real, but she likes to pretend they are. They provide her with comfort, and she likes it when I play along, telling her that I can understand their language and they can talk to her through me. I want her to enjoy childhood for as long as possible, and if that means being complicit in perpetuating this "misunderstanding" about her stuffed animals, so be it. What is wrong with having an imagination, especially when you are a child?

Rowan brings Ellie the Elephant with us down to the pool. Suddenly, she races up to me, hysterical, tears streaming down her face, almost hyperventilating. My first thought is that she's broken a bone or stepped on chards of broken glass. I am immediately frantic.

"Ellie! Ellie fell into the pool and now she may be dead!" she cries out. Tourists around us are staring now, and Boyfriend's children are gawking at us, their mouths agape. They can't believe my daughter is crying over a stuffed animal that she thinks is real and that she now thinks is dead because she dropped it in the pool by accident.

"Don't worry," I say, grabbing for a hug. "I'll do CPR." I proceed to give Ellie the Stuffed Elephant mouth-to-mouth resuscitation. Yes, maybe you're thinking that, at age seven or eight, children shouldn't believe stuffed animals are real and most certainly shouldn't believe that they have feelings or that they could drown. Boyfriend certainly does. But I remind him that he's probably forgotten how a seven-year-old acts. His youngest daughter is just over two years older than my daughter. His eldest is four years older.

"My children never believed that stuffed animals were real," he says. I look at him like he's just murdered the Tooth Fairy and kicked Santa in the nuts.

Boyfriend's children can't believe what they were seeing. Rather than concern for Rowan, they seem embarrassed, and they're stifling laughs at the freak-out over the "drowning" and my subsequent valiant attempt at resuscitation.

"See? She's fine!" I say to Rowan as I wrap Ellie in a towel. "She's breathing now. She's fine." Rowan eventually calms down. Ellie is alive and well.

I have raised my daughter to use her imagination, telling her that "only boring people get bored."

"It's not normal," Boyfriend says to me. "She's too old to believe in stuffed animals."

"Says who?" I retort. Hasn't he seen any of the *Toy Story* movies? They're awesome!

"Says everyone."

Here we go again, the bullshit invocation of "everyone."

"Who is 'everyone'?" I retort.

"Just everyone."

"Everyone can fuck right off. If my daughter wants to believe in the fucking Tooth Fairy until she's forty, I couldn't care less," I say, with my unwavering loyalty to my daughter.

"I don't think it's healthy," Boyfriend says to me. I want to laugh in his face. Who does he think he is, being judge and jury over what is healthy for a child? My child, my rules. Your children? Your rules. *So take your opinions and shut up*, is what I want to say, but I don't.

"You raise your daughters the way you want. But don't criticize the way I raise my daughter," I say, anger brewing inside me like a pressure cooker.

"I'm not criticizing your parenting," he says. "I just don't think it's healthy for a seven-year-old to cry over a stuffed animal."

I don't get why he can't just let this go and be okay with how I'm parenting Rowan. Like, don't we have enough shit to figure out without trying to fix what isn't broken? I have zero issues with her loving her stuffies like I love her. If I don't care, he shouldn't. Let's save our arguments for real shit, shall we?

All the girls go back into the pool to play while Ellie sunbathes on a lounge chair beside me. Boyfriend and Bonus Children are entirely unsympathetic and give each other sideway glances, like, "Who the fuck are these idiots who believe that stuffed animals are alive? Did I just witness a grown woman actually give mouth-to-mouth resuscitation to a fucking stuffed animal? Is this for real?" They seem downright entertained by the fact that not only does Rowan still believe in stuffed animals, but she believes they can die if they are dropped into a pool. I get it; they're pre-teens. So to them, this is entirely ridiculous and probably embarrassing. I'm annoyed by their lack of sympathy for how my daughter is feeling and how she had reacted, though, and I want to say, *She's still young! Don't make fun! It isn't nice.*

Even worse, my daughter *noticed* their disbelief, them trying not to laugh, and their WTF glances to each other. Thank god for our code words.

"I really feel like a mango, Mommy. And maybe a pineapple," my daughter, who is now holding my hand, announces. My mind races. Right! Mango = *I feel left out!* Pineapple = *They're making fun of me!*

I tell Boyfriend and his girls to go back to the room and get ready for dinner, while I talk with my daughter to find out why she's feeling "Mango" and "Pineapple." I give her a squeeze and ask why she is feeling left out.

"They were laughing at me," she says, tears welling in her eyes. It brings me to tears, because we are just embarking on our family blending, and I'm not sure how to handle my daughter's first real meltdown on our first blended vacation.

"So what? They're just not *believers*," I tell her. "Like I've always told you, there are people in the world who are believers, and there are people who aren't. They aren't believers, but that doesn't mean you can't be. I still am!"

I suddenly feel like we're living in a laboratory and that some scientist is watching us for clues on how to create a successful blended family and marriage, given different styles of parenting, age gaps, and the intricacies of the modern family — which, in my family, includes having secret code words with my daughter.

Rowan's mini-meltdown is just a minor blip in our otherwise lovely holiday. She only cries this one time. The fact is, everyone just wants to feel like they're always someone's priority and to not feel left out — and there's no fucking way I'm ever going to let my daughter feel that way. I remain unapologetic about that, too.

It is the first time, in hindsight, that I realize that Boyfriend and I have differing parenting styles, probably something we should have discussed before blending. I put that down on my mental to-do list, which means it will never happen. I have an aversion to to-do lists, one just as powerful as my aversion to change. *Apple*, I think whenever my daughter is hurting, or when I am. Apple = *I just want to be with you.*

· SEVEN ·

Before our first blended vacation, of course our children had already met. Whether you like it or not — rather whether you agree with it or not — we live in a fast food culture, one in which we move at an incredible pace, and consequences are afterthoughts.

Boyfriend and I never think of the consequences of introducing our children to each other really early on in our relationship, because why would we? We are happy. And our relationship has gone from zero to sixty like a fucking Lamborghini, so why wouldn't we continue to move our relationship at the same pace?

Boyfriend first introduces me, by myself, to his children at the house he rented after his separation. I make the almost hour-long drive in traffic. I'm not nervous. I'm excited to see Boyfriend and meet his children, but I'm also annoyed at the traffic getting there. Very early on, when Boyfriend first invited me over to his place for dinner, I remember very clearly thinking our relationship was not going to work out because the drive from the city to the suburbs took fucking forever. I actually did think about dumping him after my first drive to his house. Luckily, he wooed me and, more often than not, would make the drive and come see me.

Boyfriend's girls are extremely welcoming when I walk in and we first meet. They are outgoing and objectively beautiful. I play a karaoke video game with them, hoping that they'll think I'm cool, despite the fact that the last time I played a video game I was a child and the game was Frogger (Google it!), plus I'm completely tone deaf and trying way too hard.

I feel like I've just arrived at a cocktail party where I don't know anyone, and pray that someone will talk to me, except there's no alcohol. I want Boyfriend's children to like me. Like, really, really like me.

I don't spend the night, but Boyfriend and I manage to sneak into his washroom and have sex before I leave. So maybe that's why I'm glowing. Or maybe it's because my first meeting with his children went off without a hitch. In fact, it was a success! I am beyond happy and relieved that his children seemed so open to meeting me.

There was no big conversation about how we should get our children to meet (shocker, right?) or how they'd get along, although there may have been conversations about how excited we both are to have our respective children get together. That's almost like actually talking about it happening, right? We both agree that if we make it a big deal, it will become a big deal, so we keep the evening when we finally pull the trigger light and easy. *Just another Thursday night, people. Move along.*

Boyfriend, like I've said, is blessed with outgoing, friendly, and talkative children who are young enough to integrate. I am blessed with a daughter who is up for anything, including meeting Boyfriend's children. She, too, is also young enough to easily integrate into a new family makeup. I think it becomes harder on children to assimilate into a blended family when they are older, because they can really speak their minds and overanalyze things. Our children are young enough to, well, not overanalyze anything.

We all pile into the kitchen at Boyfriend's house to make our own pizzas, because who doesn't like making their own pizza? It's an easy activity that we can all enjoy together. The night is, mostly, a success. There are no tantrums. No one storms off. But I have to pull my daughter aside once after she says "Banana." My mind races to remember what the code word means. It comes to me within seconds. Banana = *I'm sad and I don't know why.*

I know why. The girls all seem to get along, except for a few minutes, when Boyfriend's girls give a sideways WTF glance at the pizza creation my daughter has made, which is a fucking disaster. She's seven. I'm not totally sure what kind of masterpiece pizza they were expecting, but clearly she's not quite ready for a Michelin star, as far as they're concerned.

I can tell she is a little jealous, not because I'm conversing with Boyfriend's children or she doesn't have my sole attention, but because Boyfriend's children's pizzas are so perfect it makes even me wonder if they work part-time at Domino's. Rowan's subpar pizza being compared to his daughters' isn't a blended family issue. It's a sibling jealousy issue, and I sort of treat it like that. I take her aside, into the bathroom.

"Why are you feeling sad?" I ask, even though I know why. I can read my daughter's mind and her facial expressions like I can read a book.

"I don't know. I just am," she tells me.

"Are you sad because you didn't like your pizza?" I ask.

"I don't know," she says.

"Just tell me the truth. You're a little pear, aren't you?" Pear = *I feel jealous.*

"Yes, Mommy," my daughter admits, tears welling.

"Oh, who cares," I say to her. "It's just a pizza. They taste the same no matter how they look."

"But did you like my pizza?" she asks.

"Your pizza was perfect!" I say. "Should we go back now and join the others?"

After we eat our pizzas and clean up, all the girls watch a movie together. Boyfriend and I sneak off to have sex in the washroom again. Like a porn star, he can cum on demand, so we are quick. At the end of the first get-together, Rowan is happy. When we leave and I ask her how she liked Boyfriend's girls, she answers, "I liked them. They were nice."

When our children meet, it really isn't a big deal. At least it doesn't seem that way to Boyfriend and me, or to the children either. We don't think "this is too soon," because we want all of our offspring to spend time together so we can spend time together. After, I wonder whether Boyfriend and I would still be together if our kids didn't get along. This meeting is a much bigger deal than any of us realize. Classic us. What about our relationship isn't?

One of my friends, who is a single mother and is on many dating apps, refuses to divulge on her profile that she has a child. "I want them to get to know me first," she says. I don't judge her, but I can't help but think, *Why wouldn't you want potential dates to know you have a child? You're hiding the most important part of your life!* Maybe she thinks that if she says she has a child, her odds of meeting a partner will be lower. Truth is, if the man she meets is turned off that she has a child, is that really someone she wants to entertain as a partner? Seems like a big waste of time to me.

Another mother I know is divorced and dating a man who has children. I call her my soccer mom friend because our daughters are on the same team and we sit together on the sidelines, half watching our girls play, but mostly talking to each other. Each week, she gives me updates on how her relationship is progressing. It's going well, although it seems to be progressing as slowly as a garden snail.

"It's great. But I still don't know when I should introduce him to my daughter," she tells me, one evening, while we're on the sidelines.

"Hasn't it been almost a year since you started dating him?" I ask, hoping to not sound judgmental, because judging another mother is just plain wrong and I'm trying to be objective. I'm also trying to understand why!

"Yep! But my daughter is overly sensitive these days, and she already is slamming doors in my face, so I don't want to rock the boat even more," she sighs.

While many would think that Boyfriend and I are moving way too fast, introducing our children to each other within a handful of months, I would have a few questions for Soccer Mom Friend, if I had the balls, no pun intended. Like, won't your daughter be super pissed that you hid the fact you've been seeing someone for more than a year? Also, it's probably the advent of puberty that is causing her to be so sensitive, so why not just let her in on it?

I don't ask her, because I like her, and if it doesn't feel right to her, who am I to judge? No one's windows are clean. Mine certainly aren't.

Still, it sheds light on the fact that there really is no right or wrong way to introduce children to each other, be it two months into a relationship or two years. Who knows what the outcome will be? All of us dating who have children or are dating someone with children are confused and winging it. Maybe there is a right way and a wrong way, but there's no one to direct us. If you want to know the right time to introduce you children, you may just as well look at your watch, because there isn't a universal right time. Even a broken clock is right twice a day.

We ignore all so-called experts and well-meaning friends, who say you should wait at least six months to a year before introducing your respective children to your new partner or to each other. What makes them the experts, anyways? Am I an expert because I am embarking on a blended life? So-called experts can fuck right off with their advice, because waiting six months to a year doesn't feel right for us. And it's not like I'm dating someone in rehab who's been told not to date anyone for a year so they can focus on their recovery. I'm simply a woman with a child moving forward in life with a man who has children of his own.

Another friend who blended families also introduced her children to her now husband's children after only a couple of months, believing that she and her boyfriend needed to see how their children would get along before their relationship could advance, something I hadn't even considered when I first met Boyfriend's children.

"We introduced our children after only a couple months of dating. Our children were very young. Mine were two, five, and seven, and his were three and six," she says.

At first, she tells me, they would hang out socially with other divorced friends and their kids. "We all had a barbecue together with a bunch of other couples and divorced families. I think in the beginning, due to their young age, it was easy to integrate the kids as 'Mommy's friend,' as I had a few divorced friends at the time and we ended up doing things together. This was about two months after we first met."

As things got more serious between them, they started spending more "deliberate" time with all their children together — going for ice cream and dinners, and eventually spending entire weekends together. They are now married. But she, too, had wondered what would have happened if their kids hadn't gotten along and if they would have chosen not to move forward if that was the case.

"I remember it being slightly tricky because I wanted to have a chance to experience what it would be like, not only if we were together with all of our children, but also how it would impact the kids if we ended up breaking up, after a few months," she says.

This is also not something I'd ever thought about. What would I have done if Boyfriend's and my children hated one another or constantly fought? Would I have broken up with Boyfriend? Would Boyfriend have broken up with me? Personally, I didn't even think about how the children would react if we broke up after a handful of months.

"I definitely wanted to see early on how well we blended. I used to tell my husband that if we had no kids there would never be a reason to get married," she laughs. "He used to say if we had no kids we would be married already."

Another friend of mine, who is divorced, tells me that when he introduced his three children to his girlfriend, who he had been dating for less than two months, at a restaurant for dinner, it pretty much ruined his relationship with his kids.

She came on way too strong, way too fast, with his children, which made them feel uncomfortable. "She practically demanded that I had to introduce her to my children after just knowing each other for two weeks," he tells me. "I should have seen that as the first red flag. They didn't like her at all. They detested her and I knew that wasn't going to change, especially since she tried to act like their mother from the minute I had introduced her, as if she were in some sort of competition with my ex. Even I was sort of horrified when she handed my daughter an expensive piece of jewellery on the day they met, after I had casually mentioned that her graduation was coming up and she had asked for this one thing. My daughter was fifteen at that point and saw it for what it was. No, it wasn't a nice gesture. It was clearly bribery, and my kid was way too old for such outrageous bribery. Also, they didn't like that I was talking with them about the women I was dating, like they were my friends and not my children. My children didn't want me to be their friend. They wanted me to be their parent."

My friend was more than dismayed — he was gutted — when his daughters sent him a long, heartfelt email the day after meeting his girlfriend, pretty much saying they didn't want to hear about anyone he was dating until it was serious, and, in fact, they no longer wanted anything to do with him if he was with her. They wrote him, "We are not your friends." They didn't give him an ultimatum, exactly, but they refused to talk to him for months, all because they hated the woman he was choosing to spend his time with, a woman who was trying to force his children to like her, a woman so thirsty to blend, it was like she was dehydrated.

"I did break up with her because of my children, after they sent me that very hurtful email, which broke me to my very core. But we were not getting along anyway. We were fighting every day because she wanted to rush our relationship. I knew I had to break up with her, not just for my own sanity, but to work to earn my children's trust back. They refused to talk to me for six months. It was the worst six months of my life. It was torture." So, at least in this area of blending, Boyfriend and I are lucky. Our children are still young enough to be open to dating and don't really even know there's an option to speak up. When your children are young, they still think you're the boss. Ah, the all-too-fleeting glory days.

My friend introduced his children to the woman he was dating really early on, and it bit him in the ass. From then on, he refused to rush into any relationship, and he stopped talking to his children as if they were girlfriends at a sleepover party. "I continued to date, but wouldn't tell them about it. It didn't matter anyway. I haven't found anyone yet that I would want my children to meet."

But Boyfriend and I are two grown adults and want our new lives to start stat. We want to be together all the time. We want our children to become and eventually act like true siblings. I want to marry Boyfriend and he wants to marry me, because we know that, together, there are more pros than cons. Call it making a compromise. Call it placing a bet. Call it crossing our fingers. Call it wishful thinking. We don't care what you call it. Whatever we're doing seems to be working. That is, until I invite Boyfriend and his children over to my house for the first time so that we can take them to a nearby museum, a place I've taken my daughter every month since she was three years old.

Boyfriend's children are immediately bored. As soon as we buy our tickets and start walking through the museum, I can tell they don't care about any of the displays. Their pained expressions make them look as if they are being punished. I realize, even at their young ages then, nine and eleven, that going on cultural excursions, like to the museum or an art gallery, is just not their thing. Neither, for that matter, is seeing people who happen to be homeless.

My daughter grew up passing homeless people every day, since she was three. The small private school she attended downtown was a ten-minute walk from the condo we used to live in, before we moved into our house, and we would pass the same homeless man every day for the four entire school years. She knew his name. He knew her name. She knew that he liked to fish on weekends. He always had a lollipop to give her, and I always kept change on me so my daughter could drop it in the bowl by his feet. She liked petting his dog, too.

Meanwhile, when Boyfriend's children come to our hood, it's like they have never seen someone who lives on the streets, with a handmade sign asking for money, because, well, they haven't. They have always lived in a quiet suburb and haven't actually seen anyone beg for money. They are scared, acting like they've seen a huge spider, and they point out the homeless people as we pass them.

I'm astonished at their reaction to people less fortunate than them, but I don't say anything because, well, I don't know what to say and I'm still in shock that it's their first time at a museum. Boyfriend doesn't tell them, "Don't stare." I have practically just met his kids, so I keep my trap shut. I'm not about to lecture them on the importance of gratitude or the reality of mental health issues or why people end up on the street, as I've done with my daughter. Boyfriend's girls were already bored enough at the museum. The last thing they need is a lecture on how blessed they are.

It hits me, suddenly, that Boyfriend's daughters and my daughter have had very different upbringings. Boyfriend's girls would rather hang out at a mall. My daughter likes learning about history and wants to (and has) invited homeless people to come live with us.

Not surprisingly, we don't last long at the museum and head pretty quickly to a nearby restaurant. It is a first for all of us, dining out in a restaurant, and I laugh with the girls when they make fun of the waitress for having a strange name and acting a little strange. They just don't seem to know … better? Even as an adult, I felt peer-pressured into also mocking this waitress. It was my first time eating out with them, and, while far from my proudest moment, we do bond over this experience.

On the way back to Boyfriend's car, I run into an old friend in the parking lot and give him a hug. I'm at a loss when it comes to explaining who all these people are with me. So I just introduce them by their first names. I feel uncomfortable introducing

Boyfriend as "Boyfriend" in front of all our children. What if they don't think that we're "Boyfriend" and "Girlfriend" yet? What if they don't know how serious we've become? It's the first time I also recognize that there will be many future occasions, being in a blended family, when I don't know how to explain what exactly we are. When tourists ask me for directions in my own city, I probably more often than not send them the wrong way. Anything navigational is not my strong suit. Including navigating my blended family.

· EIGHT ·

It wouldn't be a mother-daughter vacation if everybody else came along, now, would it? Rowan's world changed a lot after we blended, and not just because Boyfriend has taken her spot in our bed and she can't barge into our bedroom without him huffing. So I make sure that at least one of our mother-daughter rituals, the most important one, stays the same, no matter the backlash I get. Boyfriend knows that nothing is going to get in the way of our annual mother-daughter trip, when, every year on her birthday weekend, we head to Miami. I also live for these trips, when it's just the two of us, like the old days — just me and Rowan, before I had to take other people into consideration. Boyfriend knows it's futile to try and get in the way of our mother-daughter vacations, which essentially exclude not just him, but his children as well.

Recently, a friend relayed to me a story of how one of her girlfriends, who has one biological daughter, married a man with three children of his own. She booked a trip, overseas, with just her daughter. So I'm not alone. But, apparently, her bonus children were so upset that their dad had to plan an extravagant weekend of fun for them to make up for the hurt they suffered because they weren't invited to come along, and this just shortly after they married.

Old habits die hard when you blend. I refuse to even entertain the idea of not going on these annual trips. Never once do Bonus Children seem to be unhappy about this. Never once do they say anything except, "Have a good time." I'll never really know if they feel jealousy or anger that I only take my bio daughter on these trips. But that doesn't mean I forget about Boyfriend's children when Rowan and I take off. It's kind of impossible to do so, especially when people I just meet ask, "How many children do you have?" which, when you're in a blended family, isn't as straightforward a question as you may think. In fact, it makes you seem like a complete moron.

·   ·   ·   ·   ·

I'm sitting on the balcony of our hotel room in Miami. My daughter — the epicentre of our family unit, me and my girl — is inside ordering room service for us. It's October and her birthday weekend. Our four-day vacation is how we celebrate her birthday; we've done so since she was three years old, long before I met Boyfriend and his children and we blended houses, and even after having Baby Holt. It's not that Boyfriend doesn't understand the importance of having one-on-one time with our own biological children, but when Rowan and I took off for our first mother-daughter trip after we had blended families, he didn't quite understand why everyone couldn't come along, or at least why he was quite clearly not invited.

First, there's the issue of money. Rowan and I are blessed to be able to take these vacations. We both know that we are fortunate enough that these trips are both a luxury and a necessity for me. Boyfriend's children have gone on vacations before, when their parents were still together, but, unlike Rowan, who travels all the time, mostly with her father, they weren't given the opportunity often. When those vacations took place, their parents had to plan in advance. Tropical vacations are an extravagance for his children.

Also, I'm not sure if Boyfriend is jealous of being left behind and left out of our mother-daughter vacation, or if he's just jealous that we are someplace warm with a beach, staying in a fancy hotel. I don't bother trying to pretend that I care his feelings are hurt, because he's somewhat judgmental about our trips and, even after years, still can't seem to grasp the situation. Make no mistake, Boyfriend isn't angry about the annual ritual. He honestly doesn't understand how, after we've blended families and had a baby together, I can still do this, leaving everyone else in our family out while Rowan and I take off.

"How would you feel if I just planned a trip with my kids and didn't invite you and Rowan?" he asks me once, after I've planned our mother-daughter trip without telling him. It is kind of a dick move, to book plane tickets and reserve a hotel room without asking or telling him first. I think. But I lived independently for so long before meeting Boyfriend that I am just used to doing things without having to ask for anyone's permission.

"In normal families," he tells me on more than one occasion, "we'd discuss if we had the money to go away. That's what me and my ex did. And everyone would be included. And you wouldn't just take off somewhere without letting me know first."

I don't know how to answer Boyfriend's question on how I would feel if he planned a trip with his kids and didn't invite me or my daughter. On the one hand, yes, I would feel like shit if he booked a trip with only his biological daughters, told me about it only afterwards, and then told me I wasn't invited and neither was my daughter. On the other hand, I think it would be good for them to have some alone time for a longer stretch than forty-eight hours. So, I really don't know how I'd feel. If I'm being honest, I don't think I'd mind if he wanted to go away with just his bio children. The truth is, he doesn't have the money or job flexibility to take off whenever, like I can, so it's a moot point.

"We've been doing this forever on her birthday. It's just our thing," I tell Boyfriend, who is big on avoiding exclusion, at least in the beginning and middle of our relationship, but not so much as the years go by. In theory, I am against exclusion too. In practice, though, there's no fucking way I'm not going to go on our traditional birthday getaways.

But after blending, it's hard not to forget, even on our mother-daughter vacations, that there are other children in my life now, especially when people ask, "How many children do you have?"

· · · · ·

Rowan and I decide to take a yoga class together at the hotel, and a friendly older woman asks where we're from as we're setting up our mats. I answer and add, "We're on a mother-daughter vacation." This woman *loves* the idea of a mother-daughter vacation and fawns over my daughter, by far the youngest person in the class, who she says reminds her of her granddaughter. As we stretch, the woman asks if Rowan is my only child. When I don't answer her immediately, she looks at me with the same confused expression I must have when I look at my daughter's math homework, which I stopped understanding after grade two. People in non-blended families obviously *know* how many kids they have. All my married friends with children can easily answer this question, without hesitation.

But in a blended family, this question is far more complicated to answer. You'd think I'd have the answer knocked by now — a quippy one-liner — but my answer changes depending on the situation, how I'm feeling at that particular moment, who is asking the question, and who is around.

I never forget about Boyfriend's children, of course, but am I even allowed to say they are my children when they are really Boyfriend and his ex-wife's children? Would Rowan jump in, saying that her mommy has only two children, her and her brother?

"I have a son, too," I tell the friendly woman, giving my daughter the look that says, *Shhhh!* "But he's still a baby. He's at home with my husband," I say.

That last bit's also a white lie, because even though Boyfriend has proposed and I am now his fiancée, we haven't actually gotten married. We did talk about getting married or eloping at one point, but we couldn't figure out how to pull it off, because we want the kids to be there. Certainly I'm not going to get married without my daughter being my maid of honour. Certainly Boyfriend wants his children there. But then Boyfriend and I thought that our parents would be offended if we eloped and just took the kids. Plus, Boyfriend's parents are split up, which means not only would my parents need to be invited, but so would two sets of parents from his side. But then Boyfriend said he'd feel bad leaving his sister out, which means I would have to invite my three brothers. Suddenly eloping, getting married barefoot on a beach, seemed more trouble than it was worth. There are way too many people whose feelings would get hurt if we eloped, just the two of us.

In traditional marriages, where there are no children involved yet, eloping is easy. But when you already have kids, you, of course, want them to be a part of the wedding, because you're not just marrying each other, you're marrying their children as well. So we stop talking about our wedding altogether, content with our common-law status — marriage now just another thing to add to our never-to-get-done to-do list.

"Aw," the lady in the yoga studio responds after I tell her about my son. "That's so nice. A girl and a boy! You have a million-dollar family."

Sigh. *Lady has no clue!*

Thankfully, class is about to start, so I don't have the chance to explain that Daddy at home is not my daughter's real daddy, nor is he actually my husband, let alone mention Bonus Children. But the class is a bit wrecked for me. The moment that I let out that I only have a son back at home may have passed, but I feel incredibly guilty, visualizing Bonus Daughters' faces with what-the-fuck expressions.

The rest of my family is *not* out of sight, out of mind, even on these mother-daughter vacations. I miss Boyfriend on these trips, and we talk throughout the day and every evening before bed. And, yes, we are still sending each other cheesy poems, although they are fewer and farther between. I also think about his children and always buy them some sort of souvenir. But that doesn't mean I am any more capable of answering the simple question, "How many children do you have?" No matter how I answer, it doesn't seem quite right, sort of like seeing a very slightly, but most definitely, slanted painting hanging in your house. No one else may notice, but you do.

Yes, I gave birth to two children, so I have two biological children. But Boyfriend is the biological father of three children. We are a family of six. Even the math sounds wrong. It's ... *weird*. But it seems inaccurate (and a bit of a fabrication) to say that I have four children, *especially* when people respond with, "Wow. That's a lot of kids. You look fantastic for having four children," as I lie by the pool. And because Boyfriend had children earlier than I, when I do include Boyfriend's children in my answer and say, "My eldest is sixteen," people tell me I look "so young" for having a sixteen-year-old. I always feel like I should fess up. *Of course* I look fucking fantastic. I only gave birth to two children, almost ten years apart, not four children. *Of course* I look young for having a sixteen-year-old. I didn't give birth to her!

But it also feels wrong to say, "I have two children," because although I may not be related to Boyfriend's daughters by blood, they do live with us half the time. I am watching them grow up alongside my biological children, in my house. I suppose I could answer, "I have two children and two bonus children," but many people don't know what a "bonus" child is, and I still would have to end up explaining, again, about the makeup of our modern family and how we came to be.

Plus, many people don't understand what a blended family is, and often I see, or think I see, looks of judgment after I do explain it, as if I'm the only woman in the world who — gasp! — separated, and then nine years later — *nine years later* — had a baby with a different man. I don't think Boyfriend faces this kind of judgment for having children with different women. It must be nice to be a man in this situation. I also now wonder how Boyfriend answers the question of how many children he has. I make a mental note to ask him later. But, of course, I forget.

For other people, my having kids with different fathers is compelling. I'm fascinated by their fascination. People seem to like to think I've fucked up my life — which is bullshit — because I'm on my second marriage and have children with two differ- ent dads, perhaps so they'll feel better that their own relation- ship has lasted, even if they are unhappily married. Sometimes I think I get actual looks of pity. That, or they put me on some sort of weird pedestal, like, "Wow! You must live such an interesting life. You go, girl!" People seem to want to know where I went wrong, or where I went right.

No matter how I answer — *I have two children! I have four children!* — neither answer makes me feel completely at ease.

Being in a blended family makes you feel fucking clueless, incapable of answering what is, really, a fucking simple question, like, "What do you do for a living?" I also wonder how my daughter or Boyfriend's children answer the same question. Does my daughter say she has three siblings, or just one? Do Boyfriend's children say they have three siblings, or two?

Although I may not know how to answer the question outside the home, inside our household I have tried to instill, and pound into our children's brains, that they don't have a halfbrother, they just have a *brother*. They are not stepsisters. They are *sisters*. The only steps in my house, I like to say, are the stairs. I'm not forcing them to love each other, even though that's what I hope for. I just think that using the words "half" and "step" is so outdated. Sure, you could say that I'm Bonus Daughters' stepmother, but really, I'm just another female adult, more like a friend than I ever am a parent. Even calling myself a step-parent makes me feel like a bit of a liar, since I've never "parented" them. Sure, I keep them alive under my watch and sometimes help with their homework, but mostly, yeah, we just gossip about their lives and their friends.

Even though I feel like a nitwit for not knowing how to answer the question of how many children I have, I am not the only one who finds herself somewhat bewildered when asked questions about blended families. One friend who is in a blended family, and also grew up in a blended family, says her biggest pet peeve while growing up was what to call her stepfather.

"We weren't going to call him 'Dad,' so we called him by his first name. It was hard to explain to people who he was. I hated saying 'stepdad' or 'stepfather,' because of the negative connotation around that word. Step-parents are always portrayed as evil, and he really was not at all. It was also hard to buy a Father's Day card because I didn't want one that said 'Dad.'" So, yes, when you're a child in a blended family, you are also faced with other questions that are hard to answer. "He wasn't my dad, but since I hated the word 'stepdad', I didn't know how to answer when friends would ask me if that's my father when they saw us together. It always made me uncomfortable, especially if he was near me," my friend shares. "He was a great father, even though he, technically, wasn't my father."

Never in a gazillion years would I have imagined that such a straightforward question of how to refer to others in our blended household would bring on so much confusion. Are the children just as confused? Most of the time, I say I have four children, mainly because I feel less of a liar. And, of course, I do like hearing how *fantastic* and *young* I look for having so many children. Who wouldn't?

The yoga teacher ends the class quoting the Buddha in a soft voice: "What you think, you become. What you feel, you attract. What you imagine, you create." I find her words calming. Who wants to go up against the wise words of the Buddha? Does this mean that if I *think* I have four children, then I *will* be the mother of four children? If I *feel* I have four children, I *do* have four children? If I *imagine* that all the children came out of me, does that mean I really *can* say I have four children, without feeling like I'm deceiving others? After class, as we walk back to our hotel room, I can't help but wonder if the Buddha would have changed his tune if he'd had to live in a blended family. *Just asking.*

· · · · ·

Organizing travel for a family is a pain in the ass at the best of times. Travelling with an entire blended family is a whole different ballgame. First, Boyfriend and I have to make sure that our exes agree we can have the children on the same week so we can take all of them away to our place in Mexico at the same time. That's the first hurdle.

Then I need to get a travel consent letter from my daughter's father. Boyfriend needs to get a travel letter from his ex. Boyfriend pays for his plane ticket and his two daughters' tickets. I pay for my ticket and my daughter's ticket. And we both share Baby Holt's fare. It's harder, of course, on Boyfriend, because while I only have to pay for two and a half tickets, Boyfriend has to pay for three and a half. This seems fair to me. It's not that I haven't spent money on Bonus Children, with gifts or cash or cheques on special occasions, or even not-special occasions when we find ourselves shopping. But when it comes to the larger ticket items for his children, like plane fares or class trips to Ecuador, I leave it to Boyfriend and his ex-wife to come up with the money for their children, just as when it comes to big-ticket expenses for my daughter, her father and I take care of her.

Boyfriend doesn't have the same freedom I have to travel — I can work remotely, while he has to run his business — so I take many, many mini-vacations, either alone or with my daughter, as I did before we all blended. It especially irks Boyfriend, over the years, when I travel alone, especially when I just tell him, "I need to go away," and add, "I booked a ticket." But why should I change everything about my pre-blended life? Travelling is a huge part of my life. Maybe it's not "normal," but for me it has always been the norm.

But travelling with a blended family doesn't just come with logical and financial issues. Like the Hi/Bye Fight, travelling can lead to some pretty nonsensical arguments. Beyond absurd!

After one March break, one of my male friends, who has two biological children and is married to a gorgeous woman who is child-free, tells me that whenever they travel, the bullshit-of-all-bullshit argument arises between him and his wife. Trust me, it's even sillier than the Hi/Bye Fight, an example proving reality is stranger than fiction. The cause of their fight is probably the stupidest one I have ever heard, yet at the same time I don't judge how someone feels within a blended family, because it is hard, especially if you don't have children but have married or are dating someone who has. And, yes, it does make me feel better, since I thought I was the only one who had to deal with the bullshit fights that pop up in my blended family.

"There's always a fight over seating arrangements on the airplane," he tells me. "Always! My kids want to sit with me, so I get three seats and sit in an aisle next to my wife on an aisle across. That makes her feel left out and not part of the crew." My head spins when he goes on to say, "The alternative would be two on each side, but then I am far from one of my kids and they hate that."

So before my friend, his kids, and his wife even arrive at their tropical destination, the bullshit of blending while travelling rears its ugly head. Listen, I'm the first to know what it's like to feel left out and "not part of the crew" in certain situations, like when all his kids are on the couch with Boyfriend and there's no room left for me, literally and figuratively, but I'm certainly not going to whine, "Where am I supposed to sit? On the hardwood floor?" It's these little issues — like feeling you're left out because you want to sit with your husband but can't because the kiddos want to sit with their father — that sting and lead to feuds.

"Now that is a crazy stupid fight," I say to him, trying to contain my laugh. On the other hand, of course, I can't believe his wife would care about where she sits on a less-than-four-hour plane ride. In fact, I think that in most traditional families, at least one parent would *love* to not sit with their kids on a plane ride. They'd love the break, just to be able to sit alone, reading a trashy magazine, instead of catering to their kids for hours in the air.

"I was surprised she was so pissed. But she felt shunned," he says. "So it's always rocky when we travel, and the trip never starts well, because I'm not sure how to make both her and my kids happy on the plane. And, yes, I get an earful for it and reassure her that she's not being left out. So neither of us is happy."

Yay! I'm not the only one who is woefully unprepared for the silly fights that feel like slights.

When you're travelling with a blended family, you do really wonder, *In the event of a drop in cabin pressure, whose oxygen mask would go on first?*

· NINE ·

Because I'm a journalist, I like to read and research and interview people. You'd think I would have done this before I got involved in a blended family. I was too busy enjoying life with my new guy and his children, while also taking care of my daughter and Baby Holt. I didn't spend time researching because *I was living in the moment*! I was happy!

But I start reading up about blended families, years after we have blended, when things start to get worse, not better, and Boyfriend and I are now fighting — over the money I think he owes me, about who takes more care of the baby, over the fact his dog has ruined yet another pair of underwear, and over how we can't seem to fit in one date night a week. The backyard fights are almost daily now, away from the ears of our children but probably to the delight of our neighbours, who, too, are in a blended-family situation. I often wonder if they overhear our heated arguments, and if so, do they think what we're fighting over is insane? Do they get bored of our fights? Often we fight over things we have already fought over. We have "discussions," as Boyfriend likes to call our disagreements, over discussions that we have already discussed. Or maybe our neighbours are all like, "They are so like us!"

My neighbour entered her second marriage with one child, marrying a man with no children. They went on to have two children of their own. But I never hear them arguing in their backyard. I hear them yell at the kids when they are in the pool, but I never hear any arguments between them. Perhaps it has something to do with the fact they bought the house next door together, as opposed to her moving into his house or him moving into her house? They started fresh.

Experts, as I've said, profess it can take up to five years for everyone in a blended family to feel truly relaxed around each other and in their new roles. So why, I have to ask, are things getting worse after five years of blending in my household? Why does it seem so much harder than it was in the early years? When did everybody start tiptoeing around each other? When did I turn into such a nag? When did Boyfriend's actions, or lack of action, start to exasperate me? And when did I start not wanting to come home at all?

.   .   .   .   .

I've become obsessed with my Google searches. I search phrases like "blended family problems," "successful blended families," and "why blended families don't work." I even search "when to leave a blended family." I get caught in the vortex of the internet, finding either nothing that applies to me or stuff that seems to apply but then provides advice that is just common sense or vague. I start to wonder if "experts" are on acid when they write these articles and blogs handing out "advice" and "tips." Like, I know Boyfriend and I moved fast, but advice like, "Don't expect to fall in love with your partner's children overnight," or, "Insist on respect," or, "Limit your expectations" doesn't seem all that helpful or insightful or even doable. It's not only that it's easier said than done, but who can give advice when they don't get down to the nitty gritty of what it's really like to blend? Or what you should do after you've blended and didn't discuss anything? Sure, I've read about the problems we will most likely face, but there's nothing on, "Why you feel like you're lower a priority in your blended family than the dog." There's not much on how to "fix" a blended family when it starts to break apart. There's no warranty. I can't get a replacement for free, to start all over again with, like I did when my dishwasher broke down. There's no repairman for blended families. No one really knows what the fuck to do with us *after* we have already blended!

So I also Google search "blended family statistics," which is a colossal mistake, kind of like reading *What to Expect When You're Expecting* and being left thinking, "Well, thanks for telling me the millions of ways I've already screwed up my fetus! Thanks for also letting me know the millions of things that can go wrong with my pregnancy." Or like searching for "headache on left side of eye" on WebMD and thinking you have brain cancer, possibly MS, and also blood clots.

The statistics on blended families are eyebrow raising at best and dire at worst. They are definitely a wakeup call. Again and again, I read that 66 percent of blended families don't make it. These are pretty shitty odds. I don't want to be part of that cringeworthy statistic. But I also realize that we are far from unique.

I read that more than a *thousand* blended families are formed every day — every day! — in North America. I am too lazy to do the math, but that means that of the 1,300 blended families forming each day, more than half of them will end up divorced *again*. And who wants to wear that as a badge of honour? Who wants to be a serial divorcee? What kid wants to see their parent break up a *second* time? But I'm starting to get why the statistic is so fucking high. Something has shifted in our relationship, and even I don't understand why. Sexually, we are completely compatible, and I still find him extremely sexy. But little things have started to bug me. I feel that I am often reprimanded for just being ... me. My quirks that he once found cute, he doesn't find so cute anymore. Mostly, we have become less kind to each other, and our loyalties to our children are even more divided. But doesn't every marriage have its ups and downs?

Apparently, nowadays, 75 percent of us who remarry will end up with someone who already has children. The statistics also show that almost half of North American children under the age of thirteen are currently living with one biological parent and that parent's current partner. Clearly, blending is an *epidemic*. Clearly, people need help! Including Boyfriend and me. We still love each other. We fight a lot but, I think, we fight for "us." We fight for our blended family. Even when we yell, "This is just not working out!" at each other, we continue to fight for us, day after day, week after week, year after year.

Fucking experts. They really don't know all the bullshit that goes on behind the closed doors after years of blending, and that it seems to get worse for many of us, not better. No one can tell us why or even warn us that this can happen. I make myself stop these Google searches, instead opting to take quizzes on what cheese best suits my personality. At least, then, I get an easy answer. (Brie!) I still think Boyfriend and I will be the exception to these statistics. Sure, we basically just jumped off a cliff to blend our families. So fucking what? *Wheee!*

· · · · ·

Remember the couple who set me and Boyfriend up back when I was just looking for a distraction and a one-night stand? Well, they are now going through a horrific breakup, so ghastly it's as though their relationship has been murdered. There is figurative blood splattered everywhere. They are part of the 66 percent who couldn't make blended work. Their breakup is the type of epic breakdown where you feel pressured to choose sides and are forced to listen, awkwardly, to rumours (that aren't really rumours) about midnight stealing of patio furniture from their once-blended house's backyard, along with defamatory accusations about each other's character. After years of trying to blend, our friends now truly seem to detest each other. Around the same time, another friend escapes her blended family — yes, it does feel for many like they have escaped — and is on her second divorce.

"If I could go back in time, I would never have moved in with him and blended our family," this girlfriend tells me in one of her many late-night, drunken, post-breakup phone calls. "I did everything around the house, and there was no appreciation. He knew I didn't make a lot of money, so I tried to make up for it by making dinners and grocery shopping and cleaning the house. He would literally hand me receipts for things like mouthwash, that cost less than ten dollars, for me to split with him."

As with the friends who set Boyfriend and me up, she'd moved in with him and the house was his. This is the first I hear of how they had split the bills inside their house, and I wonder why her soon-to-be-ex asked her to pay for half of everything, including fucking mouthwash. Apparently, from his point of view, they *both* used the mouthwash, so they *both* should split the cost of it. From my girlfriend's point of view, she couldn't believe, especially when they were still happy, that he would dare ask for three dollars and twelve cents when he came home with a receipt for something as small, for example, as toothpaste. Obviously, unlike in my blended household, the fact that she cleaned, made the dinners, and did the grocery shopping didn't seem to matter at all to him. Early on in their relationship they had agreed to split all household items, though how could my friend ever imagine that would include every damn thing, from big grocery shops to items as small as dental hygiene products? I'm actually embarrassed for her ex-husband, but at the same time, I know what it's like, whether it's based in reality or not, to feel like your partner isn't splitting things evenly. This is a constant argument between Boyfriend and me. He doesn't pay rent or chip in for the mortgage or pay the insane property taxes, because he takes care of the groceries. He says it equals out. I don't believe it.

It doesn't matter what my friend says to me during her drunken late-night rants or that they had agreed to split every damn household item fifty/fifty, even though he earns probably a hundred times more than what she makes. I doubt she'll even remember these rants. Their breakup has left my friend broken and broke, and she needs to find another home for her and her two children.

The girlfriend who set me up, meanwhile, who now also detests her now-ex, luckily finds a nice place she loves quickly, and just like that, she is no longer living in a blended household. Poof! Just like that, she is no longer part of a blended family. Poof! Just like that, she's back to being a single mother ... and back on the dating scene. I'm sure there were months, if not years, of fights leading up to their final demise, but not only did they blend quickly, they *un-blended* just as quickly. In the months and years to come, she will no longer have anything to do with him or his children. Poof! Just like that, she no longer has bonus children. I tell her she's lucky they didn't have a kid together — a platitude, but one she adamantly agrees with.

"No, I don't keep in touch with his kids," says another one of my friends who couldn't make blended splendid. "They are still pretty young. And I don't think that will work anyway. We can't stay in touch. It was very unhealthy for me. And I just wanted to move on as quickly as possible."

For many in a blended family, once you decide to break up, you're not just breaking up. You're un-blending, which takes even more of an emotional toll than a regular breakup, because you're not just breaking up with you partner. You're breaking up with a number of people. While you may think blending is hard, and it is, un-blending seems even more painful.

Even if you do want to keep in touch with your once–bonus children, sometimes you don't get to make that choice. Take one of my girlfriends who married a man with two children. The went on to have a son together. When they broke up — she didn't feel appreciated, her husband would never interfere when she needed help disciplining his kids, and, also, like me, she let *a lot* slide because he gave her a baby after professing that he didn't want more children when they first met — it was her ex-husband's children who wanted nothing to do with her, even though she's the mother of one of their siblings and treated them like her own.

"They refuse to talk to me. They blame me for the breakup. We even tried to go to family counselling, after we split up, to figure out how to move forward and maybe keep in touch, since they are the brothers to my son. But it didn't work. His kids thought I was the bitch that ruined the marriage. Now I have nothing to do with his children. I wanted to keep in touch with them, but they didn't want me in their life anymore."

As the saying goes, "When you get married, you are also marrying their family," but when it comes to divorce in a blended family, you are also divorcing their family. When traditional couples with children break up, parents keep in touch with their children, and children, usually, want to keep in touch with both parents. But in blended families, you lose the family you gained when blending, including children who may have been in your life for years, children who may be related, by blood, to one of your children.

For months after their breakup, my girlfriend who had set me up with Boyfriend, self-medicates, both by using hard drugs and by going home with bartenders with hard abs, to help her "cope" with going from being in a far-from-splendid blended family back to a single household again.

When I find out they are done for good, I should be sadder about their breakup than I am. Surprisingly, another emotion takes over: jealousy. I'm not envious about my girlfriend's indulgence in self-medicating or free love after her breakup — I'm concerned, but I get it — but I am also, frankly, envious that my friend no longer has to deal with arguments over money, the division of chores, logistics, managing expectations, how his kids treated her, how he treated her, how their kids treated each other, how she treated her partner, and how each day brought on something new to argue about. So, yes, I'm fucking jealous, especially when Boyfriend and I fight about all of the above, plus who takes care of the baby more, and my immediate reaction is to tell him to get the fuck out of *my house*. No longer does my girlfriend have to live under the same roof with a throng of kids, not all of whom share the same DNA. No longer does she continually have to "work" on their relationship and make sure everyone is happy blending, trying to treat his kids equally to her own. No longer does she have to self-medicate to fall asleep after another day of blending. Above all else, no longer does my friend even have to try to pretend to enjoy being in a blended family. *Lucky bitch.*

Learning of their breakup is kind of like finding out that a celebrity is headed to rehab for "exhaustion." Not exactly earth-shattering news. It may make for good gossip within their circle of friends, but it is far from a surprise, especially after I saw and heard how they treated each other in the early days. If they were comfortable enough to bicker in front of me and Boyfriend on our double date, I could only imagine what their fights were like when no one was around. Death, taxes, and their breakup, I kind of knew in my gut, were three things that were inevitable.

I feel a dull melancholy for weeks when I learn about it, though, as I do when I hear of anyone I care for breaking up, but I'm even sadder about theirs because they couldn't make blending work. Their issues weren't just between them. Their issues included all their children, arguments over who paid for what, and her feeling unappreciated and taken for granted. I know they truly loved one another when they first decided to blend. So what the hell happened to them? I don't wonder if my blended family will eventually follow the same fate and demise, because although Boyfriend and I have started to argue over perceived slights and unresolved issues, more often than not we are, for the most part, still happy living together. Plus, after seeing my friend's family implode and hearing about the disaster of them un-blending, breaking up a blended family seems dreadfully grisly.

In fact, un-blending is even harder than a breakup, because you don't break up with just your partner. Suddenly, the children that were part of your life when you blended no longer are. Suddenly, your children, who have already gone through one divorce, are now going through another one, but they're not just losing their mom's or dad's partner, they're also losing siblings, whether related by blood or not. I do think that after a traditional breakup, one that involves no kids, there should be a no-contact period. But when you've known your partner's children for almost as long as you've known your partner, it feels absolutely wrong to ditch the kids, who never asked to be in a blended family and certainly didn't ask to go through un-blending. And when you also share a child together, obviously there needs to be contact.

"I kept in touch via text with my ex's two children," says one of my friends who is also part of the 66 percent of couples who don't make blending work. "And they were kind to my texts, always responding, thanking me for checking in on them, or saying 'thank you' when I would send texts wishing them good luck for things like the start of the school year or when I heard that one of them got a part-time job. But the texts became less and less frequent because, truthfully, I had moved on with my life and had slowly started to forget my old life. My ex's children never reach out to me. I don't think it's because they hate me. I just think it's because we all moved on, and they did, too. Once my ex had a serious new girlfriend, I felt like my texts to the kids were an intrusion. It became just awkward, too, because I wasn't talking to their father. All I can say is that it is a blessing in disguise that we didn't have a bio child together, but that doesn't mean that his children weren't an important part of my life. So, yes, it was like a triple breakup, all in one."

She says she still often thinks about her bonus children, but the thoughts are fleeting. "It kind of feels like thinking of my best friend from when I was ten years old who I lost touch with. I think of our childhood memories fondly, but we went in different directions. We don't dislike each other. We just have nothing in common anymore. What I had in common with my bonus children was their father, and we don't have that anymore. But even if I don't reach out, I still think of them fondly. I definitely didn't think I'd miss them as much as I do, because my ex and I definitely weren't on the same page when we were all together." Now when she thinks of reaching out to them, something stops her. Mostly, she feels wistful that she has no idea what is happening in their lives anymore.

"It didn't seem like they minded when I used to text them right after their father and I split, and I let them know that they could always reach out to me. What more could I do? I had to accept the fact that they may not want me in their lives and were just too polite to say so. For nine years we were in each other's lives. I encouraged my kids to keep in touch with his kids. And they did for a while until, I guess, life got in the way and they were busy with their friends and school work. It didn't seem that my children cared that much to keep in touch with his kids. Maybe they found it awkward too." Also, she adds, while she had closure with her ex after breaking up, she didn't feel as if she had closure with his kids, who weren't around when she moved into her own place again. "That always makes me sad, when I think that I didn't even really get the chance to say goodbye."

· · · · ·

So, yes, I admit, I often find myself extremely jealous of my friend who set Boyfriend and me up. I look back at that night of our double date and think, "Oh, okay, *now* I get it! I get why you bickered so much." Smug me is now humbled me. That's for fucking sure. I have started to resent Boyfriend over many issues, mostly those that stem from financial disagreements and feeling as if I can do no right, that I'm always being reprimanded for something, like I'm a child. I have a myriad of complaints and hurt feelings, and I no longer trust Boyfriend's promises that things will get better. Boyfriend has a myriad of complaints about me and my expectations, and he doesn't understand why I lash out. It turns out that Boyfriend's financial condition wasn't situational, and I've become like my girlfriend's ex, reminding him about how much I shell out for our blended family compared to him. I know what triggers my anger and am self-aware enough to know why I've started to feel unappreciated, which leads me to feel resentful and Boyfriend to feel disrespected. He doesn't always deserve my wrath, that's for sure. But I can never seem to get him to see my side of things.

From my perspective, I've let a lot of things slide — truthfully, because Boyfriend gave me the baby I was so desperate for. When I cry to one of my friends after an epic fight with Boyfriend, years into blending, she actually says to me, "If you two didn't have a baby together, I think you would have been done with him within six months." I don't know whether to agree or not — I can't think of life now without Baby Holt in it — though I do often think that if Boyfriend and I had no kids, there would be a hell of lot less arguing and we'd be truly happy. Fuck, when I think about the early days, when we were just dating, when we had no issues and it was glorious, when I did really feel like I had found my soulmate, I felt like I was his priority. I felt wooed, and he showed it. And I showed it. But it is entirely true that I let a lot slide with Boyfriend that I never would put up with from any other man because he gave me Baby Holt, and what better gift is that? So many times, I guess, I feel like *I owe him.*

. . . . .

By the time the friends who set up Boyfriend and me break up and she has moved out, I am catching up, understanding now how hard blending can be, how it affects everyone in the family, and how much extra effort you have to put in to make blending work, to make it so that, if everyone is not necessarily blissfully happy, they are, at the very least, *reasonably* happy. Yes, I'd settle for reasonably happy. So while my friends' relationship has been beaten to shit and is dead and buried, some part of them must feel a huge relief that it has ended, as if both of them have been acquitted on all counts of murder. *It was self-defence.*

My friend is free! She. Is. Out. And on some days, this makes me green with envy. My shrink tells me that "jealousy is also a fear of comparison and insecurity." I find myself comparing my girlfriend's once-blended family to mine, which is dumb for a number of reasons. I don't know exactly how much of a role blending played in their breakup, because my friend has never really told me the entire story of the demise of their relationship. Plus, I don't want to pry, and — *La la la, I can't hear you* — do I really want to know? Mostly, on bad days in my blended household, I torment myself by comparing our lives, despite the fact that all families, blended or not, have their own unique issues.

I know Boyfriend really loves me, and I love him, but I have started to feel insecure in my relationship and am starting to wonder what the hell we've gotten into. On many days, I wonder when I turned into such a bitch, seething with resentment, jealousy, and insecurity. What has happened to the lighthearted, witty, independent woman I once was? I wonder why Boyfriend can never, *ever* say he's sorry. Mostly, I no longer feel like Boyfriend's priority, or a priority at all. The more I tell him how I'm feeling, the more defensive he becomes. I feel a lack of appreciation for all the things I've purchased for him and our family — the condo in Mexico, the motorcycle I bought him for his fortieth birthday, the piece of expensive artwork I bought for our anniversary, the leather motorcycle jacket he wanted, the designer sunglasses he wanted, the $500 bottle of cologne he wanted, the house they all are living in. I've started to feel like a walking bank machine. All I really want is either a genuine "thank you" or a genuine "I'm sorry."

Because we never can seem to resolve our issues when we argue in person, the arguments often continue throughout the following days by text or email. I get a lot of emails from Boyfriend after I tell him how I'm feeling. "We can speak about everything in detail: driving Rowan, food in the fridge, paying bills, vacationing, taking care of Holt, paying for Holt, the house, repairs to the house, the condo in Mexico, showing thanks, managing and splitting time with kids, time and money spent with our own daughters, division of time, my business," Boyfriend writes to me in one text. So it's not like he doesn't know what bothers me or what our relationship issues are. I stare at the list of issues he's written out that clearly need to get resolved. Boyfriend, yes, is aware of how I'm feeling, but will anything change? Because I need them to.

But, at the same time, I wanted all of this, right? I was the one who invited my partner and his daughters to move in. I was the one who brought up the idea of having another baby. On many, many occasions, I can't help but think, "We thought blending our families was a great idea! We were so in love! Having another baby was a blessing! So what the hell happened to us?!"

"At least you are dedicated to your nights playing soccer or badminton," I find myself complaining to him, jealous of how he can find a dedicated time to play his sports, while I can't even lock him down for one date night a week. We try, of course, to have date nights, but we can't quite fit it in with all of our kids' schedules and with the baby. Of course I was a priority when we first met. We were trying to impress each other and we wanted to spend all of our time together. But now, I just feel taken advantage of. I wonder how much more I have in me to make us work, considering nothing really ever gets resolved and I find myself criticizing more than complimenting. He has started criticizing more than complimenting as well.

Bonus Daughters aren't staying with us as much anymore, and when they do, they bring friends and boyfriends. Since their friends, boyfriends, and part-time jobs are near their mother's, that's where they stay most of the time. So now, to see them, Boyfriend must drive to them and take them for dinner near their mother's house. I start to feel less and less important to him as he starts to make plans to go out more nights than not. I find myself constantly complaining that he's not appreciative of all I have done and do. Our family is starting to unravel, because I can't seem to lower my expectations and have started to resent the fact that I'm always being told to "be the bigger person" and that I'm being "unrealistic." I wonder, *Are we fighting to continue to blend, or is this the start of us un-blending?*

Thanks to my friend and her newfound freedom, I now also can't stop asking myself, *If I had to blend again, would I?* The unpleasant feeling in the pit of my stomach is now constant.

· TEN ·

There's subversive disparity not just within the four walls of the house, but also within the snack drawers and refrigerator. I've started to notice how Boyfriend magically turns into a short-order cook when his children are with us, buying groceries he knows they like or have asked for and practically making three-course meals when they are staying with us. On the days they are not with us, Boyfriend doesn't seem to care as much about what we — Rowan, me, and him — are having for dinner. He's more than happy leaving our nanny to make us something and leaving the fridge almost bare. Boiled pasta is as fancy as he gets for Rowan. There are still nights, of course, when he does make dinners for the two of us, when the children aren't around or on our date nights we have promised to have once a week. But mostly, on the nights without his children, dinners are pretty plain.

It's unfathomable, isn't it, to be jealous of children who always have the groceries they enjoy in our house and to resent the fact that their dad spends an hour preparing a meal for them as if he's on a cooking game show on the Food Network. But I often am jealous when I see that Boyfriend — what, *tries harder? Puts in more of an effort?* — as he stocks the cupboards and fridge and makes home-cooked dinners, from scratch and, of course, with love, mostly on the days when his children stay with us. So, yes, we even argue over groceries.

Boyfriend, by default, is in charge of the grocery shopping, his way of contributing to the household. We never talked about the division of household chores before we blended, but we both know it's his way of chipping in, while living without paying rent or the mortgage or property taxes or the gardener or the internet or cable bill. I hate grocery shopping, so I think it's a fair trade. But it does bother me that, if it's just my daughter at home, he'll boil her pasta, while he puts on an elaborate dinner when his children are with us.

While my feelings may be irrational, it's nice to know that I'm not the only one who goes through this. "Sometimes it does bother me that my husband does things for his biological son that he never does for our two kids, because I'm the primary parent," one of my friends tells me, once I start noticing how, when Boyfriend's children are over, our house turns into a five-star restaurant. "For instance, he goes to his son's doctor's appointments and buys him birthday and Christmas presents and clothes, and he's never done any of that with our other two. He's happy to let me be the primary parent, whereas he's somewhat competitive with his ex-wife, who he has a very strained relationship with," she says. "Part of it is also that he feels terribly guilty about his son, which I understand. So he plans special activities with him and tries harder to have quality time, and makes him meals that he'd never make for us. I do understand why this is the case, but sometimes I can't help but feel that he treats his kids differently, including when it comes to what they eat."

Unlike Boyfriend's kids, my daughter lives with me and Boyfriend full-time. I really don't know what it's like to only see your children half the time, nor can I really, truly, understand what it's like for his children to only see their dad part-time. This guilt and need to make up for the times he isn't with them is an emotion he keeps close to his heart — I have never actually heard him say he feels guilty — but that he shows by making them elaborate meals. Maybe his guilt is the root cause of many of our arguments, including those about grocery shopping. I do know, however, what it's like to not see your children for a while, as my daughter spends three consecutive weeks with her father every summer and during winter break from school. If the pain Boyfriend and his children feel when they don't see each other is anything like how I feel when Rowan is not with me, I feel for all of them. I miss my daughter so much when I don't see her for weeks; it feels like a part of me is missing, even though I know she's safe and happy. There's always a constant ache in my heart. Does Boyfriend feel this ache? Do Boyfriend's children feel this ache? Is he trying to show them, through home-cooked meals, his love? I don't know. My gut tells me, *Duh, obviously.*

What I do know is that I often want to scream, "Where are my staples?" when I wake up and see there is no orange juice left. Or that someone in the household has left a carton of orange juice in the fridge with maybe a teaspoon left. Boyfriend will say he shops for me, but I don't remember the last time I ate a Fruit Roll-Up or slices of ham. Of course, in a traditional family, finding an empty carton of milk happens all the time, especially if you have teenagers. The difference is, you can yell at your kid. I can't yell at Boyfriend's children, so I just scream in my head.

One of my friends, who has six children and is happily married, and not in a blended family, told me about the time one of her kid's birthday request was an entire carton of chocolate milk *just for himself.* How easy and cheap a gift is that? Alas, her kid didn't end up getting his birthday present wish, because his siblings didn't know that their mom had bought that carton of chocolate milk especially for the birthday boy. The kid burst into tears, of course, when he realized he didn't get the one and only wish he had for his birthday. That's how I'm starting to feel. I'm a grown-ass woman who doesn't get the groceries she wants. I don't cry, but I do get angry, an adult throwing a tantrum, like a kid who didn't get his carton of chocolate milk on his birthday.

How can Boyfriend remember that his daughters like a certain type of potato chips but can't remember that I need to eat a banana every morning? I've become pretty protective of the few staples I like to always have on hand.

"I'll just go grocery shopping for myself," I've huffed on more than one occasion, but I never do. Once I hid a few cans of Diet Coke in my bedroom because of all the other mouths who like Diet Coke. I have also, when there is one Diet Coke left in the fridge, put a Post-it note on it, with my name written across, feeling as if I'm living in a dorm room with roommates instead of with my family. I remember those emails sent to "all company" from a colleague at work who realized that other people in the office had been using the cream in the office fridge that they'd bought for themself. I always laughed at those company emails. Should I send out a group text to my blended family? At home, I'm the one who wants to remind people that it's my cream.

In my defence, I have to say that I felt that I needed to. However, I also have to admit that my actions might have been a bit over the top. But I want to tell you what one of Boyfriend's children does for me, because it shows that they not only care about me but also know me. One day, when I open the fridge, I see a Post-it note on a lone Diet Coke on the shelf, with "Rebecca" written on it. I didn't do it. Boyfriend's daughter did this, and even though it seems like such a small thing, it actually means the *world* to me. *She cares!* Just as little things can turn into huge arguments in a blended family, sometimes small things make you want to cry because you realize that, while it may not always seem like it, people are thinking about you.

But shopping for a blended family means integrating differences and evolving new rules and rituals. Boundaries are more fluid in our house, because, by definition, we are less cohesive than non-divorced families. When Boyfriend's girls are with us, we all eat together. "I can't think of any blended family that I know of where everyone's happy all the time," one of my divorced, and wisest, friends says. She, too, tried to blend with a man who had two children. "Maybe you should just accept the fact that he's going to act differently, and go out of his way, when his children are around. Just enjoy that he cooks for you!" she says. She has a good point. And I do enjoy when Boyfriend makes us all dinner, because Boyfriend is a wonderful cook … when his children are with us, that is.

I find it hilarious that, yet again, this common bullshit issue in blended families is something else that somehow didn't make it to the lips or fingers of any so-called blended family expert. Sure, I appreciate their advice on how not to force other children to love you — duh — but where's the advice about the grocery shopping arguments you'll inevitably have? Where's the tip warning me to not take it personally that Boyfriend is a chef part-time? It's not the huge issues that I need advice on. It's the small issues, like grocery shopping, that no one seems to talk about, that often lead to fights that can last days. *Death by a million paper cuts.* I know that others feel the same way. A coincidence? I think not.

"Oh my god," I read in a comment section on a blended family forum I visit when I need to see if I'm being totally unrealistic about something … and also, to read about others who have it worse than I do. "No lie! We almost never have eggs or pancakes or anything like that on our alone weekends, but the second it's the weekend with his children, we turn into a Denny's," one commenter writes, and I can't help but laugh out loud, not just because I haven't been to a Denny's in years, but also because now I'm craving pancakes. Still, I know only too well how she feels. "Last weekend with them, they wanted omelettes," another commenter posts. "My husband has never made me an omelette in the seven years we've been together, but that's what his kids wanted. He even had to go out and buy all the ingredients because all we had was eggs." I feel validated. I'm not alone!

"Mine, too! Husband becomes a chef when his kids are around. My husband used to make me breakfast when we we're still dating and he was trying to impress me. Now I'm lucky if he makes me a coffee. Sometimes I ask him to make me breakfast when the kids aren't around, and he whines that he doesn't want to. I'm like, 'Seriously?! When your kids are around you make eggs, bacon, sausage, pancakes, cinnamon rolls ...'" yet another commenter writes, somewhat excitedly, perhaps because, like me, she didn't know this was going to be a concern after blending, and even though we don't know each other, *we are in this together.* We aren't batshit crazy. The contempt is real!

I almost want to take a screenshot of these comments and text them to Boyfriend to say, "Look, I'm not the only one who feels this way!" because often he doesn't understand why I feel snubbed and rejected. But I know it will be fruitless (as will my fruit bowl). Boyfriend will just argue that it's not true that he leaves us to starve when his children are with their mother. Okay, "starve" may be too strong a word. But I want to say to him, "Look inside the fridge! Do you notice it's bare?" And then, when his kids are around, I also want to say to him, "Now look at it! Do you notice the difference?"

·   ·   ·   ·   ·

"Why is it you only do a good grocery shop when your kids are here?" I ask Boyfriend out of the blue one night.

I'm surprised by his response. I may sound accusatory, but he is overly defensive, as if I'm accusing him of sleeping with one of my close girlfriends, not just asking him about his grocery schedule.

"Do you know how hard it is to shop for six people who all like different things? Do you know how expensive groceries are?" he asks. I can't help but scoff. Surely the grocery bill isn't as large as what I shell out on bills. Surely it can't cost as much as I pay to keep this household running, a source of constant contention between us, especially after Baby Holt's birth.

"I also have to buy all the toilet paper and the paper towels and cleaning supplies," Boyfriend adds.

Even though I don't grocery shop, I know that groceries are expensive. I did grocery shop *all by myself* for many years before he moved in. That being said, there are many grocery store chains that are pretty cheap. Boyfriend does now go to Costco — because we've blended families, apparently we need eight thousand chicken wings. We now also, it seems, need to buy huge packages of toilet paper, as if we're going on a year-long camping trip. There are also grocery items now in my house that I don't really agree with, like the sugary cereals Bonus Daughters like, and now Holt likes, too. It doesn't help that, although Rowan won't touch any of it, it's piled high in my cupboard. Rowan is ridiculously health conscious and refuses to eat anything that is not organic. She also demands vegetables with every meal. (Thanks, stupid school, for teaching her about the importance of eating organic, leaving out the part about how much organic-everything costs. *Thank you very much!* Often I just lie to her, telling her that, yes, the chicken is organic, of course the eggs are organic, and yes, everything on your plate is organic.)

"Do you know how hard it is to cook a meal that everyone likes?" Boyfriend also asks. He's right. Although he makes home-cooked dinners that could be served at a five-star restaurant when his girls are around, he gets defensive whenever I mention it. But because he acts like a chef when his children are around, I have started to treat him like a waiter or busboy, or that's the way I think he must feel. He not only makes the dinner, but he also has to remind the rest of us to put our dirty dishes away. He, too, must know what it feels like to be unappreciated.

Behind the closed doors of blended families, the arguments over buying food that every kid likes is concealed, guarded like a secret you'd share with only your trusted therapist — which I do. Have these experts not looked at what people in blended families are talking about on comment boards? Like the Hi/Bye Fight, the grocery shopping argument is a real thing in blended families — both ludicrous and seemingly trivial, but something that eats away (pun not intended) at our once splendid blended family. We aren't just arguing over what he buys and when he buys groceries. We are basically also arguing about who gets the most attention and love.

Why is this starting to bother me only now? Maybe I'm only starting to notice it now. Unlike the husband who won't even make his wife a coffee, Boyfriend sometimes still makes me coffee in the morning. Sometimes I'll make him coffee and bring it to him while he's in the shower. I know, in these instances, when he lights up when I bring him coffee as he gets ready to go to work, that I still very much love him and he does appreciate me. Even still, the resentment overshadows these small moments of appreciation and is sucking the life out of me, slowly but surely.

· · · · ·

So why do I feel such resentment toward Boyfriend after years of blending? Thanks to my therapist, I think I can say with confidence that, in my opinion, it's Boyfriend's seeming sense of entitlement that really irks me. (Boyfriend, of course, will have his own opinion on this.) When a big-ticket item breaks down in the house — the furnace, for example — he expects that me and my ex will pay for it, since it's not his house (although he lives in it). His action — or inaction — leaves me in a panic to pay for it. And as everyone knows, big-ticket items always seem to break down when your bank account is low. Mostly, I don't think Boyfriend really thinks about money in the same way I do.

As bad as this sounds, life was so much more, well, fun when I was with my ex, the father of my daughter. His income meant that I led a pretty fucking good life. When I was with Rowan's father, there were numerous trips to Maui, where we stayed at the Four Seasons. It didn't seem like a big deal to walk into a department store and buy three pairs of designer shoes with his credit card — he wouldn't blink an eye. Once, he bought me diamond earrings, which were beautiful, but I didn't wear them for months because I thought they looked too flashy. I never worried about money when I was with Ex. I don't remember paying for anything, or even seeing a bill. When our daughter was born, he didn't just buy me a Cartier Love bracelet, he also bought me a car. I'm not saying money makes you happier (although it kind of does, at least when you get a high off of buying a $1,200 pair of shoes), but it does make life easier. But money isn't a guarantee that you'll stay together, obviously.

After Ex and I broke up, I found myself actually having to look at bank statements and work on a *budget* (gawd, I hate that word!). I'm not going to lie — compared to many, I still lead a pretty blessed life. But I had to learn that, no, I could not afford to buy myself three pairs of designer shoes. Staying at the Four

Seasons in Maui for ten days was no longer an option. I learned that bills come every single month and that they have to be paid off every single month. After Rowan's dad and I broke up, I was no longer spoiled rotten with expensive gifts. I had to get used to a new lifestyle and appreciate what I had in the present, not compare what I had in the past.

Boyfriend's spending habits, however, even after his expensive divorce, haven't seemed to change at all. He'll still buy himself shoes, although he has almost as many pairs as I do. He'll still lose money at his weekly poker games. And, yeah, it really starts to bug me when Boyfriend talks about expensive cars and points out houses that are worth millions, when I think he should be happy where we are. I mean, for fuck's sake, the house we live in is worth more than a million dollars. We have a condo in Mexico! When he talks about material things, it annoys me to no end. So not only do I become resentful that I think he thinks that money just falls of the trees in my backyard. I'm also really resentful that he doesn't realize I actually have made a pretty lucrative career for myself and that I work extremely hard at it, and have for decades. He is happy the money is there but seems to give entirely no fucks where it comes from. I don't think Boyfriend lacks ambition, but we definitely have a very *different* definition of ambition.

I usually work at home, and since Boyfriend is his own boss, he can often do the same. However, it starts to annoy me when he works out of the house. I end up asking him, "Are you going to work today?" I need space and I can't work knowing he's at home, even if he's in another room. Once, I wanted to be with him twenty-four/seven. Now I want to scream, "Go to your office!"

The issues are starting to pile up. Could it be we are just … not compatible? The thought is like a knife through my heart.

When I was dating, the first thing I would do, if I went back to a guy's place, is look at their bookshelves or the books just lying around their homes. If there were no books, that was a warning sign to me, a definite red flag, and there would be no follow-up date. I'm not sure why I let this rule slide with Boyfriend. When I first visited his house and was scouting about the place, like a detective looking for clues, and didn't see any books around, I should have known that this might be a problem. But I think I excused the fact that he didn't read or have any books around, because the oh-so-handsome-but-underemployed-guy I was dating right before him read *all the time* and had *hundreds* of books, and that relationship didn't work out. I was trying on something new with Boyfriend by dating a guy who only read the *Sports Illustrated* swimsuit edition and, occasionally, the sports pages of the paper. Not that there's anything wrong with that.

What is wrong, in my opinion, is that Boyfriend rarely reads anything I write, nor does he seem to notice or recognize that publishing nine books is a huge accomplishment, one that paid for the place in Mexico. He doesn't seem to care that my career allows me to buy him expensive gifts and pay for the gardener and taxes, which I was and am happy to do. (Make that: I have to do.) But because I can't seem to lower my expectations, it hurts when I don't get recognition or praise, especially from Boyfriend, who is supposed to be my number one cheerleader. Although I write a weekly blog, which I post on my social feeds, Boyfriend rarely, if ever, reads it. I feel like if he was, in fact, on my team, he'd read my stuff, taking three minutes out of his day to do so. I'd like to think he's proud of me and my work too, but, no, he isn't. If he was, wouldn't he say something to me like, "I loved your latest story!" instead of, "I haven't had time to read it." So, yes, it seems to me that he only cares about the fruits of the labour, rather than the labour itself.

I break out with pimples around my jawline. Stupid stress pimples. I make an appointment with my dermatologist, who also happens to be in a blended family.

"What can I say?" my dermatologist says when I moan about my stress pimple flare-ups and tell her I blame it on Boyfriend and me not getting along. "It's a long-term process. Believe me, I know! It's been twelve years for us. At this point, the only thing holding us together is our weekly couple's therapy."

I ask her, point blank, not just about what the hell she's going to do to get rid of the stress pimples, but also why the fuck she stays in her marriage if they are so unhappy. How much money, I wonder, do she and her husband spend on therapy just to keep their relationship alive and to feel equals in their blended households? Their weekly couple's therapy, she says, is the only place her husband really hears her complaints, mostly because the therapist sides with her and asks her husband, "Do you *hear* what she's saying?"

As she pops my pimples with a needle, I actually attempt to do the math. If their couple's therapist charges them $250 a week (a standard price for most therapists) and there are fifty-two weeks in a year, that means they spend ... wait ... still doing the math ... $13,000 a year! And they've been going to couple's therapy for two years now.

"How do I make it work and make myself happy?" she asks, after I ask if there's some manual going around that I'm missing. "I just make sure that I go out with my girlfriends every Thursday night to let off steam. And I'll go away a few times a year for girls' weekends to Vegas." So, my dermatologist just admitted that what keeps them together is not just weekly couple's therapy, but also the fact that she makes a point to get away from her husband and their blended household. Even though it is painful to have these stress pimples popped, it is nice to hear that someone else feels the same way I do and that her blended family is basically being held together by safety pins. They spend $13,000 a year to keep fighting to blend. Staying in a successful blended family, it turns out, can also be fucking expensive.

"I think everyone was just on their best behaviour when we decided to blend our families," my dermatologist continues. "Then, a couple years in … I don't know, it seemed to come out of nowhere, and things started to flare up. I became used to feeling like a stranger in my own home. I'm the one who does the grocery shopping. And I never get it right," she tells me after I have just told her how annoyed I get with the way Boyfriend goes grocery shopping. "There is always something that someone in my family finds missing. I tell them to write it down on the grocery list, but they never do, even though it's right there on the kitchen counter! More than once I've sent my husband out to buy groceries, but he's terrible at it. Honestly, I wouldn't be surprised if he came home one day with dog food, and we don't have a dog. So I just do it myself, and when the kids or my husband complains, I just tell them they can go grocery shopping for themselves."

Who knew the bullshit and — What is it that I'm feeling? Um, like I'm holding a grudge — over what Boyfriend chooses to buy while grocery shopping is a common argument on both sides. At the very least, it's irritating when he tells me that what he pays for groceries is more than what he would pay chipping in for rent. What bothers me is that I don't feel he's really thinking of me. But while I'm annoyed by how Boyfriend shops, without him recognizing that he buys a shitload more groceries and makes dinners mostly only when his children are around, others in blended families make *excuses* to go grocery shopping, just so they can get away from the craziness in their own blended households. Yes, many of us in blended families will even do outside chores to get some alone time.

Unfortunately, I can never make that excuse. Boyfriend knows I can't cook and haven't the slightest interest in learning to cook. I'd rather do anything than grocery shop for our blended family — Costco both amazes and terrifies me — so I shouldn't complain, right? But I do gripe about this. Sometimes it's warranted, and sometimes maybe not so much.

· ELEVEN ·

I am starting to get private messages from "friends" on social media, people I've never met in person but who know I'm in a blended family, because I have written about it and have posted photographs of our children.

"Hi Rebecca," one such message starts, when I open my inbox. "I believe we haven't formally met, but I read your posts and I am embarking on blending a family. So, so hard! Would love to know if you have any advice and can offer some insight into what to expect. Thanks so much and hope you're great!" It's like receiving a message from a childhood friend you haven't talked to in twenty years and they ask, "So what's new?" I mean, where would I even start?

These messages make me feel like a sought-out therapist, but one with no real credentials, except for the fact that I know, and am learning more and more every day, about the chaos and bullshit of blending families and what it is like to be in one. I'm not sure how to respond to these messages, because I suddenly remember, especially because of the message, that blending wasn't as easy a transition as I had thought it actually was.

When we first blended and Boyfriend's two daughters stayed
with us, I had, in fact, witnessed him trying to calm them down
when they had mini-meltdowns occasionally. Sometimes it was
just the eldest daughter who was in tears. But mostly, it was his
youngest daughter, bless her, who used to cry to her father, while
I patiently waited, sometimes for hours, as he reassured her that
he didn't love me more than her.

"It's not about loving someone more. It's just a different kind
of love," Boyfriend would tell her. His children didn't always believe him, as they cried in their new beds in their new bedroom
in their new house, adjusting to their dad's new life and, by extension, their new lives. And why would they believe him? His
answer, though true, sounded like a platitude. And they were
still getting over their parents' divorce when I entered the picture just two months after he had moved out from his marital
home. Plus, they were almost pre-teens, so their emotions were
all wonky, like when you update your phone and it seems pos-
sessed for the next two days. Unlike my daughter, who only ever
knew her parents not being together, since we split up when she
was just turning three, Boyfriend's daughters were still processing their parents' divorce and the fact that they were now children of divorce. They needed a lot of reassurance, a lot of extra
attention, and extra love.

And, even though he may not have recognized it, and I
didn't either until it was too late, Boyfriend, I think, was going through an incredible amount of shame and guilt, and also
enormous pressure to make sure his children were both emotionally and mentally okay. Boyfriend didn't want to be with his
ex-wife, was never going to get back together with her, but he
certainly didn't want his daughters to feel such sorrow, to feel
loved less, or to be worried that they were to blame for their
parents' breakup.

Unlike my friend who says it's silly to "pretend" that you love bio children differently than the ones who come along after blending, I felt a sense of responsibility that I had to care for Boyfriend's daughters, make them happy, and believed that eventually I would fall in love with them. But, as everyone knows, you can't force love. And, looking back, what the fuck did I know about raising children who weren't biologically my own? What did I know about being a child of divorce?

The virtual friend who had asked for advice, adding, "Blending families is so, so hard," is right. In fact, even though she's just about to embark on blending, her words resonate with me more than any expert advice I have read. Sure, saying that blending is "so, so hard," is not a very interesting description of what happens when blending, but it is *so, so* true. Blending families is so, so fucking hard!

Oddly, later on the same day, I get a text from a divorced male acquaintance who has shared custody with his children and wants to chat. We aren't exactly friends — we haven't ever gone out or even met for coffee — we're more virtual or texting friends. I tell him that Boyfriend would not like it if I met up with him, which is true, but I also tell him that I don't think his girlfriend would like it if we met for coffee either.

By this point, Boyfriend doesn't like it if I go out with Rowan and her dad when he is in town, even though I think it's wonderful for Rowan to see that her father and I can and do get along. So, no, I don't tell Boyfriend about these calls, because he'll get jealous, and then, of course, another bullshit fight would ensue about how I can't be friends with people of the opposite sex. I definitely can't be friends with people I once dated, not because I think it's wrong, but because Boyfriend does, and because I love him, I don't want to hurt his feelings.

"Call me if you can, please. I need advice!" my male friend messages me.

I hate giving advice, but I am curious to know what guidance he's looking for. I do know that, only days earlier, his child-free girlfriend had moved in with him, into a new house that he had purchased for both of them and the two children he has part-time. I also know, even though his girlfriend makes a good living, he never asks her to pay for rent and professes he never will, mostly because he can afford the house on his own and is more traditional. He's happy being the provider. It feeds his ego.

"KK," I message back. "I'm calling you now."

And so I call him, not because I think I have any words of wisdom, but because I'm just plain nosy and want to hear what bullshit has led to him reaching out to me.

"What's up?" I ask, after he picks up the phone after one ring. Clearly, he's been waiting by his phone, as desperate as if he were waiting for results from a doctor after having a biopsy ... but it's a weekend.

"My girlfriend is getting upset with my kids over the stupidest things," he tells me. "Is this normal?"

I snort. Normal? What the fuck is normal in a blended family?

"Didn't she move in, like, less than seventy-two hours ago?" I ask, trying not to laugh.

"Yeah, but last night she got upset because she was trying to watch some reality show on television and couldn't hear because my kids were being too loud and they were annoying her by jumping on the couch," he says.

As absurd as it may sound, I do kind of get where his girlfriend is coming from, even if I don't agree with her execution, which apparently involved screaming at him to tell his kids to be quiet. I simply think that his girlfriend wasn't prepared for all the life changes that would come her way after moving in with my friend, especially when his two boys stay with them. It *is* a pretty big upheaval to go from single and in charge of your surroundings, and watching a TV show in peace, to being one member of a family circus that includes two rowdy boys she isn't related to who have no interest in her addiction to reality shows. I feel for her and for him, both equally and for different reasons. Clearly, if his girlfriend was upset because she couldn't hear her show and was taking it out on her boyfriend, she is woefully unprepared for what life will be like in their house in the days, weeks, and years to come. Clearly, my friend, who is already lamenting about his hot-off-the-press blended family, is not adjusting so well either, being also woefully naive about the bullshit that pops up in a blended family. Before they blended, he probably had no idea how important it was for her to hear every single word of a show on television.

"Well," I tell him. "Your children should always come first. Child love is unconditional! Couple love is not." *Boy, am I fucking clever!*

I tell him, too, that he'd better set some boundaries from the start, which is advice I would have benefitted from hearing *before* I blended families. I actually do want to say, "What can I say? Blending families is so, so hard!" and leave it at that, because it really does sum it all up.

Still, when I've given him some advice, or reassurance, and think that he's feeling better about things, I can't help but break some bad news. At least, it will be bad news for him.

"Your girlfriend being upset about not being able to hear her show is *not* going to be your biggest hurdle. Not by a long shot," I say.

And so I tell him what my intuition is telling me. After all, if my male friend thinks that a battle over hearing the television is a big deal, I figure he better buckle up for the ride of a lifetime.

"She's going to want a baby. You know that, right? She's, what, thirty-six?" I say. "Her clock is ticking."

"So? She says she doesn't want kids," he tells me. "We already discussed that."

Rookie!

Sure, some women don't ever want to have kids, a perfectly sane life choice. But based on my friends who married partners who already had children, and based on my own experience, I believe there is a great possibility his girlfriend, still in her child-bearing years, will eventually talk him into having another baby, a baby that would be *theirs. Hers.* Even if only so she won't feel like an outsider when my male friend has his kids.

"Do you want to make a bet?" I ask him. I'm so confident that his girlfriend is going to try to convince him to have another baby that I tell him I'm willing to place a thousand dollar bet.

"I had a vasectomy," he adds. Ha! As if *that* means anything. "I'm not getting it reversed. No way!"

"Okay," I tell him. But I can't stop myself from reminding him that, months ago, after they had been dating for nearly two years, she gave him an ultimatum to marry him. And he proposed!

"I'm *not* having another baby," he says testily. "I don't want any more children. She says she doesn't want children. But what should I do when she flares up at the littlest things, when my kids are just being kids?"

"Um, you should probably tell her that kids are, um, loud. That's pretty much in their job description," I say.

Boy, I really am fucking clever!

My friend has now taken to calling *or* texting me every few weeks or so to "check to see" how *my* relationship is doing. These calls piss me off, because I know he wants to hear that I'm miserable, or at least have something to complain about in my blended family, especially since he's now in one and needs reassurance that he didn't make a mistake. He taunts me with questions like, "Who paid the last hydro bill?"

I tell him to go fuck himself, because I'm loyal to Boyfriend and I love Boyfriend. But still he continues to call and text, complaining about his girlfriend, who has what he describes as "fits of rage", when she feels left out … which is every time his children are around.

I know I'm not the best person for him to complain to, since I have had many of my own "fits of rage."

"I just can't take the ups and downs when my children are with me," he says.

"But you made the choice to live with her!" I say. I feel bad for him, so I also add, "Don't worry, you'll all find your groove." I'm not sure if this will be true, but, hey, I want to bolster his mood.

One of the reasons no one knows what really happens when you blend is because couples in blended families don't want to air their dirty laundry. Even I don't share the entire truth of Boyfriend's and my relationship, because I'm embarrassed over what we fight about. I don't want other people knowing. Yet, at the same time, I want people to speak up about their truths and the harsh reality of blending.

And so, my friend gets married. I'm not invited, but I see posts on social with photos of the wedding. I "like" their status updates.

Two months later, also on social, I see that they have gotten a puppy, an almost surefire sign that his girlfriend is thinking about wanting a baby. Pretty much every couple I have ever met who gets a dog — a fur baby — together finds themselves pregnant within the year. It turns out they are no exception. I see the announcement, months later, that they are expecting. I want my thousand bucks!

I want to tell both him and my virtual friend that it's important to let yourself admit that blending families is hard. It's like being an alcoholic: the first step is admitting you have a problem. Blending puts massive stress on your relationship, and if you don't accept it, it will only make things worse. In blended families, more so than others, it's really important for parents to acknowledge each other and show gratitude, because resentments crop up so easily over so many bullshit things, including not being able to hear a television show. Then again, I don't follow my own goddamn advice, so why should anyone listen to me?

My male friend stops calling and texting me. I'm pretty sure he just doesn't want to admit that I was right. Or maybe, just maybe, they are blended and splendid? Or maybe he doesn't want to give me the thousand dollars on the bet he lost.

· TWELVE ·

Brené Brown is a self-described research professor at the University of Houston, and she has spent the last twenty years studying courage, vulnerability, shame, and empathy. "Expectations are resentments waiting to happen," she quotes from novelist Anne Lamott.

So, while my friend's wife is expecting (a baby), I've had to tone down my expectations, for myself, of my family. Or at least I'm *trying* to tone down my expectations. I attempt to no longer expect anything, or at least to not feel disappointed, because expectations really are resentments waiting to happen. There's one problem, though. I don't know *how* to tone down my expectations. Expectations are abstract. They are not clearly defined or expressed. In fact, maybe I have vague expectations in my head that I have unsuccessfully tried to clarify, and thus have ended up disappointed.

"What is so wrong with having expectations?" I yell at Boyfriend in the backyard, on more than one occasion, when, yet again, I feel hurt. Tonight, I'm on a rampage, admittedly taking my wrath out on Boyfriend. Maybe I do have higher expectations than the average person, but who wants to be average?

Boyfriend, after all, fell in love with me and, like anyone in a new relationship, I came with expectations. To lower my expectations seems impossible, like I'd have to change my entire personality. Having high expectations is just who I am, and have always been, and I don't know how to change *me*. And, anyway, what's so wrong with being the type of person who sets goals and wants to achieve them? Trust me, if it was as easy as tapping my heels together, I would lower my expectations to not even having any at all, because it sure as hell would make life easier in my blended family. Note to self: *Stop expecting*.

"I'm cancelling Mother's Day forever," I say to Boyfriend, as we stand in the backyard on my third or fourth Mother's Day in a blended family and I'm in tears. We spent the majority of the day celebrating Boyfriend's mother and my mother at a brunch at my house, and I'm exhausted. My daughter wrote me a wonderful, heartfelt card, saying how much she loves me. My parents and Boyfriend's parents have given me cards and flowers. And, yes, Boyfriend has bought me a beautiful bracelet. And, yet, this year, it's just not *enough*. Why? It's now ten o'clock at night and I haven't heard a peep from Boyfriend's daughters, who of course are spending the day with their mother.

"They probably are just busy with their mom and grandparents," Boyfriend tells me.

"Too busy to send even a one-line text?" I shoot back. His daughters, now teenagers, are normally stuck to their phones like barnacles, so I find it hard to believe they haven't picked up their phones once today.

I'm not sure what to expect from them, exactly, but I know that I have to lower my expectations when it comes to celebrations, be it my birthday, Mother's Day, our anniversary, or pretty much any celebration. I get great joy celebrating other people, and I guess I expect the same back. *Tsk tsk, me*.

I watch Boyfriend typing something into his phone, and within seconds, my phone beeps.

"Happy Mother's Day, Rebecca," his eldest daughter texts, with a heart emoji. Ten seconds later, my phone beeps again.

"Happy Mother's Day, Rebecca!" his other daughter texts.

I stare at him blankly.

I'm not a fucking idiot. Clearly he just texted his girls, reminding them to text me. While I appreciate him having my back, I can't help but wish he said to his children, "Maybe wait a bit?" so that it wasn't exceedingly obvious that they didn't do it of their own volition.

When it comes to Father's Day, I make sure that my daughter makes Boyfriend a card. She does so without question, and what she writes to him is so beautiful and thoughtful, it melts my heart. So why aren't I getting the same kind of love back from Boyfriend's children on Mother's Day?

The texts would have been great if I'd found them as soon as I woke up. But with just two hours before Mother's Day ends, and in the wake of an obvious message from their father, the effort (if I can call it that) feels insincere. Probably because, let's be fucking real, the fact that they needed to be told makes it exactly that.

Maybe I have expectations because it wasn't always like this. One Mother's Day, I received a text from one of Boyfriend's daughters at 10 a.m. It isn't until much later, after blending, that it occurs to me that it wasn't that they didn't like me or didn't think of me, but they probably had no idea what to say to me or whether they should say anything at all. They have their own mother, who they are extremely loyal to. I'm also reminded of my friend, the one who grew up with a wonderful stepfather and still found Father's Day tricky because she didn't want to give him a card that said "Dad" on it, since he wasn't her dad. Maybe

Boyfriend's girls just don't feel comfortable giving me a card that says "Mom" on it because I'm not their mom.

"I think it takes a special person to be a step-parent," my friend tells me when I say my Mother's Day sucked because I was disappointed that Boyfriend's daughters failed to acknowledge me. Obviously, I haven't quite grasped how to lower my expectations. "You have to have an enormous amount of love and devotion to your partner and have a really big heart to really let the kids in. I always say my stepfather didn't have to love me, but he chose to," she says.

Yet, these days, blended families aren't necessarily any more dysfunctional than any other type of family makeup. Except for the fact that, in blended families, unlike traditional families, you definitely need to lower your expectations or else you're fucked. No expectations equals no disappointments. I have learned, though, even if I don't always show it, that I can't blame other people when they disappoint me. I should blame myself for expecting too much. I also have learned that you *never* get any credit for lowering your expectations. The same thing happens with a couple after a breakup, and you actually give the engagement ring back when the other person asks for it. Has anyone, after a nasty breakup, gotten credit for giving the engagement ring back? Never have I heard of someone getting kudos when someone expects them to give the ring back and they actually do. Never once has Boyfriend, or anyone for that matter, said to me or acknowledged, "Geez, thanks so much Rebecca for lowering your expectations. I'm so very appreciative that you didn't freak out, even though I know you feel shunned. Extra credit for you!"

But, sometimes, just sometimes, when you're in a blended family, you do get credit … from the person you least expect.

•   •   •   •   •

I have a friend who also hates Mother's Day, and she made the same mistake I did of not tempering her expectations when it came to her first Hallmark holiday in a blended family. She's one of my best girlfriends, and she married a man who had two children from his first marriage. They would go on to have their own son, a child she so desperately wanted. On her first Mother's Day as a mother of the biological child she had with her husband and a bonus parent to his children from his first marriage 50 percent of the time, my friend woke up, anticipating being celebrated. Yes, she did have high expectations for the day. (*No, no, no! Expectations = disappointment!*)

When she woke up, her husband was not beside her in bed. She thought — or hoped, or *expected* — that her husband was in the kitchen preparing a surprise breakfast for her. But when she went downstairs, breathless and eager to see what her husband had planned for her on her first Mother's Day, she couldn't believe or understand what she saw. She saw … nothing.

Her husband was nowhere to be seen, off on his daily morning jog. There was no card on the kitchen counter, no note telling her how much he appreciated her, no flowers, no small box with a piece of jewellery inside, and definitely no breakfast waiting for her. She had, she tells me, at the very least expected her husband to maybe go out and bring her back a coffee. Or she at least expected to wake up to hear her husband say to her, "Happy Mother's Day." But, nope. Her husband acted like Mother's Day was just another Sunday. My friend was clearly upset, but she didn't say anything to her husband when he got back home because she wanted to see how the day played out. She still had hope, or assumed, that he would do or say *something*. And, so she waited … and waited.

"I didn't say anything, because truthfully? I was curious to see how long it would take before he realized that he hadn't done anything for me," she says. "I didn't expect his kids to do anything for me. But I had cooked for his kids, cleaned up after his kids, drove his kids to activities. And, also, we had our own baby. How could he not acknowledge that? It was, in my head, my first real Mother's Day, and all I could think was, 'How can he forget me, the mother of one of his children?' It was *my* first real Mother's Day!" she repeats. Should she have lowered *her* expectations, to none at all, on her first Mother's Day? How much less of an expectation could my friend possibly have, when she would have even been happy with a damn $5.99 Hallmark card?

To make matters worse, it's not like her husband didn't *know* it was Mother's Day. They had plans to go over to my friend's mother's house for brunch to celebrate her mother. That evening, they had plans to go visit her husband's mother for dinner, to celebrate his mother. The one mother he seemed to have forgotten to celebrate was the mother he saw every single day — my friend, his wife and bio mother to one of his children!

"I was so bitter and beyond offended that my husband didn't even say 'Happy Mother's Day' to me," she continues. "But I kept a calm exterior, because I didn't want to start a fight that would ruin the entire day." To this day, I'm in awe of how she managed to hide her true feelings. I would have fucking lost my everloving mind if my husband totally didn't do a thing for me on Mother's Day.

Although she was enraged, she did somehow manage to contain her disappointment. She continued to wait for something (a card, a kiss) or, at least, for her husband to say the actual words.

Just when she was about to cave and admit that her Mother's Day was a disaster, her disappointment turned into elation. "When we got back to our house, there was a huge, beautiful bouquet of very expensive-looking flowers outside the door," my friend explains. "I thought, *Y-E-S!* My husband must have called to order flowers for me and they were just delivered very late in the day! I thought maybe he hadn't said anything because he, too, was wondering when the flowers would show up. They were absolutely beautiful. And I immediately felt like an asshole for thinking my husband hadn't thought about doing anything for me on Mother's Day."

But then she opened and read the card. She was beyond floored.

The gorgeous flower arrangement wasn't from her husband. The flowers weren't sent "from the kids" via her husband either. Guess who had sent them to her? Well, the flowers were from … *her husband's ex-wife.*

"The card read, 'Thank you for taking such care of my children when they are with you,'" my friend tells me.

My friend, of course, was flabbergasted, not just because her husband's ex-wife did this very considerate thing, but because his ex-wife was the only one in her blended family vortex who acknowledged her on Mother's Day.

"How gracious was it that his *ex* was so thoughtful, and remembered *me* on Mother's Day, and went out of her way to send me flowers with such a nice note about taking care of their children, while my husband didn't do a damn thing for me?" she asks. Of course, there was an ensuing fight.

That was the start of their un-blending, she reflects. "He didn't get why I was so upset. I just kind of thought, how can I move on from this? Was every Mother's Day going to be like this for the rest of my life? It sounds so immature, but Mother's Day mattered to me, and it should have mattered to my husband because it mattered to me. I fought for us for three more years. But Mother's Day was ruined for me. It wasn't something I could forget. I could never quite forgive my husband for what I expected to be a wonderful day. After he didn't even acknowledge me on Mother's Day, I started to see all his faults and I started to notice how much he was always letting me down. So, yeah ..." she trails off, because there's not much more to say. In this case, her now-ex's non-action spoke louder than words.

Like me, she detests Mother's Day.

So, while I also can't seem to lower my expectations, I have learned to create my own celebration, since my birthday always falls on the same weekend as Mother's Day. I simply book a ticket and head to our condo in Mexico, either solo or just with my daughter, so I'm not around and, thus, can't have any spoiled expectations, and so I can enjoy my freedom. Freedom from my blended family. Freedom from worrying if I'm going to get a "Happy Birthday" message or "Happy Mother's Day" texts. Freedom from worrying about why I was so worried about not being acknowledged. Freedom from putting Boyfriend in the middle of me and his biological children, who he would have to remind to text me. Freedom from expecting nothing and everything. Freedom from having to be the bigger person, and freedom from having expectations.

Many of my friends just *do* lower their expectations in their blended families. Or they really don't give a shit if they're acknowledged or not. Or at least they say they don't care. So either they are saints or liars. "My stepson would never make me a card for Mother's Day, which is fine because he has a mother and she should get the card," one of my girlfriends says. She has two biological daughters with her husband, who has a son from his first marriage. "I think if I didn't have any kids of my own and was only caring for my husband's child half the time, I'd feel differently about this. On the other hand, I do call my own stepmother on Mother's Day because she raised me and my sister and doesn't have kids of her own."

The secret to happiness in blended families, it seems, is to have low expectations. Unfortunately, it's quite hard to accept the fact that other people might never have intended to let me down, but that doesn't mean I'm not let down. When it comes to expectations within a blended family, sometimes you just have to pull up your ugly granny pants, be the bigger person, and recognize that what others consider their best is just ... less than you expected. But if I hear the words "You need to lower your expectations" one more fucking time, I may just explode.

· · · ·

I'm constantly reminded of my friend who told me that you have to have an enormous amount of love and devotion to your partner and have a really big heart to let the kids "really in."

I have to ask myself, *Have I truly not fully accepted Boyfriend's children into my heart, like* fully? It's definitely possible. I know they have seen it that way.

"Hey," reads a text I sent to his eldest daughter a while back. "First off, I absolutely don't hate you!! I love you and your sister very, very much!! xo. It's my fault that I've been out of it. Started writing a book and when I do that my mind is only half in reality so that's why I'm probably acting odd. I love you and your sister so very much. I probably don't show it enough, but I do. You are my family. Anyway, let's forget this and we will hang when we can for sure!! But do not ever forget that I love you."

I'm not sure what prompted the text, to be honest. I've been skimming though some old messages and stumbled upon this one, and I'm racking my brain trying to figure out what prompted it. What the fuck did I do that made her think I don't love her? I must have committed some offence that caused a slight she was feeling, which she shared with Boyfriend, who then shared it with me like we're gossipy girls in high school. I obviously, too, felt that I had done something wrong, because I had apologized.

Obviously, I love Boyfriend's children, so why don't my actions always show this? Did I not open my heart fully to them? And if I didn't, was there a way to do this, years after blending? I know that, like most teenagers and children of divorce, they can be manipulative (and I'd say this about my own daughter), but Boyfriend's children have never been malicious.

As much as I do genuinely care about them, I can see how they may think that I don't. Lately, because I can't always leave on a jet plane when the going gets tough, I only find peace hiding out in my bedroom. It may seem like I'm hiding from them. It may seem like I'm hiding from Boyfriend. But the truth is, when I'm alone in my bedroom, with the door shut, I can turn off my brain from overthinking. I think I am also depressed and on edge, and that sick feeling in my gut isn't going away. I just want to be left alone. I'm so tired of feeling let down. I'm so tired of feeling like I don't matter. I'm tired of fighting with Boyfriend over the same issues. I'm tired of worrying whether how I'm acting is normal. I'm tired of feeling like a nag. I'm tired of never getting an "I'm sorry." Pretty much, I'm even tired of myself. And I'm definitely tired of trying to make blended splendid. And so I sleep. A lot.

· THIRTEEN ·

I'm not a hoarder. But I'm now a … hider? The bedroom and my car have become my hiding spots. And I don't mean my place to hide things. I mean my place to hide myself, although it's not a very good hiding place, since everyone knows where I am.

I spend so much time in my bedroom these days that I'm starting to feel trapped. At the moment, I'm lying in my bed wondering how I can get a snack from the kitchen to bring back to my bedroom without anyone noticing me. I think of texting my daughter, "Can you please bring me up a cookie or something?" since she is at the kitchen table on her iPad, watching inappropriate YouTube videos. But I'm not at a hotel (although I often think of checking myself into one) and there's no room service, and anyway, I know someone eventually is going to need something from me and that I will feel guilty for hiding. Eventually, I will have to leave my bedroom.

Sometimes I lie on my bed, wondering how much time I have left to be alone in my bedroom before Boyfriend knocks on my door to tell me that dinner is ready or asks if I plan to get out of bed. On those nights, I have to come downstairs and face my blended family and pretend to be happy. There is something to be said for faking it until you make it. But my vibe is ... off. And I think everyone can sense it, like a dog can sense if someone is scared. I actually start to believe that, by hiding myself, it's just better for everyone.

I don't always hide in my bedroom. Sometimes I hide in my car.

"Are you coming inside?" Boyfriend texts when he busts me, watching me from a window as I sit in the driveway checking my text messages, talking to friends on the phone, anything to avoid stepping my foot in the house.

"Yes, be right in!" I text Boyfriend back, sighing a guttural sigh. I take one deep breath and slowly exhale. It seems like a very long walk to the front door, and, at the same time, all too short.

Yep, I'm a hider, loosely defined as someone who finds ways to avoid all human contact in their own home. It turns out that a lot of us who are in blended families are hiders. Many other adults in blended families also hang out in their bedrooms and their cars or take epic pees or absurdly long showers, just to avoid what awaits us. I thought I was the only one who did this, blaming it on being depressed, but it turns out I'm not that special or unique. In fact, it's a pretty typical characteristic of blenders. Some people become hiders immediately after blending houses. Some of us become hiders after years of trying to fit in and attempting to lower our expectations and finding we can't. So we hide, because it seems like the easiest option, and maybe our only option to not feel disappointed again.

Our bedrooms become both our sanctuaries and a sentence to solitary confinement. We hide to disengage, which is not a good sign.

"The minute I hear his car pull into the driveway with his biological kids," one friend tells me, "I start counting down the days until they leave. When they are here, I spend an inordinate amount of time in my bedroom alone, watching reality television, so I can see other grown-ups also acting like children, much like I act when everyone is here for the weekend."

It's not just us adults in blended families who see no other option for dealing with stressful blended families. Children in blended families, I learn, often do the same thing. "My son spends most of his time in his room avoiding his stepsisters, much like I do," admits another friend. "When they leave, that's when my son and I come out of hiding."

When I admit to a friend that I sometimes race upstairs to pretend I'm napping, she commiserates, admitting, "Some days, when I'm already home, when I hear my partner pull up with his kids in the car, I race upstairs to pretend that I'm napping too. My partner thinks that I just love napping, which I do — I consider it one of my hobbies — but really, I just need space."

Another friend, who isn't in a blended family, laughs when she happens to call one late afternoon and I whisper into the phone, "Everyone is here. I'm in hiding!" But it's really not that funny, feeling like you're cornered into hiding, paralyzed with fear because you don't know what may start another argument and are afraid you'll feel low down on the priority list.

I wonder if there is some sort of witness protection program for the times when all the kids are here or when Boyfriend and I argue. It's not that I hate hanging around his kids — they are good and outgoing — but I know that when they are around, I no longer exist. Or I do exist, but I feel sort of like a mistress — a woman who pines for a man but also knows he will never leave his wife, though he promises he will. I feel like that woman who endures excuses why he can't, but keeps hoping things are going to change. But at this point, my head is spinning, racing, trying to figure out what I can do to ensure my happiness while ensuring everyone else's happiness.

Add becoming a "hider" to the long list of things that happen in blended families that failed to make the cut in any books or articles I read from so-called experts.

I once told a friend that I hide in my bedroom, and she literally screeched like a four-year-old who hears an ice cream truck coming. "That is so, so me! I can't believe you do that too. I'll do anything to avoid being around when everyone is here. I love my husband, and he thinks I'm distant sometimes and doesn't get it, but I don't have the guts to tell him that it's not him, it's everybody, the whole situation, that makes me run and want to hide." Amen!

For many of us, we honestly can't explain why exactly we end up hiding in our bedroom. It's not like we're mad at our spouse over something and slamming our bedroom door shut. There's no one reason we hide. We don't even know how, or why, we turned into hiders. As my friend tried to explain, it's just the whole … *situation*. Even with the help of therapy, I haven't found a way to explain why I have this overwhelming urge to hide.

I know, I know. You're probably wondering what kind of woman hides from her family. But then I remember when I was a kid, how my mother would take two-hour long baths, and my siblings and I knew to stay the fuck away from the washroom. And my parents have been happily married for fifty-plus years!

Still, for me and my friends who also have blended households, the bedroom is really the last and only room that we feel is still ours, a little slice of life before blending.

I lock myself in by locking everyone else out. Blending is harder than I ever could have imagined, as is dealing with the feelings that boil over when it seems like everyone has taken over the entire house and I am like a stranger or a guest in my own house. Maybe I just feel outnumbered? Many times, I feel like the people in my family just don't care about me at all.

"Oh, I get it," one of my friends says when I tell her I hide in my bedroom but can't really explain why and I don't want to have a deep conversation about it or overanalyze it, because no matter how much I try, I can't explain it. Maybe some of us are too sensitive to be in a blended family. Maybe *I'm* too sensitive to be in one?

"It fucking stings when I see my husband and his children take over the entire couch as they watch a movie. There's literally no room or space for me. It's a double whammy because they moved into my house," one of my friends tells me. "They know I'm there, but no one offers to move over or asks me to join them. What am I supposed to do? So, yeah, a lot of the time I end up alone in my bedroom, bawling my eyes out, because I don't feel welcome, or I don't feel they care if I'm there or not. How come I feel so lonely, even with so many people around? And this is my family!"

Boyfriend and his children, and even my daughter, have started to notice that I now spend a lot of time in my bedroom. How can they not? I don't want to spend so much time alone, retreating like this, but no longer does Boyfriend bring out the best in me. So I'm proactive and hide, because I don't like who I've turned into. This way, no one has to see me in a mood or in a funk. I truly believe, at this point, I'm actually doing my family a favour, but I will realize that disengaging like this makes me feel even worse. Is it better to be the hider than the seeker? Or is it better to be the seeker than the hider?

"I either magically find errands as an excuse to leave, or I hibernate in my room. I hate it. I wish I had a time machine so we could go back to living in our separate houses and dating. That was a great time," another blended friend tells me.

I know it sounds like we do, but we don't hate our partners' children (well, maybe some of us do, but I don't). Many of us just feel … annoyance, and not for any good reason. We realize it's wrong, like being pissed off when it rains because you had kick-ass outdoor plans. It sucks and it's irrational, but that rain can fuck itself! That's kind of how I feel when my house is filled to the brim with children, and sides are chosen, and I no longer exist as I once did. So I hide in the bedroom. When I'm there alone, no one can hurt my feelings. I can't overreact or have someone lose it on me for some perceived slight. I can't get angry when I am locked upstairs by myself. The only one I can get angry with is myself, and I do. All. The. Time. Still, I am off-duty when I close my bedroom door. *Nobody's home.*

Frankly, many of us don't know what to do when shit inevitably hits the fan and you realize that all the investment you've made in the family over the years has yielded a very low interest rate. We just want to avoid the risk of any awkwardness or fights or irrational thoughts. We just want to not have to nag our partners because they aren't paying attention to us and we feel underappreciated. This is when many of us not only start to hide but also start to self-medicate. Clonazepam and Ativan, prescribed by understanding doctors, becomes our lifesavers.

Frankly, many of us just want to avoid the risk of awkwardness and fights by playing hide and seek like five-year-olds. But it's really the saddest game of hide and seek ever. While everyone knows where we are hiding, eventually, everyone stops coming to find us.

· · · · ·

Today, I'm not in hiding. I'm excited to leave the house! Boyfriend is driving me and his daughter downtown, where there is a long stretch of cute boutique clothing stores. Boyfriend's daughter has asked me to help her shop for a prom dress. I'm beyond thrilled that she's asked me to come along. This is a big deal! I think Boyfriend's daughter must think that I have good taste in clothes and really wants my opinion. Or maybe she thinks that, because I live downtown, there are more boutiques nearby, as opposed to where Boyfriend's children's mother lives in the suburbs. I am excited and up to the challenge of acting like a personal shopper for Bonus Child.

We go into a number of stores, where Boyfriend's daughter comes out of the dressing room showing off her perfect body. She looks stunning in all the dresses, each time coming out of the change room looking better than the last reveal. I gush over how beautiful she looks, feeling not only proud, but also happy that we're bonding. We're actually having fun!

Over the last little while, for some reason, while my relationship with Boyfriend's children remains civil, it seems like it has also become more ... professional? Like we're office buddies who forget about each other during non-work hours. Even our tone when we ask each other "How are you?" sounds like we haven't lived with each other for years. We sound, instead, like we are greeting a great aunt we've only met two times in our lives. That's how it feels to me. So, this invitation to help her shop makes me beyond happy. Maybe this will reboot our relationship, back to the days when we were comfortable together and chatted like friends.

When Bonus Child comes out in one specific dress — the one I think is so perfect, a jaw-dropper, both elegant and sexy — I tell her how amazing she looks in it.

"This is *the dress*," I tell her excitedly. "You look amazing! You'll be the best dressed person there."

She goes back in to the change room with me thinking that we've found The Dress. She does seem to take a long time changing into different dresses, but I'm a woman so I know that it takes time to get in and out of dresses. I wait patiently with Boyfriend, who is aimlessly walking around the store. I'm sort of perplexed when she comes out looking a little disappointed.

"Mommy thinks it's too short," she says.

I'm sorry. What did she just say? I look around the store, wondering if her mother is there, hiding behind us. How did Boyfriend's ex-wife know what the dress looked like on their daughter?

It turns out that Boyfriend's daughter has been taking selfies of herself in all of the dresses she has been trying on in the change room and is sending them, via text, to her mother for her approval. Cleary, her mother's taste differs from mine. And clearly she has the last say.

I am, quite frankly, heartbroken when I find this out, sad and let down because I thought this was the bonding moment that would get us back on track, especially after many months of feeling disengaged with everyone in my blended family. My fucking expectations got the best of me — again!

I initially try not to let on that I know I'm not really needed on this shopping trip, but, in one of my least proud moments, I sort of storm out of the store, telling Boyfriend that I'm taking a taxi back home, that I'm done shopping, that I wonder why I'm here at all. My sadness comes out as anger. I was expecting to have a great day shopping with Boyfriend and his daughter, because I thought that she cared and that she valued my opinion. I thought this dress-shopping excursion would bring us closer together, when all it really did was divide us, yet again.

"Why did she invite me in the first place if it all comes down to what your ex thinks is okay?" I cry to Boyfriend, that evening, my heart still crushed.

I feel incredibly guilty for leaving the store, and incredibly filled with rage. *My stupid, stupid expectations!* Like I said, far from my proudest moment in my blended family. Boyfriend is angry with me for storming off, saying he had to defend my actions to his daughter, who probably felt torn between my opinion and what her mother wanted.

"Can you put yourself into my shoes, just this once?" I ask him, sobbing. "Do you know what it feels like to get so excited about something, only to be disappointed *again*?"

Of course, Boyfriend tells me, yet again, that my expectations are too high, which makes me even angrier. I'm surprised that Boyfriend hasn't learned this yet. It's sort of like being told to "just get over it." I want to scream, "Has it ever worked for you in the past when you've told me to lower my expectations? Has that ever ended well for either of us?"

But, because I am in tears over this — now hypersensitive to everything that happens in my blended family — Boyfriend hugs me and says he understands why I feel the way I do, while at the same time telling me I shouldn't feel the way I do. I hate when people speak out of both sides of their mouths, which is what Boyfriend is doing.

Maybe Bonus Child had really wanted my opinion, even though she knew that it had to be approved by her mother. Maybe she felt caught between my opinion and her mother's opinion. I'm mad because of the situation. But I'm not mad at Bonus Child. She didn't choose to be in a blended family. I have never once heard any child say, "I want to grow up and be in a blended family." Not. Once. Have you?

· · · · · ·

I do get to attend Bonus Child's graduation, her last year of high school. I bring flowers. This is just one of many graduations I'll attend for his children over the years, but this is the most important one, it being her last before she heads off to college. We are seated in a gym full of proud parents, and it's hot and sticky and there's no air conditioning. Because of our blended family, Bonus Child had to ask for more than the allotted four tickets the school allows for every family. Cleary, the school system has not caught up with the times. Bonus Child needs tickets for not only her parents and for her grandparents on both sides, but also for me and Rowan. She needs *double* the tickets allotted for each family because we all want to see her graduate. But there were a few days, after she asked the school for more tickets, that she wasn't sure they'd be able to accommodate everyone. And, if she couldn't get more tickets, guess who'd be the ones not going? Me and my daughter. Fortunately, she does get more tickets, and I'm both excited and a little nervous, as if it was my own biological daughter who was going to walk across the stage and accept that diploma.

Boyfriend and I, with his mother and my daughter, sit near the back, and I tell Boyfriend to take the aisle seat so he can get a photo of his daughter walking toward the stage. Boyfriend's ex-wife is seated a few rows ahead of us. It's always awkward for me when I have to be in the same room as her. This time it's no different.

I not-so-fondly remember the time we brought Baby Holt to one of Boyfriend's kid's graduations. Bonus Child rushed up to hold her little brother and brought him over to her mom to show him off. When Ex-Wife reached out her hands to take my son, I totally raced over to grab my baby from her clutches. Who is she to *hold my* baby? Was that move immature? Sure. Human? Yes. Baby Holt is my baby. Plus, we barely acknowledge each other.

Afterwards, photographs are taken, and, yes, Boyfriend takes a photo of me and Bonus Child, which is awkward for both me and Bonus Child, as her mother stands watching us.

When I ask one of my friends, who most definitely doesn't get along with her husband's ex-wife, how she manages to remain mature when she's in the same room with her husband's ex, she says, "It took a few years. Now we get along, within reason," she tells me. "The truest thing about a blended family is that saying, 'You're marrying the ex.' I realized, and maybe I should have realized this even earlier, that if I was going to have a happy, easy family life, I was going to have to find a way to get her to trust me. I wouldn't say we're best friends now, but we are friendly and respectful. It's been hugely helpful in opening up lines of communication after what was a very painful divorce for both my husband and her," she says.

Boyfriend's ex and I don't exactly get along, mostly because I hear the stories that Boyfriend has told me about her, and of course I'm going to side with Boyfriend and believe what he tells me. When it comes to his ex-wife, I don't think, "Wait. There are always three sides to every story. His truth. Her truth. And the real truth." Plus, not only did she act completely indifferent to me when I made the call to her years earlier to come over and check out my house, but she has made it difficult for Boyfriend's children and my children to bond, especially in the early years, the most critical ones.

When we first blended households, I told Boyfriend, on more than one occasion, that it was important for his children to meet other children their age in the neighbourhood, because I knew that for them to really feel at home and want to continue coming to the city to stay with us, they needed friends to hang out with in our area. There are a lot of children the same age as Boyfriend's children who live in the area. And when we first started blending, we tried to get the girls to do things together. We didn't force them to bond, but we tried to direct and encourage them.

One year, early on after blending households, with my encouragement, Boyfriend signed his two children up for a play that I'd also signed my daughter to be in as an extracurricular activity. Rehearsals were every Wednesday night for an hour and a half. Boyfriend got into a fight with his ex about this. Since rehearsals were every Wednesday night in the city, she thought that he should pay for the cost of his two children being in this play, since they didn't happen on "her" days and they happened in the city, and she refused to drive them so far.

Because I'm in love with Boyfriend, of course I think she's a cow — Boyfriend's description, not mine — for refusing to help pay, even though their divorce agreement states that they each have to chip in for their kids' extracurricular activities. I think, in all of our years blending, Boyfriend's ex has only picked up their children from my house maybe twice. Likewise, I can count on my one hand the number of times I've gone with Boyfriend to pick up his girls. (I used to love it when his eldest would get in the car and change into an outfit her mother didn't agree with.)

When it came to the actual performance, I actually did reach out to Boyfriend's ex to ask her how many tickets she'd need, and I offered to buy them for her and said she could pay me back later. It was fantastic to see all the children on stage, but because Rowan's father and grandparents also came and we are all seated together, I was later reprimanded for sitting beside my ex and not Boyfriend.

Over the years of blending, I've never really figured out how to feel totally at ease when Boyfriend and Rowan's father are in the same room. Sure, they are civil together, much more civil than I am with Boyfriend's ex. But they'll never be best friends either. While Boyfriend is definitely friendlier with my ex, I can tell my ex doesn't exactly want to be pals with Boyfriend. I know. I know. I have heard of women, who, after blending households, actually talk to their ex's new wife, to deal with logistics, and actually become friends. Mind you, I have never met anyone like this, but like I said, I've heard stories. I kind of wish that I had that relationship with Boyfriend's ex, but it's at the point like when you don't return someone's phone call, keep meaning to, and then it just becomes too awkward to make that phone call, and so you don't, and that feeling haunts you for years. My window of opportunity for becoming friends with Boyfriend's ex has long since closed.

Still, his daughters' participation in the play is not the first time Boyfriend and his ex have gotten into fights over who pays for what or such when we try to get our children to bond. I did lose it on her, once, over email, when she didn't let one of their children come to our son's birthday party because she was on a soccer team at the time and Boyfriend's ex insisted she couldn't miss a practice. Or at least that's what I was told by Boyfriend, which led me to email her a not-so-nice note saying, sarcastically, that she was so "classy" for making her daughter miss her own brother's birthday party.

"Clearly, you have no idea what transpired," she wrote back. "It was her decision to hold her commitments with her rep soccer team." She went on to write that Boyfriend had this chat with his daughter earlier in the day, so Boyfriend knew what his daughter wanted. Furthermore, she went on, it was Boyfriend who had reached out to her to see if she would take their daughter for the night and take her to soccer. Had Boyfriend left out part of the story? After a bit of nasty back and forth, she sarcastically ended the email train with, "Good luck to you! You'll need it."

Back then, I had no idea what she was talking about. Boyfriend was perfect! He treated me like a queen! But there is something to be said for listening to your partner's ex, especially if they were together for years. You forget that they also know your partner well. They had been married for twelve years, after all, longer than I'd known him, so in a way she knew Boyfriend better than I did, and she knew what his personality was like. She was definitely sending me a warning, but like everything in the early years when it came to Boyfriend, I had no idea why she would tell me both "good luck," and that I'd "need it." Yes, I wished that I could have had a crystal ball.

· FOURTEEN ·

Every summer my daughter attends an overnight camp for one month. When I told Boyfriend how amazing this camp was and that I thought all the girls should spend a month there together, he agreed wholeheartedly. This, too, was early on, our first summer together as a blended family. Not only would it have been a great chance for our girls to spend a month together, at a camp that offers everything from golf to tennis to yoga to salad bars, but it would also have given Boyfriend's daughters a chance to meet other people their age, because many of the campers live around our area.

But Boyfriend's ex adamantly disagreed and didn't even bother to entertain the thought of her two daughters going to the overnight camp my daughter had attended for a couple of years. I'm not sure if it was because she wanted control, or that she thought the camp was too pricey. I wanted the girls to bond so badly at the beginning that I even sent her an email saying that I'd chip in for the cost of their two girls to attend the camp with my daughter. What better way for them to connect, and meet new friends in the neighbourhood, than to spend a month away together at this camp? But Ex-Wife wouldn't budge. She and Boyfriend argued over this, but to no avail. So while my daughter did, and continues to, go off to her overnight camp, Boyfriend's girls headed to a camp in an entirely different city, which made absolutely no sense to me or Boyfriend.

Lost was a great opportunity for the girls to connect and network over the summer; now, not only would they not be together at camp, they wouldn't see each other for nearly two months, as my daughter spends the second month of summer with her father in a different city. Yeah, it's a non-issue in a typical household, but in a blended one, especially in the early days, its impact can't be understated. Momentum is everything when it comes to relationships, and Boyfriend's ex-wife had put a complete halt on the momentum of our children clicking by planting her feet in the sand.

"Why does she want them to go there? It makes no sense. They can meet friends who live around us if they go to the same camp as Rowan," I said to Boyfriend.

"I agree. But she's not budging on this," he responded. I asked him why he didn't fight harder since he, too, said he thought it was a great idea.

"She's not going to budge," he tells me again, after I ask if he has tried to talk to her about it. "Trust me. I know what she's like."

So, Boyfriend, and by extension me, lost that fight. Our girls have never spent a summer bonding and have gone months without seeing each other. It pisses me off that she's got in the way of our girls becoming close. Why she refused to bend on this will remain one of life's great mysteries. It's a nice overnight camp. It's not fucking jail. But I'm pissed, too, because I've always wondered why Boyfriend never fought harder. Why did he just give up? Why didn't he really try, knowing it was something I truly believed would help bond our kids, while also knowing they'd have a fabulous time? After all, he's their parent, too, and should have equal say in what his children do. Maybe that was another red flag that blending our families wouldn't be as easy as we had believed.

"This pisses me off too," admits one of my friends, who married a man with a daughter, and then went on to have another daughter with him. "I never knew just how difficult it would be having my entire family life tied to another person who my husband used to be married to and frankly, doesn't even like very much. Every holiday, every plan has to be put past her," she says. "I never knew that it would be such an issue when we got married. We have many, many fights about it."

I just wanted our girls to blend, or at least have the chance to blend. Really, was that too much to ask?

Bonus Children love the camp their mother insists they go to, but the window of them meeting people around where we live closed before it really opened, and it was Boyfriend's ex who slammed it with a solid kick, or that's what I was led to believe. Why was Boyfriend allowing his ex to make the final decision when he knew how important it was for me, and how good it would have been for all the girls, to be together for a month? Was it always going to be this way?

After the play and the camp argument, Boyfriend's children never again tried, nor really had the opportunity, to make friends with other people in our neighbourhood.

So, yes, I blame it on his ex, but I also blame Boyfriend for giving up on the fight. I get that he may have often felt, and still feels, in the middle of me and his daughters, but why should he feel in the middle of his ex-wife and me? I am, after all, his present and his future. My daughter is his present and his future. And Boyfriend's kids are *my* present and *my* future. In a non-blended family, no outsider dictates how you raise your children.

After years of blending, Bonus Children still don't have any friends where we live, so when they are with us, they are *with* us, twenty-four/seven, and this means that they need to be entertained by us every time they are here. Usually, Boyfriend will take them to malls. They are mall rats. I hate malls, so I often bow out of their excursions, not only because I get "mall headache," but because I find it incredibly boring and can't play the charade that I'm enjoying myself. I can't hold back my feelings of resentment that, in order for us to be together, it always has to be at a mall. That, and I can't stand how, every weekend they are with us, he buys them clothes, because that's what you do at a mall. When you've blended families, you can only watch from the sidelines as Dad Guilt plays out, because dads in blended families will rarely, if ever, admit they suffer from Dad Guilt or even be aware that they have guilt. It's like their lack of ability to see a doctor or ask for directions. They basically have to be forced to acknowledge that they are sick or lost, or both! Sigh.

"I try to be sympathetic about my husband's Dad Guilt," a friend tells me. "It literally eats him alive. But, yeah, when he comes home with his son with a new mountain bike or an Xbox they bought together on the spur of the moment, it does make me want to scream! What about the two children we have together? Don't they deserve the same sort of gifts?"

But, no, they don't. Because they get their daddy full-time, so he doesn't feel the need to make up for lost time with material things.

So I complain to my friends that Boyfriend seems to have money to spend on his daughters and also himself, while I have to remind him, feeling like a bounty hunter trying to chase him down, to pay for half of the gas bill each month. The thing is, material things will never make up for lost time. The only thing material things do is out-parent the other parent, and the side effect is that they tangibly show the disparity in their dad's desire to go above and beyond for some kids and not others. It's the oil in the vinegar — the formula that will never, ever blend, no matter how hard you try.

. . . .

Camp was just one of the many times that I felt like an outsider in the lives of my Bonus Children, and that I felt like it was Boyfriend's ex's intention and desire to ensure that was the case and, by extension, Boyfriend's as well. Prom was the same. As if the whole dress-purchasing bullshit hadn't already crushed me, when the day finally rolls around to see her off to her prom, I respectfully bow out. I did it not because I'm the Bigger Person or have learned to lower my expectations, but because I know, in this instance, it's the right thing to do. Anyway, I don't feel like I have much choice to begin with. Maybe I have learned to be the Bigger Person. Maybe, finally, I have lowered my expectations.

Almost, or just, as important as prom is the pre-prom get together. All the graduates arrange to gather in a friend's backyard, and all the parents join in to take photographs of their children, so very dressed up, with their dates. Boyfriend and I plan to go. Or at least I plan on going and am looking forward to seeing Boyfriend's daughter all gussied up, with her makeup and hair professionally done. I have met her boyfriend a number of times. In fact, he has slept over at my house numerous times. The first time she asked if she could bring her boyfriend to sleep over, Boyfriend asked me what the sleeping arrangements should be.

"I don't know. She's sixteen. Just let them sleep in the same room," I said, because, well, let's face it, she's sixteen, they've been dating for a long time, and they'd sneak away to be with each other anyway. I know. I was once sixteen, too. The funny thing is, I don't think I'd let my daughter, even at sixteen or seventeen, have a boy sleep over, and certainly not in the same room. I'm more lax when it comes to Bonus Children, because I really don't care if his eldest shares a room, or bed, with her boyfriend. After all these years, while I have grown to love them, I've never really parented them, or felt like I had a say in raising them, and I wasn't going to start then. Plus, I want her to enjoy coming here, and if that means bringing her boyfriend to sleep over, and in the same room, so be it. Boyfriend agrees.

But, when it comes to me joining in with the other parents to take photographs on prom night, it stresses eldest Bonus Daughter out. It becomes obvious, although I'm not quite sure it's true, that Boyfriend's ex has told his eldest daughter that she prefers I'm not there. That's what she told her dad anyway, and he in turn told me. Again, I wonder why he doesn't fight harder on my behalf. Shouldn't he?

"I promise to just sit on the sidelines and say nothing!" I say to Boyfriend, with a heavy heart, begging to be a part of this.

There is only so much he can do to fight for my right to be there, I suppose, just as there was only so much he could do to fight for all the girls to attend the same overnight camp. Sure, he stands up for me, I think, but he also knows that his ex and I don't get along, and maybe his daughters think I'm the one who is the cause of this tension. And when Boyfriend realizes just how much this is stressing his daughter out, he finds himself caught in the middle of what his daughter wants and what I want. Or maybe he feels caught between his ex and me. Or both. He knows that I am extremely hurt by this. I was so excited for his daughter.

When she was eagerly waiting for her boyfriend to make his grand promposal, I was on pins and needles for her, nervous as I would be at an interview for a job I really wanted. Promposals these days are like goddamn marriage proposals. The kids make a huge scene and plan creative ways to ask their anxiously waiting better half, or crush, to prom.

"How did your BF ask you?" I sent her in a text, wondering if Bonus Child's boyfriend had asked her to be his date yet. There were only a few weeks left before the prom and pre-prom parties, including the part for parents to gather for photographs.

"He hasn't asked me yet (boohoo). I'm still waiting. Someone else gave a girl a box of pizza and on the inside of the box he had written, 'I know this is cheesy, but will you go to prom with me?'" she texts back with an emoji of a face laughing its ass/face off.

"Ha! WTF? He hasn't asked you! I guess he just expects you're going? When is your prom?"

"No, no," she texts back. "I know he is going to ask but prom isn't for another few weeks. Our school has only had two promposals so far. They are all gonna come soon."

It doesn't matter that I've shown interest in her prom and her promposal, or that I'm almost as excited as she is for this big night, a night that she will always remember, because don't we all remember our prom nights, whether they were fun or not? Everyone remembers their prom, and I wanted to be a part of the night, to celebrate alongside Boyfriend by joining in the picture-taking portion. The thought of being left out of this occasion hadn't even entered my mind. I simply assumed that of course I would be going along with Boyfriend.

Prom has become such a big deal these days, it almost feels as if your kid is getting married, and that's how important it has become for parents too. If my ex brought a girlfriend or wife along to my daughter's pre-prom, I, too, think I would be annoyed to share the night with another woman, although I would never say, "No, she can't come!"

But because Boyfriend has let me know that the pre-prom photo session is stressing his daughter out, I bow out, gracefully sending his daughter a text the night before prom, pretty much at the last hour, because until then I did think I was still going with Boyfriend to join in the celebration. After all, I am his better half. After all, she is my Bonus Child. The truth is, while on the outside it seems to be that I'm bowing out gracefully, on the inside I feel literally sick to my stomach. I'm only taking myself out of the equation because I know Boyfriend can't handle the stress of trying to please everyone, and, most importantly, because his daughter feels uncomfortable with me coming, and it is her night, after all. I hate it — yet again being left out — but I get why it's important that today, of all days, I be the Bigger Person. In reality, I'm forced to feel that I have no other choice but to bow out, and I can't help but wonder, *What happens when she gets married? Will I be left out of that?* In any case, I send her a text that reads, "Hey! Your dad mentioned it may be a tad awkward if I come tomorrow evening. I totally understand. I'm sad to be missing seeing you in your gorgeous gown and with your date. But I've told your dad to take a million photos so I'll get to see you. xo."

Two seconds after I send the text, Boyfriend's daughter texts back, "Thanks so much Rebecca! That was such a thoughtful message and it means a lot to me. Love ya! And I'll send you tons of pictures."

I'm sad and seething. It sucks to feel left out. It sucks to be left out. It sucks to feel like I've been disinvited at the eleventh hour. It definitely sucks to feel unwanted, like an outsider in my own family. It sucks to know that I've made a child happy and relieved by not showing up on a day that is so important to her, which makes me feel like I'm always doing wrong and can do no right. Again, I am hurt. Again, Boyfriend doesn't quite understand why, or he does understand, but feels like he can't do anything about it. I think, too, Boyfriend wants to have a nice evening celebrating, and if I'm not there, he won't have to worry about how I'm feeling and can put all his focus on his daughter. Still, I inwardly wish he would have had my back. To me, it's bullshit that he doesn't.

So, while Boyfriend's out taking pre-prom pictures of his daughter, surrounded by other parents also taking pictures of their children, I cry at home. Boyfriend knows I'm not happy. He doesn't know, however, that I spend the night sobbing into my pillow. I convince him that I'm okay with him leaving me back at home, because at this point in our relationship, I'm finding plenty to complain about and I don't want to complain about this. And so I bawl like I'm a seventh-grader and the only girl not invited to a sleepover. This is just another issue that is wearing me down. Why, after so many years of blending, does it seem like I'm more of an irritation to everyone, like a rash? Why do I feel that everyone seems to find it easier when I'm not around? Maybe I should have tried harder to be nice to his ex, to at least be civil. The second she refused my offer to see my house, where her children would stay part-time, I felt the spit in the face. It feels like it's on me that we don't get along. Maybe I'm more exhausted from the expectation I had that people would just know and see how much I wanted us to be all blissfully blended. I've been the one who's wanted it so badly all along. So why am I the one home on this big night, sobbing, left out, forgotten — *discarded*?

But Bonus Child, as promised, sends me a ton of photos of her with her date. So, no, I'm not exactly forgotten. I'm just not wanted around. I do feel slightly better that she kept her promise to send me photographs.

Still, not feeling welcome, and knowing I'm not welcome, just adds to the growing pile of blended-family bullshit that leads to more fights between Boyfriend and me. I let him know, yet again, that I feel excluded, because I am excluded. I don't even get an "I understand how you're feeling," from Boyfriend. Sure, this night was not about me, but it stings nonetheless. I will always remember Bonus Daughter's prom night, but for all the wrong reasons.

· FIFTEEN ·

Not everything is negative. Remember how I cried after telling Rowan's biological father that Boyfriend was moving in and that we were pregnant? Remember how that catch in his throat nearly broke my heart, because I thought he was worried that another man would be taking on the role of father figure, a man that would see his daughter every day, unlike him? Remember how I called Boyfriend's ex-wife too, stunned at what seemed to be her indifference to my offer to come over and see where her kids would be staying when they were with their father? Although both conversations were completely uncomfortable for me to make, I can't help but notice a positive change after those two phone calls. Namely, both Rowan's father and Boyfriend's ex-wife seem to have upped their parenting game. Both, in my opinion, have stepped up — whether unconsciously, subconsciously, or consciously — their parenting to vie for favourite parent of their biological children, or at least to make sure that other people weren't taking over their roles.

Rowan's father starts coming to town more often. He books trips to take her to Aspen, Italy, and Arizona, as well as to

Calgary, where he lives, as do her grandparents. He texts her nightly, and they have long conversations on the phone. Where once he came into town maybe once every three or four weeks to spend a weekend with her, Rowan's father now asks to take her away for weeks to travel with him and his parents during summer and winter breaks. In fact, even though he lives in a different city, my ex now spends more quality time with our daughter than most fathers who live in the same house with their children and who maybe see them for only a couple of hours at night and on weekends.

Meanwhile, Boyfriend's ex, who is pretty strict when it comes to parenting — regulating how her daughters dress, demanding high grades — has become more laid-back and, from my point of view, has started to treat her daughters more like friends, talking to them openly about everything. I remember how Boyfriend got mad at her when their divorce papers were finally signed and she took them out for a "celebratory dinner." He thought that she was trying to outdo him or make him look bad. But I, too, often treat my daughter like a friend, so I understand, in this instance, where Boyfriend's ex is coming from.

When Rowan's father comes to pick her up, he always comes in the house. When Boyfriend is home on these days, Rowan's father and Boyfriend will shake hands, each time, as if it were the first time they were meeting, acting civil but standoffish.

"How's it going?" Boyfriend will ask Rowan's father.

"Good, thanks," Rowan's father will respond. That's pretty much the extent of their conversations when my ex comes to pick up our daughter.

Sometimes, when he picks her up and Baby Holt is around, Rowan's father will look at him as if he's never seen a toddler before. Although these meetings are brief, they are uncomfortable for me. Boyfriend doesn't seem bothered at all. Rowan doesn't seem bothered at all. Holt doesn't seem bothered at all. But for me, even these brief moments make me highly uncomfortable, and I much prefer dropping Rowan off at the hotel her father stays at when he's in town visiting her.

By now, years into our blended family, I should be used to these moments, but I'm not. I think, too, that Rowan's father doesn't feel entirely comfortable in the few minutes he waits inside the house — half his house — while our daughter runs upstairs to her room to pack something she forgot. When she is finally ready to go, he whisks her out the door. I'm thrilled that my daughter and her biological father have become so close. Maybe it was the result of Boyfriend and I blending families — the fact that there was a new man in Rowan's daily life — that made him up his game, or maybe it's just because Rowan is older now and her biological father can relate to her better than when she was three or four or five. But now, he's a way larger part of Rowan's life than he was before, and it's all because he's making an added effort. Would he have made such a concerted effort if Boyfriend hadn't moved in? Whatever. The fact that Rowan and her father have become super close since Boyfriend and I blended makes me very, very happy.

·   ·   ·   ·   ·

Still, because I'm hyperaware of everyone's level of comfort, a part of me wants and does keep my ex and Boyfriend away from each other, as if I'm worried they are going to get into some physical altercation, which of course is ridiculous. When it comes to special nights at Rowan's school — there are so many of them! — I don't always invite Boyfriend to come along, because it makes me uncomfortable. I think it would make Rowan's dad feel uncomfortable too, and I'm still very loyal to him and care what he thinks. Not only does her father usually come to these special nights at my daughter's school, so also do his parents and mine. I constantly worry that someone from my past life will encounter the people in my blended family and that they are going to feel awkward around each other, making what should be a fun night into one with a shitload of pressure. The candid truth is, it *is* fucking awkward. I'm glad when, for example, my daughter is in a play or has a dance recital and there are two nights of performances. This means that Boyfriend and my ex (and his parents) can go on different nights, thus never having to see each other, let alone sit next to each other and breathe the same air. I know, from reading articles on blended families and co-parenting after divorce, that some couples even live next door to each other, even if one partner has remarried. I wonder how they do it. I wonder how they can feel so comfortable living so close to an ex who has remarried when I don't even feel comfortable with my ex and Boyfriend being in the same room for a mere two hours. Who are these people who say they get on so wonderfully with their exes? I just want to ask them, "If you get along so well, why the fuck did you break up in the first place?" I don't believe for one goddamn second that jealousy doesn't rear its ugly head when a former spouse sees daily how their ex has moved on before them. I just don't buy it.

·　·　·　·

Just a couple of weeks after Baby Holt is born, Rowan's grandparents come in for the weekend to visit Rowan, who is now almost ten years old. They pick her up at the house on the way from the airport to the hotel they are staying at. I don't doubt that Rowan's grandparents aren't exactly enamoured with the fact that a new man has moved into the house their son half owns and pays the mortgage for. I don't doubt that they worry, whether that worry is warranted or not, how blending is affecting their only grandchild.

When Rowan comes back from that weekend visit, she hands me a big box, wrapped in a blue ribbon, from Pottery Barn. Inside is a beautiful baby blanket, which Rowan tells me she picked out by herself after she asked her grandparents to take her shopping for a present for her new baby brother. I almost cry because it is beyond thoughtful of Rowan's grandparents to buy a gift for me — their son's ex — and the baby, who isn't related to them at all.

This, though, marks the first, and last, time that Rowan's grandparents acknowledge, at least to me, that Rowan has a brother.

I talk to Rowan's grandmother, Grandma, on the phone about every two or three weeks. I call her or she calls me, and our conversations usually last at least half an hour. After all, we have one thing in common that we can talk about *forever*, which is my daughter, and so we talk about her endlessly. Besides me, I don't think there is anyone more in love with my daughter than her grandmother, who loves buying her clothes and taking her for manicures and haircuts, and who can gush about how cute she is for hours on end. Even years after blending with Boyfriend and his children, we still talk on the phone, not only to gush over how much we love Rowan or discuss how she's progressing at school, but also to go over packing lists before they head off on one of their many trips.

Not once, except for that one time she bought Rowan's new baby brother a gift — a totally thoughtful gesture — does she bring Baby Holt up or even mention his name in our conversations. In our long chats she never asks how Holt is, how Boyfriend is, or how his children are, nor do I bring up Baby Holt, Boyfriend, or his children either. When we speak on the phone, they don't exist. It's like these conversations happen in some suspension of reality between my old life and the new one,

I am speaking to her as if my life never progressed after Rowan's dad and I split. It is both uncomfortable and comforting, weird but natural. I can go on endlessly about a life that doesn't include my blended family.

I know Rowan's grandparents worry about their one and only grandchild and how she's managing going from being an only child to having a new biological brother and two bonus sisters and another male figure in the house. Yet, while Rowan's amazing grandmother will ask things like, "Do you think she's made new friends?" or, "Do you think she needs a tutor?" she never once asks me how Rowan is holding up in her new blended family or if she gets along with Boyfriend's children, and never anything about her new baby brother or Boyfriend. I think Rowan's grandmother just doesn't want to seem like she's prying, or perhaps she thinks I don't want to talk to her about my present family makeup because I might think it's none of her business. Most likely, she simply doesn't know what is acceptable and not acceptable to ask.

It's not that Rowan's grandmother doesn't care that Rowan has this larger family. I think she really does care and truly worries about how my daughter is adjusting and continues to adjust. She's the most kind-hearted person in the world. I'm quite positive she wants to know how the most important person in her life, Rowan, is handling these new people in the house, or how she's dealing with life in a blended family, or how she feels about Boyfriend, because I'm 1,000 percent positive she wants to know that her only granddaughter is nothing but happy every single second of every single day. So, no, she doesn't ask, and I don't share this part of my life with her either. We are both nothing but amateurs when it comes to talking about my blended family and how Rowan is dealing with it. Often, I do want to reassure Rowan's grandparents that their only granddaughter is just fine, but that would mean I would have to bring up Boyfriend and his children, and I still keep my old pre-blended life and my new life compartmentalized.

Rowan's grandparents and my parents still talk on the phone occasionally, and sometimes, when they are in town visiting Rowan, they'll invite my parents to go out to dinner with them, or my parents will invite them out for a meal. More often than not, I'm not even invited to these dinners, only finding out afterwards that the grandparents have made plans and gone out as a foursome, along with my daughter. Maybe only once have my parents gone out with Boyfriend's mother or father. My parents, too, in many ways are still living in the past.

Rowan's father never asks about Baby Holt either. When we talk, just like when I talk to his mother, it's like Holt doesn't exist, and neither does Boyfriend or his children. I don't think this is because Rowan's father doesn't care. Rowan's dad is not one to pry, and he's also a super private person. (He's not on any social media at all! Who in this day and age isn't on social media? Rowan's father, that's who.) He doesn't interfere with my life, and, maybe a small part of him wants to forget that his daughter has all these new people in her life. It may be easier for him and his parents to act as though they don't exist and that the blending never really happened — sort of like a dream you have and you're not sure if it really happened or not.

Still, I do feel the need to reassure all of them that they need not worry, that Rowan is still very much loved and is doing well in my blended household. Even after years, they still never ask about Boyfriend, his children, or Baby Holt. Even after years, I don't bring up Holt's name. Perhaps they ask Rowan about her brother and new sisters when she's alone with them, but I do not know this for certain. I have never asked my daughter if the rest of our family comes up in conversation with her father or grandparents, because I don't want my daughter to feel like I'm snooping for information. That, and also, frankly, I don't really want to know what they truly think about the choices I've made.

This uncomfortableness, or pretending that Rowan is still an only child, never goes away. It's been there since the first day we blended, and it's still here now, years later.

One night, years after Boyfriend has moved in, I find myself in a bind. Rowan is now on a soccer team. Her father is in town and wants to see her play. She also wants me to see her play. But I don't have anyone to watch Holt this one evening — Boyfriend has plans. I don't want to disappoint my daughter, but I also don't want to bring Holt to her game because Rowan's father will be there and I don't want him to feel uncomfortable. Truth be told, I don't want to feel uncomfortable either, having him watch me mother another kid who's related to his daughter but not to him. I call my mother.

"Can you and Dad come over and watch Holt this Tuesday night?" I ask, telling her how Rowan's dad is also coming to the game. My mother gets what I'm saying immediately.

"Yes, we will come over and watch Holt. It will be way too uncomfortable for you," she says. Well, fuck, it turns out my parents do have some sense of what it feels like to be in a blended family and have your past and present lives collide.

Rowan is blissfully unaware of the uncomfortableness that we adults feel because of our blended family. She wants everyone to come, for example, to visit her at her overnight camp on Visitors' Day.

"Can Holt come?" she begs. "I really want him to see my camp."

"We'll see," I say, knowing this is never going to happen, because Visitors' Day is three hours long, and by bringing Holt along, it will take away time her father wants to spend with her. So I make up an excuse, though it is also true.

"You know how he is. Holt gets bored easily. And you know how he is when he gets bored. He'll want to leave after twenty minutes," I tell my daughter.

At my daughter's overnight camp, there is another day for divorced parents — exes who can't get along, even for three hours, for their children. But Rowan's dad and I do get along, and so the outside world, or at least her counsellors, have no idea that Rowan's father and I aren't together and that back at home I have another family, and so does Rowan. I don't invite Boyfriend, either, to Rowan's Visitors' Day at camp because I don't want her father to have to share these three precious hours with Boyfriend, even if he has been part of her life, and my life, for years.

I don't know if Boyfriend feels left out on Visitors' Day. Maybe he does. Maybe he feels like I felt on his daughter's prom day. Some days are reserved for biological parents. That has been my experience, even if I wish it could be different. But I guess that's how it should be, even though it fucking sucks when you're the one left out. Boyfriend doesn't bow out of Visitors' Day, nor does he really press to come. The difference, though, between prom and Visitors' Day is that Boyfriend was never invited in the first place. But it still sort of stings when he doesn't even bother to ask if he could tag along. Maybe he knows that I'll just say no. Or maybe he just doesn't miss my daughter like I do, or like he misses his kids when they are off at camp. I'd say it's fifty/fifty.

· · · · ·

Back at home, my bedroom still offers me respite when I'm in hiding mode, but it is now causing issues with Boyfriend and my daughter. She's now used to not sleeping with me anymore, but she still comes in every night to cuddle with me before she heads to her room. She comes in more than once to say goodnight, lingering like the last guest at a party. While personally I don't mind how often she comes in to say goodnight or the fact that she wants to cuddle until I have to kick her out, which always makes me melancholy, Boyfriend gets annoyed with how many times she does it, always coming to my side of the bed and trying to sneak in under the covers. And he doesn't bother to contain his annoyance. Coming in to say goodnight once is okay. Even twice is fine. But, by the third time my daughter comes in for one last goodnight, or if she overstays her welcome when she says she just wants to cuddle with me for *one more minute* but ends up staying for ten, Boyfriend gets really miffed.

"Rowan," he'll say, peeved. "You've already said goodnight four times. It's enough already!" Boyfriend is much more comfortable trying to discipline my bio child than I ever am with his. I don't think I've ever once even tried to discipline his children.

"She just wants to stay for one more minute," I'll say, irritated with Boyfriend's irritation, feeling a powerful need to stick up for my daughter, as always. I want to make it clear to my daughter that it's not me who is making the demand that she stop coming in, but I also want to make it clear to Boyfriend that I understand why he's frustrated. As an outsider, I do understand why he gets annoyed. But as Rowan's mother, I really don't think it's such a big deal that she wants to say goodnight numerous times.

So, while Boyfriend often feels torn between his children and me, I, too, often feel torn between my daughter and Boyfriend, especially at nighttime. I love cuddling with my daughter, but I also know that I need to spend some adult time with Boyfriend, watching one of our favourite televisions shows together, without interruption, without having to pause what we're watching every ten minutes as my daughter constantly pops in and out of our bedroom to say goodnight *one last time*.

Researchers or so-called experts on blended families and relationships speak out of both sides of their mouths, too. Many say you need to make your partner a priority when you're in a blended family. Other "experts" say that kids should always be the priority. So which fucking is it?

It annoys Boyfriend when my daughter interrupts us while we're watching one of our shows, so should I be making him a priority and tell my daughter that she can only come into my bedroom to say goodnight to me *once*? Or should my daughter remain my priority, and I should tell Boyfriend to "chill the fuck out" when my daughter wants one more cuddle with me? The truth is, I like when my daughter comes in to cuddle, and so I need to find a way to show Boyfriend he is a priority, even though, obviously, if push came to shove, I'd take my daughter's side, and Boyfriend, deep down, knows this. Just like, deep down, I know that if push really came to shove, Boyfriend would, and does, take his children's side. I mean, I've seen it too many times to count: he says he's on "my team," but his actions show otherwise. There are many nights he spends with his daughters in their bedroom, watching a movie with them, without asking me to join. I don't think he realizes that he's making the assumption that I don't want to join them. Either that, or he simply doesn't want to extend an invitation.

"How would you feel if my children were constantly coming into the bedroom every night?" Boyfriend asks, his tone filled with disdain, when my daughter enters our room for a third time one night.

"That's a moot point," I tell him. "You always go downstairs to say goodnight to them. They have never come in here to say goodnight. Rowan is younger than them and has always come in to say goodnight to me."

This routine of Rowan coming in and Boyfriend being annoyed by it has been going on for years. Nothing changes. I wonder if it ever will. I don't know why he doesn't just get the fuck over it. But Rowan knows he's annoyed. She only kind of cares, though. But she does leave, saying goodnight only to me before I remind her to say goodnight to Boyfriend, too.

"Goodnight," she'll huff to Boyfriend, clearly pissed off that she's being kicked out of the room, holding her head and slamming the bedroom door behind her.

I feel Boyfriend tense up when Rowan whispers, not so quietly, into my ear, "If I can't sleep, can I sneak in bed with you?" And I whisper back, "Of course!"

· SIXTEEN ·

I should pad my bedroom walls. I'm on the brink of a blended-family-fuelled mental breakdown.

When Boyfriend's daughter gets her driver's licence, I'm extremely proud of her. Before she goes in for the driving portion of her test, I text her very early in the morning: "Happy driver's test day! Just flash them a smile. And soon you'll be free! (Driving that is!)," adding a heart emoji.

Early that afternoon, I receive a text back from her with one word: "PASSEDDD!"

"Woot!!! Congrats!" I text back, super pleased. Boyfriend is both happy and sad. As with most parents when their children get their licences, Boyfriend is noticing now how quickly his girls are growing up, so this is a bittersweet moment for him. But now that his daughter can drive legally and has been given a used car that belonged to a family member who passed away, his eldest child can now drive herself and her sister to us, which will save Boyfriend hours and hours of driving them back and forth, stuck in traffic, getting his children from their mother's house to ours. Perhaps now his chronic back pain from sitting in the car so long will go away. But I know, even if he doesn't realize it yet, he will also miss out on the hours he spends in the car talking with his daughters, since he no longer has to be their chauffeur — something you don't think you'll ever miss, but suddenly you want that chance back because you know it's no longer an option. His daughter wants to drive, of course. She's a teenager.

By now, we're in year seven of our blended family. After seven years of ups and downs — nothing that wasn't fixable — Boyfriend's daughter and I get into our first wicked fight. Soon after she gets her licence and her car and has driven to our home, I overhear her complain to Boyfriend about how the car sucks. I can't help but think, *Isn't the gift of a car, whether brand new or used, something she should be grateful for?* We don't live in Beverly Hills, where getting a Porsche for your sixteenth birthday is a given. Most sixteen-year-olds do not get their own car as soon as they get their licences, so I'm taken aback by what I perceive to be a sense of entitlement, or maybe lack of gratitude that she has her own car at all.

"First world problems," I mutter under my breath, because I do think so, as I head up the stairs, not realizing that Boyfriend's daughter heard me. But she has and she's beyond pissed, and Boyfriend demands I apologize and make things right.

I'm not against apologizing, but not before I ask Boyfriend, "But don't you think it *is* a first world problem?"

"You need to apologize. She's really upset," he says, ignoring my question entirely. Again, without meaning to, I have put him in an uncomfortable position, which makes me, again, feel like I'm the fuck-up, that whatever I say is taken out of context, and that someone is always mad at me.

I've started to notice, as his girls get older, that Boyfriend has become much more protective of their feelings and less protective of mine. His Dad Guilt seems to me to have intensified over the years. I think, mostly, this is because they are spending less and less time with us or him. They may spend the odd night here, usually now bringing friends or boyfriends, but Boyfriend just sees them once or twice a week, driving to them to take them out for dinner and, of course, a visit to the mall.

So I go on my apology tour, not because I think I need to apologize, but to keep the peace. In fact, if my daughter had moaned about a car, *any* car, given to her for free as soon as she got her licence, I'd say the exact same thing to her. I'd have no problem telling her that she was acting like an entitled brat and that it is a "first world problem." But because Boyfriend's children are not biologically mine — and, again, I've never attempted to parent them over the years and have never once disciplined them — they complain to him about me, and then he complains to me about their complaints about me.

What can I say, except thank god for text?

"Hey. Your dad tells me you are upset with me for using the phrase 'First world problems,'" I text to Boyfriend's daughter. "We had been joking about it earlier, because at my office we are always saying 'First world problems,' and so I said it when u were talking about your car. I really don't get cars at all, so I didn't realize that it could hurt you. In fact, I care about cars so little you can have my old BMW if you want. I'm getting my new car next week. First world problems! But in no way did I mean to hurt your feelings or anything like that. For all I care you can drive a Bentley! Anyway, I'm sorry if I hurt your feelings. Wasn't intended at all. Maybe you'll come see the car next weekend and your parents can think about buying it for very little :)"

My car, which I have been driving for almost seven years, is still in great condition, with less than 50,000 kilometres on it, because I rarely seem to drive any farther than four blocks from the house.

My text apology, and maybe — probably! — the fact that I offered my car, works, and she seems to have forgiven me. "Thanks for the apology Rebecca. I guess it was just a miscommunication. And that would be awesome (smiley face, smiley face)."

What teenager, after all, wouldn't want to drive around a BMW?

"You excited to get your new car?" she texts me.

"To tell you the truth, I know what brand of car I'm getting but I've never driven one. I just picked the colours (grey outside, brown inside). Supposed to be the hottest car right now which is why it took four months to order the damn thing," I text back. I add, "See? First world problems," with a smiley face emoji.

"Haha, that's too funny. But it sounds very nice," she texts.

When I tell Boyfriend that we've made up and that everything is good again, I can tell that he's relieved, to say the least. I expect him to thank me for being the Bigger Person and apologizing, but all I get is, "Good." Just once, *once*, I'd like to be the one who gets the apology, not the one apologizing. But by now I know I have a better chance of winning the lottery or getting struck by lightning than to ever get an "I'm sorry" from Boyfriend. He doesn't realize that saying, "I'm sorry you're feeling that way," is not a true apology. It's like he's allergic to the two-word sentence. And I'm wondering if I've become allergic to being in a blended family. I may not break out in hives, but the stress pimples break out more times than I can count.

·　·　·　·　·

It's heartbreaking when you realize you aren't as important to someone as you thought you were. Or when you know you were extremely important at one time in your relationship, but you don't know how to get back to that happy place.

The merry-go-round of attention in blended families is a cy-clical hell, and as time goes on, it seems to go faster and faster, like a carnival ride that spins so fast you don't know if you'll be able to hold on. Your second spouse wants your attention, your children want your attention, you want your spouse's attention, your spouse's children want your spouse's attention. There is a finite pool of attention to go around, so it is likely that someone is going to feel neglected at one time or another.

At some point, everybody is going to get dizzy, lose their balance, and lose their grip. It becomes a ride that was super fun when it wasn't broken but no one is enjoying anymore. Now that it is broken, everyone wants to get the fuck off and run away, arms flailing.

"I still love you very much and I really want us to be great again," Boyfriend writes to me in an email, years after we've blended, after another wicked "discussion" that we never re-solve. When we are angry with each other, it's sometimes eas-ier to write out our feelings, because we usually get off track when we argue in person. Lately, I've been feeling like we're never going to be "great" again and that perhaps we should call it quits.

Ironically, I happen to be out with one of my closest friends, who is also thinking of splitting up with her husband and who also wants relief from all the blended family bullshit behind her closed doors. They eventually will break up, and she will go to court to fight to have her son 60 percent of the time, because her son doesn't like staying with his father, who also has two other children from his first marriage and now has a new girlfriend, who has kids of her own.

Because the message arrives when I'm with my friend, I read the rest of it aloud to her:

I realize relationships take work from both sides and I am willing to do my part. I do understand that you need to feel and hear that I appreciate you and the things you do more than I do. I am not belittling that nor am I saying that I cannot try harder. What I was trying to say earlier is that I know why it has been harder for me to do or show this. We both need and want each other to be the way we used to be. I am confident that we can get back to that. By remaining confident and positive I think we can get there. You are by far the person I have loved more than anybody else in my life.

I wish I could be the type of person who is confident and remains positive about relationships when they turn sour, but I just can't let things go that easily or start fresh. Honestly, how many times can we start fresh? I'm just waiting for a simple "I'm sorry," not an entire runaround about how we can get back to the honeymoon phase or how confident he is about us, while my confidence in us is waning. I truly don't believe that we can get back to "be the way we used to be." This relationship, and, in turn, this blended family, has drained me emotionally. I'm out of fuel.

Still, I have proof that we are, in fact, trying. At the same time, the proof shows that we are falling apart. Boyfriend wrote that we need to try even *harder.* But what does trying harder actually mean? How much harder do we have to try? What does he think I have been doing all these years? *Not trying?*

Many of us, like my friend who used hard drugs and slept with men with hard abs, self-medicate, which is what I'm doing tonight with my girlfriend. I have one goal tonight and that is to get stupid drunk and not have to think about whether it's ever going to get better between us or if this life I'm now living is the life I'll always be stuck in. I'm not usually a drinker, but tonight I understand what exactly women mean when they say, "I need a drink!" at the end of a long day.

I now have a regular prescription for Clonazepam, in my purse, to be used, as the directions state on the plastic bottle, "as needed." Well, fuck. I think, given the state of my family and my relationship with Boyfriend, the directions really should be more like, "whenever the hell you want to take it."

My friend also has a prescription for Clonazepam, but she finished hers almost a week earlier than she should have and can't get a refill for another five days.

"Clonazepam is my lifesaver at the moment. I know I need to cut back. I'm using way more than I should be," she says, also telling me she, more often than not, feels left out in her blended family. The stress of blending has gotten to her, too, and she is self-medicating to keep calm, ignoring the "as needed" directions because, fuck, in a blended household, it's always "needed."

In fact, when I need something to calm my nerves, all I have to say to my doctor is that I'm stressed out because of blending and fighting with Boyfriend. She is very sympathetic to my lot in life. Eventually, my "as needed" directions turn into "twice a day."

My friend and I also agree that we don't know how or when the hell we became — What's the opposite of enamoured? That word! — in our blended families.

"How did we become interlopers in our own homes?" she asks.

"I have no fucking clue," I respond. We are not just out tonight because we are friends but also because we both need a night away from the stress and arguments we're having within our respective households.

And so we drink and laugh together over the insanity of how much we need our bedrooms to hide out in and our prescriptions on us at all times, and how great it is that we can ask each other for pills when we run out before our refill is due. At least my girlfriend and I are on a good schedule when it comes to our drugs. Just as she finishes her prescription, I get mine. Just as I'm running low, she gets hers. We have the ideal custody schedule when it comes to our prescriptions.

The night with my girlfriend feels both liberating and cathartic. Maybe my dermatologist was onto something when she said the only way her blended family works is for her to get the hell away from it once a week to party with her girlfriends. I can't remember the last time I had a good laugh with Boyfriend. I don't remember the last time I smiled so hard. I needed this night with my girlfriend. I needed to remember how to laugh.

Before we part ways, my girlfriend and I decide to do one more shot of tequila. We hold up our shot glasses and make a toast.

"Here's to hiding in our bedrooms," I say.

"Here's to prescription drugs," she says. We clink our shot glasses. After we pay our bill, I hand her a few of my Clonazepams. Survival drugs.

· SEVENTEEN ·

"I'm selfish, impatient, and a little insecure. I make mistakes. I am out of control and at times hard to handle. But if you can't handle me at my worst, then you sure as hell don't deserve me at my best." The internet says Marilyn Monroe said that, but the internet is probably wrong. Whoever said it, though, is one smart person! That particular quote really resonates with me, especially after Boyfriend and I argue and he accuses me of going off on too many tangents.

Something has definitely shifted in our relationship, but I still don't think it's unfixable. Even though I've been thinking of calling it quits, I'm not a decisive person. I don't honestly know what to do. I'm not happy with him, and we fight a lot. That being said, I still think about him all the time. We are still very sexually active. Plus, certainly, if many of my married friends can remain married to their spouses for fifteen to twenty years, obviously with ups and downs, Boyfriend and I can as well. There is no one single thing that's happened that's led to me hiding out in my bedroom or to my unhappiness. It's not just the Hi/Bye Fight, or the unfairness I see when he grocery shops, or the fact that I do not feel like I'm his priority and feel unappreciated, or that I'm not welcome at certain family events. I'm simply just not happy anymore. I know, I know. You can only make your own happiness. But if I were to "make my own happiness," I would probably break up with Boyfriend. I expect — await, unfairly — Boyfriend to make me happy again, as he has promised. Meanwhile, I sink deeper and deeper into a depression about the state of my life.

This was not what I signed up for, I think. I try to be easy on myself, because just like no child chooses to be in a blended family, no one I know ever said as a child, "I can't wait to grow up and live in a blended family so I can tiptoe around like a tightrope walker, trying to please everyone, only to realize I can't." This life was not a childhood dream.

Maybe, just maybe, when things seem to fall apart, they will eventually fall into place? At least that's what I'm hoping for, or convincing myself is possible. Maybe the better comes after the worse.

Before blending, I never imagined just how many emails I'd eventually get from Boyfriend with the subject line "Us." I start getting almost as many emails with the subject line "Us" as I did ones with the subject line "Poem" when we first started dating. Obviously, I much prefer the subject line "Poem." I know, before even opening the emails with the subject line "Us," that Boyfriend will promise to change and see things from my perspective, and, also, that he'll say he loves me "more than anybody." Still, there's never a simple "I'm sorry." There are a lot of promises, always broken. And there's no "I'm sorry!" when I bring up his broken promises.

In one email he sends with the word "Us" in the subject line, he writes, after an argument in which I say something nasty to him,

To say this is extremely upsetting would not do justice to how I am really feeling. We have been through more in five years than most have in a lifetime. I know you don't think we are a family, but we are. There are lots of blended families that work, but it takes some give and take. I understand why you are upset about some of the things, but they are things that can be fixed and made better if everyone was more conscious of each other. It may never be perfect, but it can definitely get better. I vowed to work through things with you through the good and bad and I am willing to continue to fight ... I know people say love cannot conquer all, but I think it can. Love still requires work, but without it there is nothing. I am willing to go to all ends of the earth to make us great again, because when I say you are my heart, "you are my heart." It feels broken right now and it does seem clear that your heart is in the same place ... We have a lot to lose and I don't want to lose you. If you do not feel the same way anymore and don't want to be with me, I will walk away gracefully. I think we can get back to "great again." It just needs some effort to do it. I love you and you are my heart.

Sure, the words are lovely. But actions speak louder than words, and the only action Boyfriend seems to be doing is sending me more and more emails with the subject line "Us."

Yes, even when we threaten each other that this is "just not working" and we should call it quits, we keep making up, fighting to make our blended family and "Us" work. By now, I'm like the girl who cried wolf. I've threatened to kick Boyfriend out

numerous times. It doesn't seem to be getting better. Even after
we talk things through, I now know that within days we will be
fighting about something else. I don't even know anymore if it
has to do with blending, or if we are just two people who have
changed. I hate feeling like a lost dog that just needs some love
and attention. I hate having to wonder if it's better to be alone
than feel lonely in a relationship. I hate that I have reverted to
begging for attention. I don't recognize myself anymore.

Having these "discussions" — I call them fights, regard-
less of what Boyfriend wants to call them — is like texting
with someone who types faster than you. Before you can finish one thought, you receive another text about another issue.
Sometimes our discussions get so far off track, it's like missing
your exit on the highway and you're in the next fucking town
before you realize how lost you are. I hate to admit how often we
forget what we're fighting about in the first place.

Sometimes I am so depleted by all of the arguments that I'm
left feeling like a turtle who has just smoked a joint or like I'm
running with bricks on my feet, not actually getting anywhere.
Sometimes I do wonder how he puts up with me, especially
when I'm depressed. But then I remember that I put up with
him and his broken promises and his inability to apologize, and
in that sense, we're even.

The stress of our relationship, and my depression, is getting
to Boyfriend, too. My therapist says that my depression is situational and suggests that I go on an antidepressant. But is being
in a blended family situational? Isn't it just my fucking life? I
don't take the antidepressants. Still, I know Boyfriend, who likes
to say things along the lines of, "I live for today and tomorrow
and don't dwell on the past because I can't fix it or change it," is
becoming more than frustrated when I tell him I'm down and I
don't really know why. I don't expect him to rescue me, but I do

expect that he at least be empathetic because he's my partner, he says he'll do anything for me, and we are for better or for worse — or for better or for blended.

Boyfriend doesn't understand what it's like to be depressed, so he gets frustrated when I just want to be left alone. He's not meeting my needs, although I have spelled them out, again and again, and he has promised that he'll fight for us. I'm not meeting his either. It's almost as if our relationship is like a dropped phone call. We are disconnected from each other. I start sending Boyfriend articles in hopes of him understanding that much of my irritability is due to my depression, to show him that many who suffer from depression also have feelings of isolation that can be crushing. While I hide out in my bedroom or car, Boyfriend is probably experiencing an internal battle over what to say or what not to say, wondering if something he says or does will set me off, and starts making plans with "friends" so he doesn't have to deal with me. That's how I feel anyways.

I think I can speak for both Boyfriend and myself when I say we are so very tired and frustrated by the merry-go-round of fighting over the same issues over and over again. Now, every time we fight, he blames it on my depression, but he never quite understands what has put me into a depressive state. I miss the person he used to be. I miss the person I used to be. I miss how he used to treat me and look at me. I think I still love him, but I no longer recognize him. I'm both happy and sad when he makes plans to go out. When he's out, we don't argue. But when he's out, we're also growing apart. I start to accuse him of not wanting to be with me.

Later, I will learn how he really feels about our relationship when I receive a text that oozes with annoyance: "Here we go again, with you accusing me of something, which was what I lived with for years with you. It was either taking money, not paying rent, hiding your pills, not treating you like #1, blah, blah, blah."

Well, yeah, I want to scream, *because it's all fucking true.* He *didn't* pay rent. He *did* try to hide my pills. He most certainly *didn't* treat me as number one. His *dog* got more attention than I did. So, *blah, blah, blah* to you too!

I think, at this point, we both feel that we are putting overtime into this family, like a job, but without additional pay or benefits. Who the fuck would we even invoice for all this extra time and effort we've put into working on our relationship and our blended family? Apparently, in my eyes, Boyfriend cannot handle me at my worst. But, again, he gave me Baby Holt, so I should be eternally grateful.

So, what exactly are our issues?

1. Money
2. The division of chores
3. Money
4. I feel unappreciated
5. Money
6. I feel he treats his daughters, and even the dog, better than me
7. Money
8. Boyfriend feels he does most of the heavy lifting when it comes to the baby
9. Money
10. Boyfriend doesn't like feeling like he's stuck in the middle between me and his children
11. Money
12. I'm no longer a priority
13. Money
14. He can't say he's sorry even if he knows I deserve an apology
15. He may lack the empathy gene

I start to type into my laptop things like, "Signs your marriage is falling apart"; "Is my marriage falling apart quiz"; "My marriage is falling apart and I don't know what to do"; "Marriage falling apart after baby"; "How to stay positive when your marriage is falling apart"; and "My marriage is falling apart and my husband doesn't care."

This is never a good idea. When I read about "signs your marriage is falling apart," I realize that, yes, there are some signs our marriage is falling apart, but not all the signs apply to us, so maybe there is hope. For example, we may not have sex everyday anymore, but we still have sex a couple of times a week. So, instead of reading articles on whether my relationship is over, I take a quiz, meant for teenagers, to see if I'm still "into" Boyfriend. These are bullshit quizzes, not meant for those who are parents, but the results are not good.

So, yes, I have proof that we both aren't as happy as I thought we were. The division of money, always an uncomfortable topic, is a big problem — the main source of our unresolved issues — but it is not the only problem. As Boyfriend did, maturely, text, "blah, blah, blah."

I know things have gotten really bad when Boyfriend and I no longer head up to bed at the same time, which is one of the things we have always done and once promised each other we would always do. We used to enjoy watching Netflix together, and we used to wait to watch new episodes of our favourite shows together. No longer. Now I head up to bed earlier, and Boyfriend watches "our" shows downstairs. This is truly a modern sign of a relationship falling apart.

So, yes, I still find him incredibly attractive. But are we happy? And am I an evil person for wanting to stab a knife in the eye of a so-called expert on blended families, while I'm on my Google hunt for help, when I come across an article saying how important it is to determine right from the start how you plan to share your money with your new partner? Fuck. Right. Off.

Like I said, we didn't discuss even how much closet space he needed. We decided to have another baby after Boyfriend played a round of golf. He met my daughter on our first date. So, no, we did not fucking discuss financial decisions. We are a family with two piggy banks. And, now, two Netflix accounts.

·   ·   ·   ·   ·

We're headed to therapy. Whoopee! We are mainly going because there's an issue with a loan I gave him to help with his divorce, now years ago.

"I know you are very upset and that the underlying issue is money and the money I owe you. Everything seems to be super amplified because of it. It seems that the everyday things we are normally able to deal with are causing you angst and upsetting you. It is important to remember that everything in your life is not bad, it just seems like that right now because of a string of bad luck and you are stressed about money … I am going to make an appointment with a therapist for us and I will pay for it," he writes to me in another email with the subject line "Us." "I think it is important we sit down with someone to referee the situation and our feelings and help us get to the root of the problem, which sounds like it is money. At worst case, they will make sure we are listening to each other and not getting upset and turning it into a shouting match.

"My love for you has never wavered," he writes. "If money is the root of our evil, we can certainly work through that. We come from different backgrounds and have different situations, and although your money is none of my business, it is important for you to realize where my money goes, especially if you are upset that I cannot pay you back right now in one lump sum.

It is extremely hard owing you money, and being put under a microscope whenever I buy anything is very hard as well. I try and hide it because I don't want it to affect us, but it is obviously affecting you, especially right now that money is tight for you. It had been tight for me for a while, but things are starting to happen and money will not be an issue anymore in the not so distant future. I guarantee that."

By now, I don't trust his "guarantees," and I tell him so. In my head I think, *If you're not making enough money from your company, why don't you man up and get a real job?* Boyfriend, I believe and have seen, would make a brilliant salesperson working for another company. In fact, he started out as a salesman, making a lot of money, before he started his own business and the economy went to crap. But now Boyfriend is too proud to work for someone else. I can't force him to stop being an "entrepreneur" and start working for someone else or another company. By even suggesting that he gets a job, working for someone else, I think he feels I'm emasculating him. He knows it. I know it. I feel sick thinking about emasculating him, which I don't want to do and isn't my intention.

Boyfriend's texts go on to say that it crushes him to think that I think he's taking advantage of me, and he adds that he has never felt this deeply for another woman. He also, finally, admits that he sometimes keeps more inside than he should, but he doesn't want to "burden" me with his own stress when it comes to money because he knows I have my own to deal with.

He professes, too, that he will be more open with the money and his stress. "I have hit a few walls with getting loans, but I keep my head up and keep going. I didn't want to tell you about everything because if they didn't come through you would be upset. That is my bad for thinking that, but I don't want to let you down. I am still very much pursuing other means to get money and I will not stop until I pay you back every penny. I can promise you that."

All this, and still no apology! Again, all I really want is an apology, something like, "I'm sorry I can't pay you back. I really am." For years now, there have been these guarantees and promises, but they are never fulfilled. How can he not see that all his broken promises are breaking me?

So he doesn't apologize; instead, he goes on to say how things will change when he starts making money. "I have no problem paying for more if not eventually paying for everything. I know money is extremely important in a relationship, but it shouldn't dictate how much we love each other ... People say that love is not enough, but without it what is there? Many couples have much less than us but they are happy because they love and support each other unconditionally ... I am going to make an appointment to see a marriage therapist because I would do anything to keep us together and I agreed to fight for us when I proposed to you ... I will pay for it, but I think it would help us actually absorb what we are saying to one another."

At this point I will try anything — walk over hot coals, eat a carton of worms — to save our relationship, even though I have always sort of believed that going to marriage counselling is just a step toward a final breakup.

I like to think back, though, to the night Boyfriend proposed, because it makes me happy. I want and need to remember the good times, so the bad times don't seem so bad, and to remember how much we once loved each other. I was in the very early stages of my pregnancy and we were going to Mexico for a vacation. Boyfriend had booked us into a fabulous hotel. On the second night we were there, I followed Boyfriend as we headed to dinner, but instead of going to a restaurant, I realized we were heading to the beach. My mouth dropped and tears sprang to my eyes when I saw a lone table, overlooking the beach, covered with a white tablecloth and with rose petals and candles everywhere. The scene was nothing short of dreamy.

I knew then that he was going to propose. And I really hadn't expected it. In fact, I was blindsided. It was a complete surprise! It was obvious Boyfriend had put a ton of effort into organizing this night and his proposal to make it special and romantic and memorable. Definitely memorable. It was, and remains, the most romantic evening of my entire life.

He picked up his phone after we finished our first course and said he needed to read something to me. I could tell he was nervous, and so was I. And, because we were still writing poems to each other, he read me the following off his phone:

You are the love of my life, my best friend and my soulmate
Everything we do together is simply great.
I know this may seem sappy
But you make me so happy.
You are so sweet
And without you I don't feel complete.
I feel like you're always on my team
And when you smile you give off such a special gleam.
Even though you've been complaining throughout the day
There is something I have to say.
There is one thing that I've never been more sure about in my life
That is, to ask you to be my wife.

Of course, tears of joy sprang to my eyes as a bottle of champagne was popped open, the cork flying and landing somewhere on the beach. I said, "Yes!" and we kissed and I wiped away tears and he wiped away tears. And we both took a sip of the champagne. His proposal was absolutely perfect. I had a baby growing in my stomach and a gorgeous ring on my finger and a man I loved deeply.

The next morning, I told Boyfriend we needed to go back to the beach to find the cork that had flown into the dark night so I could have a keepsake of the best night of my life. I found the cork within seconds and thought, *We are definitely meant to be*. I was so fucking happy that night, deliriously happy, truly believing there wasn't a happier girl on the planet than me.

It really was like a fairytale. So how did we go from that, and sending notes to each other with the subject line "Poem," to sending each other notes with the subject line "Us"?

We just did, and so, yes, years into blending our families, we are headed to couples counselling. I'm not opposed to seeing a therapist with Boyfriend. I'm tired of his promises and guarantees that never seem to come to fruition, which makes me act like a total bitch. I think he must definitely be tired of my constant complaints over his broken promises. We do need someone to referee our fights. Boyfriend, as I've mentioned, is a salesperson at heart, and I find it truly frustrating to argue with him because he can sell his way out of everything, making me think that I'm the crazy one for having the feelings I have and that my perceptions are not based in reality. *Let him think I'm crazy*, I think to myself. Doesn't every guy, at one point, think his spouse is crazy? I'll let him think that, because I'm not crazy, I'm just super self-aware and wear my heart on my sleeve.

Boyfriend argues that my accusations, distrust, and whatever other insecurities I have are "always projected" onto him.

He will tell me that I get so "irate" and that I react and don't think of the consequences or damage I cause, and that trying to "deal" with me is "mentally and physically draining." I, too, feel mentally and physically drained. When we argue, I bring up things from the past, and the subject of our argument gets lost in a bigger argument about other slights, which leads to arguments about other issues. We can't seem to deal with one issue at a time because we never truly resolve any of our issues before moving on to the next ones. We both agree that our "discussions," or arguments, are never constructive. So therapy, here we come! Boyfriend finds a therapist on the internet, and he makes an appointment for us.

This should be fun.

· EIGHTEEN ·

Even though my blended family can often seem far from blended, what with all the bullshit that rears its ugly head, often when
I least expect it, other people have figured out how to make
blended splendid for the long term. I'm extremely jealous of
these people and wonder if I don't have the right genes in me
to be in a blended family, especially when I feel that Boyfriend
thinks I'm selfish, impatient, and a little insecure. Yes, I make
mistakes. Yes, I am out of control and at times hard to handle.
And, yes, I'm starting to feel that if Boyfriend can't handle me
at my worst, then he sure as hell doesn't deserve me at my best.

I want so badly for us to get back to the way we were. I want
to be at *my* best. Yet the harder I try, it seems the harder I fail,
which of course makes me feel like a failure. I start to hate looking at social media, where every day I see other couples writing
sappy "Happy Anniversary" messages for the world to see. I get
annoyed by these posts, like I get annoyed by people who constantly post about their workouts. Actually, they make me sad. I
want to know their secret to making it to twelve years, twenty-
four years, while I'm trying to make it to seven.

As I mentioned, some of my friends who grew up in blended families were perfectly happy. One such friend tells me it was an a-okay way to grow up. "When I was about ten or eleven, my mom meets this man at Sunday school. They started up a friendship while we kids were in class. She started to talk about 'my friend Mike.' He was married. He has three kids, younger than me. This didn't concern me until I was about twelve or thirteen. He left his wife, moved into a basement apartment, and started hanging out with his kids at our house."

It was fine, she explained. In fact, she *liked* having kids around her after being an only child for so long. She says he was a great guy. But when he started sleeping over and it became apparent that they were more than just friends, my friend started to feel really threatened. "I got very insecure and needy. I put myself between them and forced my mother to choose. I was rude and obnoxious to him. We all fought a lot. Finally, my mother, who never got angry with me, said, 'This man is the love of my life and my chance at happiness as a woman. I am more than just your mother. I need a life too.'"

It was a conversation, my friend says, that "woke me up."

"I then went to overnight camp with my three 'siblings' and was one of their counsellors. We had a great summer. We were really close," she says. I try not to let the fact that she bonded with her stepsiblings at summer camp make me feel angry yet again, never forgetting that Boyfriend's ex may have stood in the way of this opportunity for my own blended children to bond.

She also "finally" allowed her stepfather into her heart and realized how wonderful he was. "The only dad I ever knew. He treated me like his own child. No struggles. No arguments. It was a very successful blended family. He called me his daughter, not stepdaughter."

Now, looking back as an adult, she says she realizes that she had a model blended family. "We were lucky. We all got along. His kids loved my mom and I loved their dad. No one was left out. No one was jealous."

But, while she was having a successful blended experience, the unthinkable happened. Her mother passed away in a fire at their home. It was just the three of them that night; his kids were elsewhere. "My rock was gone. My stepfather was beyond depressed and guilty. It was a terrible time for all of us. We did our best to stay together over the years, but now I felt like I had no place in 'their' family. Our blended became unblended," she says.

Over the years, they drifted away from each other, especially after she got married and had her own son. "My stepdad was still a rock for me, but now it felt like a 'duty' instead of real love. He met a new woman and got married. Now, I had to blend into his family. We had to re-blend." But it was too much, and my friend started to pull away. "I had some very long-standing and deep relationships, and those people became my family. For a while I had a relationship only with my stepfather, behind his wife's back. He helped me financially and emotionally. He was a really good man. I love him to this day, but we are all estranged and have been for the past decade."

Five years ago, she reached out to him. Then again, three years ago. "But he wasn't receptive anymore. I think I hurt him. I know he hurt me. It's been a long time now."

Upon hearing her story, I, too, feel that I should be grateful. It also makes me wonder what would happen to my daughter if Boyfriend and I broke up. Would she still have a relationship with him? Would I still have a relationship with his children? Unlike nuclear families, with two parents of biological children, when a blended family breaks up, you not only lose your partner, but you also lose a lot of people who have been in your life for years. When you're in a traditional marriage and break up, you'll still see your kids at least 50 percent of the time. I'm not ready to give all that up — the thought of losing not just Boyfriend, but also his children, his parents, and even the damn dog, seems sadder than sticking it out.

· · · · ·

The therapist Boyfriend and I see works out of her house. She is older, but I'm glad to learn that she knows what comes along with a blended family, because she is in one and has been for years. Certainly she can understand what we're going through and what our issues are. Surely she can give us directions and advice. I pray she has answers for us. I pray she will get Boyfriend to see why I end up acting the way I do and why I react the way I do. I pray that she can tell me why I'm so sensitive and take things so personally. I pray, too, that she can make Boyfriend see that he can't always be right when we argue.

I've seen a lot of therapists over my lifetime, and this one is a mediocre therapist, at best. Friendly enough. I don't leave feeling better about things afterwards. But I don't feel worse either. To tell you the truth, all Boyfriend and I did was talk over each other, with the therapist occasionally asking questions. On our way out, we make another appointment, in which we will again air our grievances, often forgetting that the therapist is in the room and that we are paying her to referee. I do, however, leave feeling better about our money arguments, because Boyfriend says *in front of the therapist* that he will chip in more and pay back the money I lent him way back, in installments. But then we start arguing over the therapist — rather, who is going to continue to pay for the therapist who is helping us get to the root of our resentment, which seems mostly to stem from money. Trust me, the irony is not lost.

Although Boyfriend has promised he will pay for the therapy, after only our second session he says he can't afford it and asks that I pay for half. Therapy, I will admit, is fucking expensive. We originally saw the therapist to help us figure out our money issues and how Boyfriend can make me feel less taken advantage of. I refuse to chip in because he promised to pay, and I feel again that another promise is broken and that Boyfriend assumes I have an unlimited amount of money in my bank account. So, after just two sessions, we never go back. For months, before this therapist gives up on us, I get emails with invoices for our two appointments, which I forward to Boyfriend. Somehow the invoices arrive in my inbox.

· NINETEEN ·

I don't remember the exact day that I told Boyfriend that I was in love with him. But I do know the exact second, and will always remember the exact day, when I fell *out* of love with Boyfriend. Maybe it wasn't love at first sight with him. It might have been lust at first sight. It started as a rebound relationship, but it rapidly turned into the real deal, not just a fling.

"I think I'm falling in love with you," Boyfriend announced less than three months into our relationship, one night after we had sex and I was lying on top of him. We started kissing, and he turned me over so I was on my back and he was on top of me, looking me right in the eyes.

"I'm not quite there, but I am getting there," I told him as he hovered over me. Less than twenty-four hours later, I told Boyfriend that I loved him too.

That was then.

After "then," even when we had been fighting for months, I still loved him and thought things would eventually get better, that we were just in a slump.

Then one day, things change. *October thirtieth*, the day before Halloween. That is the day I know it is more than a slump.

What happens that leads to me to not loving Boyfriend anymore?

He is on a plane coming back from a business trip, and we have planned to meet up at a Halloween costume party later, one that friends of his hold each year at their home. I, meanwhile, am heading to another costume party first. Nana is babysitting Baby Holt. Rowan's father is in town to visit her, and they are out for dinner with him and some of his friends. I'm dressed as a sort of sexy Batgirl, wearing a tight corset with the Batman logo, paired with a black skirt, and I complete the costume with a cape that covers only one shoulder.

Five minutes after I arrive at the first party, I get a text from Rowan's father, who never texts me when my daughter is with him. "I'm taking Rowan to the hospital. She is doubled over with stomach pain and I am with a doctor friend. He said her pain is not normal and to take her to the hospital," he writes.

I call him immediately. "What's going on? What's going on?" I'm fucking freaking out.

"She started to complain of stomach cramps and she's in a lot of pain," he tells me. "My friend checked her out, and felt around her stomach, but says that she shouldn't be in so much pain. We're on the way to the hospital now." In the background I can hear my daughter crying hysterically.

"Put me on speaker phone," I demand, and he does.

"Rowan baby. Rowan baby. Listen to me. I'm coming, okay? I'm coming!"

All I can hear is her sobbing.

"What hospital are you going to?" I ask Rowan's dad.

I get an Uber and leave the party immediately, racing to the hospital. I text Boyfriend, telling him where I am heading, but he's still in the air and won't get my desperate texts for another hour, when his plane lands. At this point, he's still the first person

I go to when I have good news and the first person I run to when there is bad news.

I am freaking out, as any mother would be. The Uber driver is taking forever, I think, when in reality the drive takes less than ten minutes, the longest ten minutes of my life.

Because it's not actually Halloween, I must look nothing short of a lunatic running into the emergency room, where I find my daughter lying in a hospital bed, doubled over in pain, as the nurses take her vital signs and hook her up to IV lines. I burst into tears when I see her writhing in agony.

"Make it go away, Mommy. Make it go away," my daughter screams out. Although I'm dressed as a superhero, I feel like anything but. Rowan's dad is calmer than I am, but I can tell he's worried because of the sweat stains under his arms, just as he had the night before our daughter was born via C-section.

My daughter is admitted to a private room, where nurses pump morphine into her IV line, a Band-Aid for her pain that also makes her loopy and somewhat hilarious, asking nonsensical questions. By now, Rowan's father and I have been here a couple of hours. Every forty-five minutes or so, my daughter's pain comes back with a vengeance and she starts crying out, holding her stomach as tears stream down her face. I am beyond desperate. I feel helpless.

So where is Boyfriend during all of this? His plane landed over an hour ago.

"Since you'll be there waiting a while, I may as well go to this party," he texts me.

Um, what?

I'm floored. If this were one of his biological children, I'm 100 percent confident that he would be racing over to the hospital to be with them. But while I'm freaking out at the hospital, watching my daughter in agony, he's at the Halloween party. To say

I'm beyond disappointed in him would be the understatement of the century. He should have come to her. He should have come to me. He should be there for us. I think he may have offered to come, but after I read his text, I don't want him around. It is clear to me that he really wants to go to that Halloween party.

But I can't think about how disappointed and angry I am. My thoughts are on my daughter, and I'm running around asking nurses for more hot packs to place on her stomach. Blood work has been taken. We're waiting for her to have an ultrasound, and I'm hoping that my daughter has appendicitis, because at least we'd have an answer.

The fact that Boyfriend has gone to a party, knowing where I am and that something is wrong with my daughter, breaks my heart. Falling in love is a process. Falling out of love can also be a process. But like those who profess they fell in love at first sight, I know I've fallen out of love in an instant.

I know, after he texts that he "might as well" go to the party, that I no longer love him. Or, for that matter, even like him.

October thirtieth is the night I clock out of my blended family. I'm simply done with the bullshit. It's not blissful anymore. It will never be blissful again. If anything says to me that he's not all in, it's him "might as well" going *anywhere* but straight to the hospital when he gets my text. I. Am. Done.

It's not only that he goes to the Halloween party. I expected him to at least stay at home in case I need him to bring something to the hospital or just so I can talk to him, to have a shoulder to cry on and help calm me down. But he isn't there for me or for Rowan. He is not there for my family, in my opinion, when we really need him. It's not "ours" anymore.

My daughter is having stomach attacks every half hour or so, and not even morphine is working anymore. She's admitted to the hospital for three days as they do tests, her biological father and I switching off nights and days so our daughter is never alone, not even for a second.

Boyfriend has a different take on this night. When I confront him, he says that he had too much to drink on the plane, which to me is a pretty pathetic excuse. What else sobers up a parent than their child being at the hospital? Not just at the hospital, but admitted! Hospitals don't admit people unless it's fucking serious.

Perhaps it's also true that I told him not to come because Rowan's father was there and it would make us all uncomfortable. Even still, I did think, even if I did tell him to stay away, that maybe he would, or should, at least come and sit in the waiting room, showing his support for me, or even offer to bring me a change of clothes, since I was still dressed as sexy Batgirl. He says that he offered to do this, and maybe it's true that he did and maybe I didn't hear him, because I was beyond distraught.

For three days, I barely see Boyfriend or our son, spending all my time with Rowan, who is still in pain, still undiagnosed. Boyfriend doesn't visit once. Neither do his children. The two times he drives me to the hospital, I have to ask him to do it. During these three days, I try not to focus on the fact that I hate him. I lie beside my daughter. I hold her hand when she's in pain. I scream for nurses to help. All my energy is on my Rowan, and I don't really have it in me to try and figure out why Boyfriend would go to a party instead.

But, once we think we have a diagnosis and are discharged and back at home, I do allow myself to think about my feelings for Boyfriend and how they changed with that one text.

How could Boyfriend enjoy himself at a party knowing how worried I was and that my little girl — my everything — was in such pain? I know that if either of Boyfriend's children had been admitted to the hospital, and even if it would be awkward to be there, and even if Boyfriend had told me not to come, I still definitely wouldn't attend a party and get drunk with friends. I'd be waiting by the phone for updates. I would offer again and again to come be with him. I would drop off food for the nurses to give to him, even if he didn't want me to come.

Even though he says he wanted to come and that I told him not to bother, how could he actually have fun, and get even drunker, while I was watching my daughter double over in pain? Why wasn't he preoccupied with worry? It's like he gives entirely no fucks about the person in the world I give the most fucks about. I am ... beyond gutted. I know I will not be able to forgive him.

Exhausted beyond belief, I finally lose it on Boyfriend, who for the first time, actually apologizes. Or maybe he says he was "wrong." But, still, it's a defensive apology, as he reminds me how long things take in the ER (so what's the rush, I guess?) and that he was drunk and wasn't thinking about much more than continuing to party. Over Halloween weekend I finally see his mask come off, literally and figuratively. The fact that he said he "might as well go to the party," since my daughter's father and I were both with her and the wait would be long, is not something I can forget. So I yell at him for choosing to go to the party. I yell that I would never do such a thing if it had been one of his children. Life is a series of choices, I howl.

"You made a choice," I scream. "First, you made the *choice* to go home and change into a costume. Then you made the *choice* to go to the party. You made a *choice* to order an Uber to go to the party. Then you made a *choice* to stay at the party. Then you made a *choice* to continue to drink at the party. What if I needed to get in touch with you?" I ask him, sobbing because I am beyond hurt and exhausted. I may have slept for four hours during the past three days. I feel broken.

"Well, I did have my phone on me," he says.

Wow. Just ... wow.

Boyfriend digs himself into an even deeper hole. There are no words to describe the depth of my disappointment. Whenever his children were sick, with fevers or sore throats, it was me who demanded that Boyfriend or his ex take them to the doctor.

"So, over the noise of a party, you think you would have heard your phone ring or hear an incoming text?" I scream in disbelief, since I know how loud this house party gets.

Eventually, Boyfriend realizes that, or at least says that, his decision to go to the party was wrong. In fact, it's the first time in our years-long relationship that he actually says the words "I'm sorry."

But, really, it's too late for an apology. I'm not longer interested in hearing the words "I'm sorry," the words I've waited to hear our entire relationship. The damage is done. I don't tell Boyfriend that, much like when you squeeze too much toothpaste out, you can't get it back in. Our relationship will never be the same. I lose all respect for him. Once you lose respect for your partner, there's no turning back.

I think of the costume that I was wearing as I raced to the hospital. I know about Batman because of Baby Holt, who is now a toddler and is obsessed with superheroes. Batman's greatest weakness is also his greatest strength. He doesn't have superpowers, but he still has the courage to face crazy villains and dangerous criminals. Batman will not stop, and he will take on any and every challenge thrown at him, but he can be worn down.

I was once up to the challenge of being in a blended family, but now I feel extremely worn down, not just from the emotional toll of watching and trying to figure out what was the cause of my daughter's stomach pain, and not because I haven't had more than four hours of sleep in more than three days, but because I would do anything, like Batman, to save my daughter from the pain she was experiencing.

After much crying and asking Boyfriend what the hell he was thinking, I think he finally understands why it hurt me so much. Still, I ask myself why I even need to explain this to him. I mean, isn't it common sense? Could you imagine a parent in a traditional family who would think it was okay to go to a party, knowing their child was in the hospital with unexplained, agonizing pain? How could I not question just how much he truly cares about both my daughter and me? And I don't think I will ever forget that when I really needed him, he wasn't there. What hurts even more, though, is that he wasn't there for my daughter. And, with one foot in a relationship and the other foot out, I am stuck in limbo.

I know Boyfriend didn't *mean* to hurt me. I know Boyfriend is regretful and remorseful. I know that people don't make the best decisions when they're drunk. But it's too late. I'm beyond disenchanted with him, believing that our relationship is now past repair.

Falling out of love with someone is so fucking sad, because at one point I thought Boyfriend was my soulmate — The One. How could someone I was once so crazy about now suddenly make me feel that our relationship is an emotional flatline?

For months after, I treat him like dirt. For months, I will look back on that night in October and think, *That is the night I should have ended our relationship.* I no longer believe I can rely on him. No longer can I hear any love in his voice.

Yet, for the next two years, I stay with him in our blended family. Why? Well, it's a good question. Maybe a part of me hopes that, after that night, I could forgive him. Some people who are cheated on in marriages seem to find it within them to forgive, so me moving past this indiscretion is always a possibility, theoretically. Part of me is just indecisive, believing that I will regret ending the relationship I put years of effort into. So, I hold on to see if I can, once again, be the Bigger Person. But being the Bigger Person has made me feel small. It's made me feel invisible. I can't pretend anymore. I won't.

· · · · ·

Relationships, especially in a blended family, never die a natural death. They are murdered by ego, attitude, lack of respect, and lack of giving fucks. Our home is a crime scene. And I'm somewhere between giving up and seeing how much more I can take. I find myself asking, *Was this really ever supposed to be more than a rebound fuck, a one-night stand?* Maybe, at the end of our first date, I should have handed him the meatloaf, walked him to the door, and never looked back.

There are many more notes sent to me with the subject line "Us."

"I would like to finish our conversation. I am not trying to blame you for where we are. I want to be clear on that. I am having a hard time understanding why you sometimes talk to me the way you do. I do still really love you and want to be with you, assuming that you won't talk to me the way you sometimes do. I am not perfect but I never rip into you like that, so it is extremely hard on me when you do it, and my coping mechanism is to walk away and seek companionship from friends," he writes me in one text. He continues, "Neither of us wants that, so the question is this: Is what I do or how I treat you so bad that I deserve to be talked to like that? If the answer is yes, then we should not be together. If the answer is no, we have to learn how to cope with things when they happen and deal with them in a calm manner so shitty things are not said. I think that is the key, and if there is calm I really do think it will have a more positive effect on me and I will want to hang and do more things with you. Does that make sense?"

Another note he sends: "You are coming down on me again and giving me shit again. I understand life can get hectic with the kids, but we are parents and choose to have them, so we have to deal with them when they are around. You say you are a single mom, but don't forget about Holt. I do tons for him so if you want me to help and do more with Rowan, you can lessen my load with him. There are still two kids that need us. I think you just feel overwhelmed because you are tired."

Yes, I am tired. I'm tired of him "diagnosing" me. I take care of my daughter almost twenty-four/seven. I had thought, early on, that once Boyfriend moved in and witnessed me having to drive my daughter everywhere, he'd offer to help. On the handful of occasions I can't get my daughter or I ask him to drive her to school, which is located less than five minutes from our house, it feels like I'm asking for a favour, one that I will have to pay back. Very, very rarely do we take care of each other's children. I have never once picked up his children from school, not only because it's at least a forty-five-minute drive each way, but mostly because Boyfriend has never asked me to. Later, I will find out that Boyfriend will use this against me as one of the reasons for the demise of our relationship.

But he refuses to acknowledge that it takes two to tango and to break up, and that I shouldn't always be the one apologizing, and why, why, why can't he say he's sorry when his actions, or lack of action, upset me? By the end, I also think it's hard for him, being his own boss during work hours, to come home and be treated like an employee, not just by me, but by the children as well.

After October thirtieth, I no longer care that I hide in my bedroom. I no longer appreciate the little things he does. I start to tell Boyfriend that I'm sleeping with my daughter because he snores, but really, I'm just not into him. I make plans with my friends and tell him afterwards. I stop calling his mother regularly. I stop going out with Boyfriend and his children. Quite frankly? I no longer give a shit. After that night, I'm not even going through the motions. I have already given up in my head. But my heart likes to romanticize our history together.

For the next two years, it's wash, rinse, and repeat when it comes to our arguments. It really isn't a matter of *things will change*, or that we are *just going through a rough patch*, or that *our relationship just petered out*, as with many other married couples. After that night, at various times I ask myself, *Do I really want to make this work or not?* I'm sure Boyfriend must also be asking himself the same question. I realize, for me, that the answer was already solidified that night my daughter was admitted to the hospital, when Boyfriend wanted to go to a party. No, we can't and won't ever make blended splendid again. The lid is off. Shit is flying everywhere.

For the next two years, we push through. We are as delusional to think we could make our blended family work now as we were when we first entered this insanity with zero forethought about what it would mean. I think we stay together because we both have already been divorced and neither of us wants to be seen as a serial divorcee. We know how taxing divorce is. We both have already had marriages that crumbled, and once you've been through that, it's hard to make the decision to split up again. You do wonder if you've tried hard enough in this relationship. You believe that, this time, you are going to fucking make it work.

Interestingly, I also don't want to break up for our son's sake, though I am a firm believer that sometimes divorce is better for the children. I also worry about what kind of role model I am for my daughter when it comes to relationships.

One night, at a cocktail party, I meet a very friendly young woman who, when I tell her I'm writing a book on blended families, tells me that her mother has been married three times, and that in two of her mother's marriages she had stepsiblings. She is best friends with the child of her mother's second partner but not close with the children of her mother's third marriage. She offers me her mother's number so I can ask her questions about blending, but all I want to know is if her mother, by having two divorces, has skewed her daughter's view on relationships. I want to know if she believes in happily-ever-after, or if going through two divorces has made her scared of relationships. I'm beyond relieved when she says, "No, not at all! My mom is and has always been my best friend. Her breakups didn't really affect me at all." I want to cry tears of relief when I hear this. I give her a hug. Mentally, I'm collecting a pros-and-cons list of staying in my blended family and, also, of Boyfriend.

But Boyfriend and I will never get back on track. Too many things have been said, too many promises broken, too many accusations made, too many expectations never met, on both sides. Of course, as with everything, there is my side, his side, and then the truth. Still, certainly, I couldn't always have been wrong in the seven years we were together. My feelings can't have been wrong *all the time*. Sometimes, all a partner needs in the relationship is a genuine "I'm sorry." But it took him entirely disregarding me and my daughter to finally get one out of him.

I realize that maybe we are just too different for each other, with two different sets of values and philosophies on what makes or breaks a relationship, on work ethic, on parenting, on ambition, on money. Simply, we have different expectations and outlooks on life. No longer are we are talking to make "us" better. We are fighting to make the other person feel bad. We are, most definitely, not the poster children for "opposites attract." That's for damn sure.

· TWENTY ·

It's over.

There are no truer words than, "You don't really know a person until you divorce them." After two years of fighting a losing battle, Boyfriend and I are now part of that cringeworthy statistic. We are part of the 66 percent of blended families who have broken up. We have followed in the footsteps of the friends who set us up.

We have a final fight in which I tell him to start looking for another place. This time he does. I'm beyond devastated at the demise of our relationship, but at the same time, I'm looking forward to having my house back, my smile back, and, most of all, peace. I'm looking forward to not always having that damn pit in my stomach. I don't want to say that the last two years have been torture — that's being too dramatic — but I feel like I have suffered … a lot.

Like most people who decide to split up, and especially if you're in a second-chance marriage, I'm still not entirely sure if breaking up is 100 percent the answer. I talk to Boyfriend about taking a break from one another, that he should find another place but we should continue to try and work on our relationship and maybe we will realize that we miss each other. Maybe we just need some distance from each other.

I don't know why I think this, because, while I may at least have the good memories of Boyfriend and the early years of blending — how we went to yoga classes together and couldn't keep our hands off each other, how we brought a baby into this world, the proposal, that night I got drunk with his daughters in Mexico, the night I took one of Bonus Children to a movie, just the two of us, the numerous times I took Bonus Daughters for manicures, our family vacations — I'm romanticizing the past and I know it.

Within a couple of weeks, he has found a new place, magically, it seems, coming up with enough money to pay for rent, including first and last months. I know he pays more than $3,000 in rent. And I'm resentful of that. There is no way he spent more than $3,000 a month in groceries. I suggest we see a couples therapist, but he's not game. Admittedly, I think I want to see a therapist so I can at least say, "I tried everything." I'm still hoping and waiting to see if he'll put in the effort that would match my expectations. Maybe he realizes it's fruitless. And it is. But after all of the bullshit, don't I deserve for him to try?

Even though I'm the one who has told him to get the fuck out, I will soon learn that he is telling our mutual friends he left me. I will let him have that. Go for it. I'm not concerned about what others think about who broke up with whom. I'm too old for that kind of bullshit.

One night, when I'm really doubting my decision, idealizing our past as I look at photographs on my phone, I ask my daughter, now a teenager, if she thinks that Boyfriend and me breaking up was the right move.

"Mommy, I think a lot of the stress I've been feeling for the last two years is because you guys were always fighting. And it's not good for Holt, either, to hear that," she responds immediately. Rowan is my little therapist, smarter than us adults and also concerned. She's a mini-parent to Holt.

Her words make me feel like I've been stabbed with a sword. How could I have not seen how all this fighting has affected our kids? After what my daughter has just told me, I know with 100 percent certainty that breaking up was the right move.

Boyfriend will go on to tell people that we broke up because of my "mental problems," and that I am "irrational." I also will let him have that. Go forth! I do not care if people think I'm the crazy one in the relationship. I'm far from the first woman who has been called crazy or irrational by an ex. In fact, if he didn't use the excuse that I am crazy and irrational, I'd be shocked. If it makes him feel better to think that I'm the irrational one, that's fine by me. I think it's "crazy" and "irrational" to leave a sick child in the hospital to get drunk at a party, but what the fuck do I know?

So, the good news is that he's moving out. The bad news is that he can't move into his place for another few weeks, so we tiptoe around each other in the house. If he's in the kitchen, I'll head to the bedroom. He leaves without saying goodbye. I come home and barely say hi. He starts sleeping in the basement, where his children once slept. He has moved all his clothes down there, too. Although he tries to make plans at night not to be home, as I do too, we still manage to argue when we do find ourselves in the same room. But, now, it's like arguing with a stranger. And so we begin un-blending. I will learn immediately that the process of un-blending, like the process of blending, also brings on one shit ton of bullshit.

·   ·   ·   ·

Our first argument after we break up, but are still in the same house, is over the fucking mattress. He wants it. I remind him that he's the one who made me get rid of a perfectly good mattress and tell him that unless he can get me that mattress back, this mattress should be mine. Also, his mother bought us a couch, about a year earlier, but in order for the couch to fit, I had to get rid of my old couch. I tell Ex-Boyfriend to get my couch back, which he has given to a friend.

I'm not in a very generous mood anymore. Just weeks before we break up for good, I got a new car, and because his lease on his old car was over, I gave him my oldish but still very functional BMW. I could have sold it for at least a few thousand dollars, but, again, I let any sort of payment slide. It now makes me sick to see him drive it, because he took it without offering to pay for it and, in my opinion, without much gratitude. I may have not taken his money if he'd offered, but an offer to pay for it would have been nice, although I'm no longer surprised that he just doesn't give a shit and that I feel like he takes and takes and takes.

When, shortly after he moves out, it's our son's birthday party and I have to tip three DJs because it's a dance party for about fifteen kids, Ex-Boyfriend tells me he "forgot his wallet." Looking back, he forgot his wallet numerous times throughout our relationship.

I wonder how he can drive my old car without thinking that over the years he, literally and figuratively, has had a pretty good ride. It makes me sick to think of all the things I have bought him over the years — the motorcycle, the $500 bottle of cologne he wanted, the expensive sunglasses, the leather jacket, the fucking *condo* in Mexico. What sort of person lives for seven years, rent-free, even if he does pay half of some of the bills? What kind of person doesn't chip in for a vacation property bought for the *family*? Ex-Boyfriend, of course, will have a different opinion and honestly believes that, over the years, we've spent the same amount of money. I'm going to call it "creative accounting" on his part. I think, too, that it's his lack of gratitude that I feel and his sense of entitlement that will forever annoy me. And my high expectations and disappointments will always annoy him.

In any case, since we blended households, there are a lot of things we need to split up. Who owns the kettle? Who owns the paper towel holder? Who owns the microwave that one of us bought a few years ago after the old one broke? Like getting a vacuum cleaner from your husband on your birthday, our email exchanges are now the complete opposite of our once-romantic ones. Not surprisingly, he sends me an email with the subject line "Household items." It's a detailed list of all the things he thinks belong to him. I look at it and think, *If only he had put as much effort into our blended family.*

This is what I open:

Shed
- Everything in the shed other than Rowan's camp stuff. Tools, sports equipment, etc.
- Depending on the size of my place, was wondering if it would be okay to leave some stuff in the shed until I figure out what to do with some of the larger items.

Kitchen
- The stuff on the black shelf that is mine — printer, internet extender, etc.
- Mini Dyson vacuum
- My pictures — ketchup bottle pic, family pic in grocery store, etc.
- Clock in kitchen
- Knife block

- Coffee machine, coffee grinder, a handful of glasses and mugs, half of the plates, half the knives (only want the ones I brought or bought), half the utensils (there is almost two of everything so it won't be an issue)
- Couple of the large serving plates (the ones I brought)
- Sandwich maker, grill, slow cooker, and blender
- Paper towel holder and half of the mixing bowls, plastic bowls, popcorn bowls, two of the frying pans I bought recently – you can keep the majority of all the pots and pans (I only need a few)
- I will get a new toaster, kettle, cutlery, etc. There is a Keurig coffee machine in the dining room. You can have that, and I have a half dozen boxes of pucks for it — you can have all of them.

Dining room
- Black two drawer unit and wicker basket dresser and any of the stuff in the drawers that is mine.

Holt's toys
- We can figure that out and just split it up — he has tons so it won't be an issue

Holt's clothes
- We can split his clothes so he has clothes at both houses

Living room
- Silver and white round table, TV, bracket for TV unit, unit under the TV, couch, round wood drum table, NY and watercolour pictures, stereo, speakers, Xbox, filing cabinet, heater, and green desk chair
- If you want the couch and/or the TV (with mount), I am

willing to leave them for you if you agree to give me the replacement cost

Basement

- Basically everything in the girls' room and the downstairs closet
- I might need the tall white standup unit in hallway but if I cannot fit it in you can have it
- I would like the downstairs fridge but I may not be able to take it right away. If I don't have room for it, I wanted to know if you would be okay if I grabbed it later.
- My suitcases, sport bags, and sporting equipment

Family room

- The only thing I want is the "Live, Love" picture on the wall

Master bedroom

- Black bedside table on my side
- You can keep my TV. You'll have to get an Apple TV — I can help you with this and set it up if you want. They are around $100.

Holt's room

- Since I will have to furnish an entire room for Holt, I think it is fair to either split up the furniture or go fifty-fifty on stuff that he will need for my house. If we split up his stuff we will both have to buy stuff, otherwise I can just go get him the stuff and his room will remain the same. Not sure what is best for him; he might be more comfortable if he brings some of his stuff to my house but not sure. I am open to either.

- I would like the recliner chair in his room; would be nice for him to have something familiar and it just holds his stuffed animals now. If anything it will make his room seem bigger.

Bathrooms
- My toiletries and two of the metal garbage cans with the pop-up lids — prevents Toby from eating the garbage
- The shower caddie in our master bathroom
- Half the towels — we have tons so this won't be an issue
- Bathroom rug — white fluffy one I bought for the spare bathroom

When I first open the list, I am both amazed and appalled by some of what he's asking for. The shower caddie in the master bedroom that probably cost $25? Is he fucking kidding me? Is he really asking for garbage cans that cost about $7 at Walmart? And the paper towel holder? This really is fucking bullshit. And where does he find the gall, I wonder, to ask me for "replacement costs" for things I may want to keep? And is he really asking for the "Live, Love" painting that I bought for "us" on one of our anniversaries, which cost *me* a small fortune? Is he really going to take the *internet extender*? Does he not remember that, when he moved in, I already had a fully furnished house? Enjoy the fucking ketchup bottle picture and the cheap plastic popcorn bowls. It's all fucking yours.

In the end, I let him take whatever he wants, except the "Live, Love" painting. My lawyer tells me that to get him out faster, just let him take what he wants. It's just stuff. A television can be replaced.

Now that we've broken up, I'm also getting emails with the subject line "Spreadsheets." Our relationship has gone from being romantic to strictly professional. It's not an even remotely comfortable kind of relationship, however; it's like having to work with someone you don't really like, but have to put up with.

He continues to send me so many emails with spreadsheets listing which items he thinks are his and which he thinks are mine and what he's willing to leave me "for a price." They are so confusing that I stop opening them and end up yelling at him, "The purpose of spreadsheets is to make it easy to figure out for the other person. Your spreadsheets are so fucking complicated!"

I burst into tears when I see that he's "offering" to sell me the large couch his mother bought us, because he doesn't think it will fit into his new place, adding on HST as if my house were a store. As if he's going to remit that tax to the government. His audacity, I'm seeing, knows no end, and it's laughable at this point. But I feel ashamed and embarrassed, and I wonder if I ever really, truly knew the real him. The guy asking for the bathmat.

I know I fell out of love with him on the eve of Halloween, but now I'm seeing his mask come off. I'm starting to understand why his ex told me in one of our heated exchanges, "Good luck. You're going to need it."

I have the urge to call her and say, "You were right. I'm sorry."

.   .   .   .   .

Of course Ex-Boyfriend's mother helps him pack, just like she helped him unpack when he moved in almost seven years ago. I wonder if she's sick of packing up and unpacking her adult child's life, but mostly I think she enjoys keeping busy and helping her children, the people she lives and breathes for.

Just as I couldn't stand to be around when he drove up with the moving truck years ago, I can't stand to be around when he packs up to move out. Again, I need the Clonazepam. I feel the same angst and dread I felt when I saw the moving truck pull up, but a deep sadness too. So I book a last-minute solo trip to Mexico, asking my daughter's father if he can come in to watch her. He does. My friends, who know Ex-Boyfriend is moving out, think I'm batshit crazy to leave him at the house alone, with his mother, to pack. They offer to stay at my house to make sure he doesn't take everything.

"What if he takes something that's yours? Have you hidden your jewellery? Have you hidden all your important documents?" all of them ask me, concerned.

"Definitely lock up or bring over here anything that you don't want him to see or have," one friend offers. I love my friends and how they are looking out for me.

But I'm practically paralyzed — *What happened to us?* — and while I think that, yes, for sure he's going to take things we didn't agree upon, it's just stuff. Stuff, like my lawyer says, can be replaced. The goal is to get him out, sooner rather than later. The sooner he's out of the house, the sooner the arguments will end.

When I get home from my five day trip — I can't exactly call it a vacation — I walk into my house, which now looks like a rental storage space. There are dozens and dozens of packed boxes, taped up so tightly that it would take me days to open them all to make sure he didn't take anything that we didn't agree upon. I'm sure this was done on purpose. And there's still more to pack.

I'm back before he's actually moved, and I get to watch in awe as his mom nitpicks over things to put in the boxes. I almost lose my shit when I see her packing a pair of *scissors*. I grab them from her, like a kid who grabs a toy out of another child's hands. I am no longer a loving daughter-in-law. And, I know, I no longer have a mother-in-law who likes me very much. But she even has the gall to take half a box of ice cream bars that are in the freezer. I hope they melt all over the other shit she's taking. Will she remember trying to take a pair of scissors and the ice cream bars? You'd have to ask her. This is not something that I would make up.

When I tell my friends that Ex-Boyfriend has asked for the fucking bathmat, they aren't surprised at all. I'm surprised they aren't surprised. "He's always been a taker," one of my best girl-friends says. I'm surprised, too, that almost every single one of my friends, when I tell them that Ex-Boyfriend is moving out and we are separating, doesn't seem overly shocked, or shocked at all, just like I wasn't that shocked when my girlfriend — the one who set me and now-Ex-Boyfriend up — was breaking up with her boyfriend.

"You haven't been happy for years," every single one of my friends tells me. *Years?* Most of my girlfriends admit, only after we break up, that they have never been exactly fans of Ex-Boyfriend. It's not only that they are loyal to me and have heard my complaints over the years. All of them think he had a good ride with me, as if I was some sort of sugar mommy. Do you know how crushing it is to hear this? I hope you don't and never will. Also, I feel incredibly stupid to have not seen what seemingly all my friends had seen in him. And, so, yes I'm ashamed of myself.

Maybe the biggest perk for him was the almost-free ride, at least when it came to living rent and mortgage free. But I don't want to think that, especially because he's the father of my child. And Ex-Boyfriend doesn't see it that way, and he never will. But when I see yet another spreadsheet in my inbox — maybe the eighth or ninth — with him demanding that I now owe him money, I break down. My friends rally around me, taking me out, calling me every day, asking how they can help me. I owe *him* money? He can't be fucking serious. Does he not remember, even during our worst times, that only a handful of weeks ago I gave him a *car*? Does the man have zero pride? The answer, from all my friends, is a resounding, "Yes!"

It's hard to explain what it feels like when you realize you've been used for years — or at least that's how *I* feel — and when you've tried your best at something and failed. It's hard to admit defeat. It's hard to think of someone who I still care about being described by friends like that.

On the other hand, for reasons too complicated to get into, he disliked two of my best friends, friends I had known for twenty-plus years, and over the years made that clear to me, often making me feel bad for being friends with them. Meanwhile, my friends always supported me and my relationship, even though I learn, only after we break up, how much they dislike him, his attitude, and his lack of appreciation of me.

I want to yell at the top of my lungs, "*Why didn't anyone tell me?*"

.   .   .   .   .

I hope that this will be an amicable divorce, that we will move forward to "positively" co-parent Holt, who is now almost six. After all, "positive co-parenting" is what everyone tries to do when they have children and split up. I get along with Rowan's father, after all. So why shouldn't I be able to get along with Ex-Boyfriend? But I can't. Every time he sends me a note with the subject line "Spreadsheet" or says I can "buy" a piece of furniture from him, my heart sinks and I lose a little more respect.

I am not overly concerned over how our split will affect our son, the baby who was our co-venture, the baby who will tie us together for life, even if we aren't together. The baby I wouldn't have if Ex-Boyfriend hadn't agreed. He gave me a baby, one who was meant to be, even if Ex-Boyfriend and I weren't.

Holt has grown up seeing all of his sisters go from one house to another. He knows that Ex-Boyfriend's other children have another house, their biological mom's house. He knows that Rowan goes off with her father or grandparents often, to their houses. To him, having two houses is … normal. So I'm not particularly worried about his adjustment to our new *new*. Having two houses, to five-year-old Holt, is fun and exciting! Now he's *just* like his sisters! Holt truly doesn't seem affected at all. When he's with me, he doesn't ask for Daddy. I'm assuming that when he's with Daddy, he doesn't ask for me. We have let his teachers know, so they can keep an eye out for him, to see if he's acting any differently. He's not.

The un-blending of our blended family, at least when it comes to the move, seems very quick, just as quick as when we decided to blend families. We got together fast, and we ended things fast.

Once Ex-Boyfriend moves into his new place, we make our first co-parenting trip with Holt to Walmart, where we pick out cute paintings for his walls and cute carpets. And, yes, because he is *our* son, I pay for half of everything. Back at my house, I can finally see the dining room table again. I hire a professional cleaning service and have five people come to "deep clean" my house, including steam cleaning the carpets that the dog has shit and peed on. It takes the five of them almost nine hours to scrub my house from top to bottom. I'm sad, because I know I'm trying to scrub Ex-Boyfriend, and any memory of my once-blended family, out. At this point, I want them erased. Nothing compares to the feeling I get when I walk in. It's like a new house; it's so organized and clean. There's no more clutter. A clean slate.

The basement, where Bonus Children used to sleep, is completely empty, and I promise my daughter that I'm going to decorate it for her so it can be her hang-out when her friends come over. I spend a small fortune turning what was once Ex-Boyfriend's children's room into a room with a trundle bed, a pullout couch, funky wall paintings, and many fun and colourful shag carpets and pillows to make the new decor "Miami chic." My daughter loves it and will host many sleepover parties down there.

It is me, now, who asks my daughter if I can sleep with her or if she can come sleep with me, on days when I'm heartbroken over the breakup and my son is with Ex-Boyfriend. Just because I know it's the best, and only, option doesn't mean I'm not mourning the demise of our relationship and what we once had. It doesn't mean I don't sometimes miss him. I question if we ever really loved each other, or were just in love with the idea of family and moving forward from our exes. We were each other's rebounds. And maybe that was all it was ever supposed to be. But, no, I know I truly loved him. I know I once believed in "Us." I believed we would grow old together.

One day, about a week after Ex-Boyfriend moves out, he comes over to pick up the rest of his shit. Rowan is at home and in the front hallway. He barely says goodbye to her (again with the Hi/Bye Fight!), which leads her to a sudden outburst of sobbing. Ex-Boyfriend just leaves.

"Does he not like me anymore?" she asks. "He didn't say goodbye to me." I feel sick to my stomach and start to cry too, and I hate him in this moment. Blending affected everyone in the family, so I shouldn't be surprised that un-blending will do the same. Un-blending is like a death-defying act in Cirque du Soleil.

Ex-Boyfriend has taken the dog, which I'm happy about, but Rowan wants him to visit. Over the years, she was the one who gave him the most attention. She was the one who fed him, the one who took him on walks, the one who rubbed his belly. I now remember many, many times having to remind

Ex-Boyfriend to get his daughters to walk their dog when they were over. Now, Ex-Boyfriend doesn't think it's a good idea for the dog to go between houses. I want him to know that he's not punishing me — I can finally leave the bathroom and bedroom doors open and can leave food on the kitchen table — but that he's punishing Rowan. Again, because he has let my daughter down, he's let me down.

"I feel bad Rowan was crying," he texts me shortly after he leaves. "I tried and gave it everything I had. Once my mental wellbeing was being affected, I didn't have a choice. Your day-to-day thinking really differed from mine with respect to what or how partners are supposed to act toward one another. I deserve to be happy. It is more damaging to kids to see that than live between two parents' houses. I wish things were different, but as I mentioned before, you never listened to reason and the damage caused eventually was too hard to overcome. People have the odd bad day or two or month or two, but this was going on for years. Things were getting worse and worse. We deserve to be happy, and this was the only way to move to fulfill that goal. I don't think you are a bad person by any means, you just have some shit to deal with and figure out why you were so belittling to me for years." These words I've heard too many times to count, so I'm not sure why he feels the need to continually send me these types of notes.

Again, he feels bad about Rowan, but he doesn't apologize for leaving even after seeing her cry. *After knowing her for seven years, he could have talked to her for five fucking minutes*, I think. And, again, I'm the one who has some shit to deal with? There's no accountability on his part, but I know him, and I know he will never take any accountability for his actions, or lack of action. And of course, according to him, he has nothing to figure out. Because of his actions, broken promises, and lack of appreciation, I may have been belittling to him with my choice of words. But him leaving my daughter crying, without bothering to talk to her for even a minute, proves again that we aren't on the same page, especially after he moves out.

Still, the next day he texts me, "I have to go to Best Buy today. I can get you two HDMI cords for the TVs if you want. Let me know." I take him up on his offer, although these texts are a mind-fuck to me. He also adds in his text, "Also can you get me the money for Holt's last two dental appointments? Half of both visits is $290." *Jesus!*

For months and months, I will receive a nice text, followed by a mean one. And the same goes for my end. For months, he will continually ask me for money. Worst of all, he refuses to get a lawyer.

So, no, this divorce is not amicable.

Still, I have encouraged Rowan to keep in touch with Ex-Boyfriend's daughters. They do, after all, have a brother in common. And so, right after he moves out, she texts them both: "No matter what happened between our parents, we will always be sisters."

All three girls, who share the same brother, agree to keep in touch. But aside from one or two exchanges and one or two Instagram likes, they seem to have forgotten that we once were a family. I do send his daughters texts, once congratulating his eldest daughter for getting a summer internship she wanted so badly and, also, to wish her a happy birthday. I text his other daughter to see how her summer job is going. Months after our breakup, I will send the odd text to them, which I always initiate. But, other than that, we have lost all contact. I'm not sure if I should reach out to them or not. I want them to know that I love them and am here for them, but I can't think of any reason they would need to come to me. I am sad, too, because while I have closure with my ex, I never had the chance to say goodbye to his daughters, really. I don't have closure with them. I have no idea if or when I'll ever see them again. My daughter seems to forget them, and even Ex-Boyfriend, entirely.

Just as when you marry your partner, you marry their family, when you un-blend, you lose part of your family, the one you gained when blending. Only a couple of months after Ex-Boyfriend moves out, it's my birthday. I get a one-line text from him saying, "Happy Birthday." By the time my daughter's birthday rolls around, five months later, even once-sweet Nana doesn't text her, nor do her once-stepsisters, the two she shares a brother with. Ex-Boyfriend says he sent her a text. My daughter says she never received it.

At present, neither my daughter nor I have any contact with Ex-Boyfriend's mother or his children, aside from the odd text I'll send his daughters to let them know I'm thinking about them. His mother doesn't like me. Shocking. She's the one who actually calls me to ask for the engagement ring that her son gave to me, back. She will always side with her baby, her son. Likewise, my parents are far from happy with Ex-Boyfriend. In fact, I have never seen my dad so angry in my entire life. I have never heard him swear before. But after another disagreement, when I am on the phone with my mother telling her that Ex-Boyfriend refuses to get a lawyer — meaning he refuses to divulge his financials, the first *legal* step in a divorce — thinking that we can come to an agreement on our own via an agreement he cobbles together off the internet, I hear my dad in the background saying, "Tell him to *fuck off.*" Blood, in this case, is thicker than water. And, reflecting, it always was as we blended families.

The fact that our children aren't in contact makes me wonder if we ever really, truly blended at all. My daughter will always have a brother in common with Ex-Boyfriend's children, but when we un-blended she lost a man and two sisters who had been in her life for years. Although "lost" may not be the right word, since she seems not to care at all about keeping in touch with them. Likewise, Ex-Boyfriend's children have also lost a sister and only see their brother if he's at their father's. Eventually, my daughter will even forget about the dog that lived with us for seven years.

I do want to reach out to them, to say that if they are ever in the neighbourhood and want to drop by, my door is open. I will do this when things calm down. I hope we will eventually have some sort of relationship, though I don't know what that will look like. In the throes of our far-from-civil separation, I don't think much about Ex-Boyfriend's children, busy trying to get my life back on track and getting over the pain of another breakup. Months later, I realize how much I miss them, especially when I no longer know what's going on in their lives. I also realize that two of my son's sisters are out there in the world, yet I barely have a relationship with them, nor does my daughter, who they share a brother in common with. It's fucked up.

"It took four years," one of my friends tells me about her ex–bonus child, who refused to talk to her after she broke up with their dad, even though she was also the mother of his brother. "But my ex's son just reached out to me two weeks ago. He said he wanted to come by my place to see his brother. I, of course, said yes! And it was wonderful! I think, because he saw how their dad acts around his new girlfriend, that he finally realized that I wasn't The Bad One. I think, too, he's now just more mature. We had a very nice chat and now we text back and forth." So yes, it may take years before ex–Bonus Daughters reach out to me. I will wish them happy birthday, but since I no longer know what's going on in their day-to-day life and am not sure if they are even interested in me reaching out, I'm not sure what else to do. So, mostly, I do nothing.

Ex-Boyfriend and his children also do not text Rowan before she heads off to camp for a month. I have replaced all the furniture Ex-Boyfriend has taken. I have also, because it is too painful to see, taken down the huge canvas of all the children hanging in my kitchen. I can't bear to look at it, so I hang it in another room, a room I barely use.

Now I'm a single mother of two children, who have two different fathers. Ex-Boyfriend is a single father of three, by two different women. No longer will Ex-Boyfriend's mother speak to me, nor will my parents speak to Ex-Boyfriend. Suddenly, the grandparents, too, even if they weren't super close to them, have lost bonus grandchildren. Even the dog, yet again, has a new home.

Maybe all this will change. Maybe it won't. I will always love and have a fondness for Ex-Boyfriend's children. I will always care for them. On the bright side, the question, "How many children do you have?" is now easy to answer. There are no more fights about grocery shops or who says hi or bye first, no arguing over the bills or feeling unappreciated. I no longer feel left out. Not only do I have my house back, but, slowly, I'm finding my smile.

Interestingly, Rowan's father's parents now ask about how I am, how my son is, and how Ex-Boyfriend is treating me, concerned, it seems, with all aspects of this contentious divorce. It turns out that they, too, were never fans of Ex-Boyfriend. For years they never once asked about their granddaughter's baby brother or bonus sisters or bonus father figure. Now, every time we talk, they ask me how the divorce is going, clearly on my side, probably because I'm their granddaughter's mother. But, like my friends, they only speak up when he's no longer in the picture.

· REFLECTIONS ·

If I had to blend again, would I? To answer the question I've been asking myself for a while, and that you're probably wondering about, I can't help but think back to what all of us could have done better or what we should have done to make things splendid and keep them splendid despite all the bullshit that comes with blending. I wonder about a lot of things that led our once blissfully blended family to its eventual demise.

Would we have worked out if we hadn't moved so fast? Would we have worked out if we hadn't added another baby to the mix, though he's such a blessing? Would we have worked out if we'd discussed how to handle our finances and our financial goals before blending? Would we have worked out if we had lowered our expectations from the start? Would we have worked out if, instead of him moving into my house, we had gotten a new place together? Would we have worked out if we'd instilled house rules? Would we have worked out if we'd talked about our parenting styles? Would we have worked out if we'd made more of an effort to do more as a blended family? Would we have worked out if Ex-Boyfriend and I had tried harder to make our relationship a priority? Would we have worked out if we'd discussed what we expected of each other when it came to raising children that aren't ours biologically? Would we have worked out if we'd recognized that we were more set in our ways than we thought? Would we have worked out if I was better at change? Would we have worked out if we could have forgiven each other more and if he'd managed to say "I'm sorry"? Would we have worked out if we could have handled each other's criticism? Would we have worked out if we could have done what seems like the impossible, and loved and treated children who weren't biologically ours equally? Would we have worked out if we hadn't put so much pressure on making it work? Would we have worked out if I hadn't become depressed after the birth of Baby Holt? Would we have worked out if I had really lowered my expectations and Ex-Boyfriend had shown a little more gratitude? Would we have worked out if he'd offered to chip in for the house and condo? Would we have worked out if our children had really bonded? Would we have worked out if he hadn't gone to that party? Would we have worked out, as Ex-Boyfriend now says, if I had tried harder to bond with his daughters, which he professes was my responsibility all along and not his at all? I am shaking my head as I write all of the above, because I don't know.

I feel an incredible amount of guilt when I think of the would-we-have's — so much so that on more than one night after Ex-Boyfriend moves out, I am actually sick to my stomach. I know we didn't make it *for better or for blended*. But, no, I don't feel like a failure. I feel guilty about the so many what-ifs. What if I had a different personality and was better at change? What if he had a different personality and was more ambitious and better with money? What if — and this will remain the biggest mystery — we just weren't meant to be, and our breakup had absolutely *nothing* to do with blending families?

I do know one thing. There is never a right time to blend or un-blend. If you're looking for the right time, look at your phone.

Ultimately, there are no do-overs in life. So, to answer the question, would I blend again? Yes. But not for a long while, and definitely not before I actually discuss every fucking detail or all the bullshit issues I now know will rear their ugly heads, rather than just relying on a leap of faith and glorious love. While I am part of the 66 percent of blended families that fail, there's a 75 percent chance that my next partner (and I am confident that I will have a next partner) will have children. I will not repeat the same mistakes. I will know to temper my expectations. I will know what to expect. I will make sure we discuss everything, down to what kind of deodorant my future next partner uses.

But for now, all I know is that tonight, just me and my daughter and my son are laughing together at the table over dinner. My daughter is standing on a chair and doing a silly dance, and my son is laughing. Everything feels … light. I no longer feel suffocated, and as if I constantly have a knot in the pit of my stomach. I no longer have to try and work on "Us." I no longer hide, either in my bedroom or my car. I'm now excited to walk into my clutter-free house. I buy my own groceries and, well, I've found my smile again. My kids are not only all right, they are downright happy!

Yet, for all I perceive as Ex-Boyfriend's faults, I sometimes miss him terribly. But I no longer am worried that someone, or everyone, is angry at me over a perceived slight. I no longer expect anything from Ex-Boyfriend. It turns out it is possible to lower your expectations. I do shed many tears over the breakup, and even after he moves out I wonder if we tried our best, asking him numerous times if he thinks breaking up was the right choice.

Then, one day, I wake up after a good night's sleep, eat breakfast, and head to the office before realizing that I haven't thought of Ex-Boyfriend at all. I also realize that I am, literally, skipping down the street, like I don't have a care in the world. I park my car in the middle of the two-car driveway ... because I can. And it feels so, so good.

· · · ·· ·

Boyfriend has blocked me from his social media accounts, maybe out of necessity or maybe to hurt me. I know it's mostly because he doesn't want me to see what he's doing, but also, he probably doesn't want to see what I'm doing. Still, one day, on my son's iPad that comes and goes with him from Ex-Boyfriend's house to my house, I see that Ex-Boyfriend has composed a profile for a dating website, which he obviously forgot to erase. He writes, "Young at heart, easygoing, outgoing, into music, dogs, great sense of humour, witty, travel often, athletic, love being outdoors, cards and board games in winter. Cherish friends and family. Looking for someone fun, witty, intelligent, down-to-earth, and most importantly, someone who smiles. Six-year-old son 50%."

I can't help but laugh. The person he's described and is looking to date is *me*. At least the pre-blend me. If I had not known Ex-Boyfriend and we were both on the same dating app, I'm pretty certain we'd be a match. The irony is not lost on me. Neither is the fact that he has somehow — poof! — come up with the money to pay $3,300 a month, plus utilities and internet, to rent his own place.

Because he is the father of my son, no matter how much he has disappointed me in the past, and often continues to disappoint me, I wish him the best. No matter how much he hurt me, and after all the years of suffering and trying, a part of me will always have his back. Still, aside from being the father of my child, he is now practically a stranger to me. Maybe one day we will be friends. But not today. Not tomorrow. Not for a long while. Again, this is my story. We couldn't make blended splendid, but many do. I bow down to successful blended families, because it really is "so, so hard."

For the first time in years, I feel free. I am free from all the bullshit of blending and the toll it took on me emotionally, mentally, and even physically. I feel like *me* again. I'll never be 100 percent certain if we tried hard enough, but I'm now happy. No longer are there any more arguments held in the backyard. My house is clutter-free, literally and emotionally.

I know one thing for certain, after all this blended, then unblended, bullshit. I will never, ever eat meatloaf again. *That's for fucking sure.*

· ACKNOWLEDGEMENTS ·

Thank you to the entire team at Dundurn Press for recognizing the importance of a book like this. Thank you, Dominic Farrell, for your wonderful edits. It was nothing short of blissful to work with you. Thank you, Elena Radic, for overseeing this book and bringing it to fruition, from start to finish. Thank you, Jenny Govier, for your perfect copy-edits. Thank you, Sarah Beaudin, for your beautiful cover design, which exceeded all expectations. Thank you, Sophie Paas-Lang, for your amazing work on the interior design. A massive shout out to Sarah Miniaci for your endless energy in promoting this book. You're truly the best of the best in what you do! Thanks also to publicist Saba Eitizaz. Thank you freelance proofreader Dawn Hunter for catching any errors with your wicked eye. Thank you to my agent, Sam Hiyate, for also recognizing the importance of this book. To my wonderful family, thank you for your unwavering support. To my wonderful daughter, Rowan, your maturity, advice, and unwavering loyalty kept me strong and continues to keep me strong. I'm beyond proud to be your mother. To my wonderful son, Holt, you make me laugh like no other. You are a true blessing. Thank you to all of you who spoke to me about your experiences blending. Thank you to the team at SavvyMom, who continues to inspire me to write about family. Thank you to my wonderful army of girlfriends for being there, especially when times were tough. You definitely stepped up when I needed you the most and for that I'm eternally grateful. And a sweet wink to "Badass," who helped put me back together when I was broken. For that, I am also eternally grateful. And, last but most certainly not least, a huge shout out to freelance editor Leslie Kennedy, who helped shape the book from the start, held my hand throughout the process when I slipped into insecurity mode, and who was also the first to read the chapters. Your on-point advice, opinion, and strong editing skills were indispensable, as was your sense of humour. I'm beyond grateful that you agreed to come along on this ride. You are a true star.

· ABOUT THE AUTHOR ·

PHOTO BY NEIL BASS

Rebecca Eckler is one of Canada's best-known journalists and authors. She is the international bestselling author of *Knocked Up, Toddlers Gone Wild, Wiped!,* and *How to Raise a Boyfriend.* Rebecca has been a columnist at the *National Post* and the *Globe and Mail* and her work has appeared in the *New York Times* and *Los Angeles Times,* as well as in numerous magazines and on parenting blogs across North America. She is the executive editor of SavvyMom, a website for all things parenting related. Rebecca won Best Columnist two years in a row at the Canadian Online Publishing Awards. She lives in Toronto with her daughter, Rowan, and her son, Holt.

Falling for London
A Cautionary Tale
Sean Mallen

When Sean Mallen finally landed his dream job, it fell on him like a ton of bricks. The veteran journalist was ecstatic when he unexpectedly got the chance he'd always craved: to be a London-based foreign correspondent. It meant living in a great city and covering great events, starting with the Royal Wedding of William and Kate. Except: his tearful wife and six-year-old daughter hated the idea of uprooting their lives and moving to another country.

Falling for London is the hilarious and touching story of how he convinced them to go, how they learned to live in and love that wondrous but challenging city, and how his dream came true in ways he could have never expected.

Do You Ever Cry, Dad?
A Father's Guide to Surviving
Family Breakup
I.J. Schecter

Divorce and separation are overwhelmingly sad, especially when kids are involved. In *Do You Ever Cry, Dad?* I.J. Schecter shares his experience, stories from other fathers, and insights from family experts to provide practical and emotional support to dads going through the anguish of a split, and to help them maintain a loving and healthy relationship with those who matter most in their lives: their children.

Filled with emotional and practical help, concrete research, and a deep understanding of the pain and processing marital breakup involves, *Do You Ever Cry, Dad?* aims to help dads get themselves and their kids through one of the hardest changes in their lives. Honest, heartfelt, and compassionate, this book is here to instill in any dad hope in place of the despair and hurt he may be keeping to himself.

Co-Parenting From The Inside Out
Voices of Moms and Dads
Karen L. Kristjanson
Foreword by Edward Kruk

Effective co-parenting, or sharing significant parenting time with an ex-spouse, is one of the best gifts separated parents can give to their children. The interviews in *Co-Parenting from the Inside Out* are with real moms and dads in diverse circumstances, showing them making choices, sometimes struggling, and often growing. Their stories offer insights into wise decision-making, as well as practical strategies that strengthen families. Parents can see that they are not alone as they navigate their feelings and build a future. While pain exists in most stories, there is also hope. Co-parents often feel that they have become more confident and compassionate, and parent better than before. The effects of their personal growth and their children's are the silver lining in the dark pain of divorce.

Karen L. Kristjanson has brought together real life co-parenting stories that inspire separated parents and help them understand co-parenting better, offering practical tips and tools that directly benefit families.

Book Credits
Acquiring Editor: Scott Fraser
Developmental Editor: Dominic Farrell
Project Editor: Elena Radic
Copy Editor: Jenny Govier
Proofreader: Dawn Hunter

Cover Designer: Sarah Beaudin
Interior Designer: Sophie Paas-Lang

Publicist: Saba Eitizaz

dundurn.com 　　　dundurnpress
@dundurnpress 　　dundurnpress
dundurnpress 　　　info@dundurn.com

FIND US ON NETGALLEY & GOODREADS TOO!

 DUNDURN